What the reviewers have said ab

Many families have found they don't ~~...~~
in France, villas in Italy or ski chalets ~~...~~
dose of common sense coupled with some good old-fashioned trust. . . .
Home-swapping can be a simple, satisfying and safe experience all
around.

San Francisco Chronicle

No subject brings more letters to the Good Housekeeping travel department than home exchanging. . . . There are huge advantages to taking
a holiday this way when you have young children. Everything is much
more relaxed than in a hotel—the children seem happier and entertain
themselves better.

Good Housekeeping/London

If you're the slightest bit adventurous, home exchange vacationing is
the way to go.

Washington Post

Possibly the most important reason for exchanging: money goes farther.
You can double or even triple your vacation budget. Saving money on
lodging and, frequently, a car can leave room for a more extravagant
vacation. You can go places that might not be possible without the savings. And return visits to special places are often possible once a relationship—perhaps a lifelong friendship—is established with exhange
partners.

A Better Tomorrow

Instead of being in a sterile hotel atmosphere, you're in a home. It's
easier on the kids, plus you can pack lighter because you have access to
a washer and dryer. Most people can't come up with any disadvantages.

Sunday Oregonian

Home exchanging's a lot more than just saving money. . . . It's meeting the neighbors, living the way they do, shopping where they shop,
and every day absorbing the history and the culture in which they live.

Philadelphia Inquirer

Home exchanging makes for good security, because someone is living
in your home while you are away.

Houston Post

What the reviewers said about *Trading Places,* the authors' first book on home exchanging:

Novice swappers, leery of coming home to kitchens resembling nuclear test sites, will be pleased that the book's bulk is devoted to pull-no-punches, first-person advice.

New York Daily News

Relies heavily on the actual experiences of people who have had exchange vacations.

Dallas Morning News

Its 24 chapters detail the philosophy of a "live-in" vacation: the best ways for home exchangers to contact each other and make home exchange arrangements.

Fort Lauderdale Sun-Sentinel

Trading Places is a how-to-guide to home exchanging.

Hartford Courant

Stuffed with definitive information on exchange procedures, pointing out potential risks as well as advantages.

Atlanta Journal and Constitution

A thorough examination of every aspect of home exchange, with lots of personal anecdotes.

Los Angeles Times

One of the best guides on the market. . . . Covers the swap-scene from A-Z and offers lots of practical advice on maximizing the pleasures and avoiding the pitfalls. . . . Indispensable for the novice and a bible for the veteran.

West Hawaii Today

This book is packed with personal experiences and tips of people who've exchanged homes, plus plenty of advice from the authors who are veteran exchangers.

Chicago Tribune

Full of practical information for those considering a home swap.

SHE magazine, Australia

Informative, fun to read, and . . . indispensable for potential home exchangers.

St. Paul Pioneer Press

Written on a people level and balanced by the pitfalls as well as [the] pluses.

Detroit News

Home Exchange Vacationing
Your Guide to Free Accommodations

Home Exchange Vacationing

Your Guide to Free Accommodations

Bill and Mary Barbour

Illustrated by Al Hartley

Rutledge Hill Press
Nashville, Tennessee

Published in Nashville, Tennessee, by Rutledge Hill Press, 211 Seventh Avenue North, Nashville, Tennessee 37219. Distributed in Canada by H. B. Fenn and Co., Ltd., 1090 Lorimar Drive, Mississauga, Ontario L5S 1R7. Distributed in Australia by Millennium Books, 13/3 Maddox Street, Alexandria NSW 2015. Distributed in New Zealand by Tandem Press, 2 Rugby Road, Birkenhead, Auckland 10. Distributed in the United Kingdom by Verulam Press, Ltd., 152a Park Street Lane, Park Street, St. Albans, Hertfordshire AL2 2AU.

Typography by E. T. Lowe, Nashville, Tennessee.

Library of Congress Cataloging-in-Publication Data

Barbour, Bill, 1922–
   Home exchange vacationing : your guide to free accommodations /
   Bill and Mary Barbour ; illustrated by Al Hartley.
      p. cm.
   Rev., updated, and expanded ed. of: Trading places, c1991.
   ISBN 1-55853-389-3 (pbk.)
   1. Vacation homes. 2. Home exchanging. I. Barbour, Mary, 1924– .
  II. Barbour, Bill, 1922– Trading places. III. Title.
  HD7289.2.B37 1996
  643'.2—dc20   95-51059
                                            CIP

Printed in the United States of America.

1 2 3 4 5 6 7 8 9—99 98 97 96

*This book is dedicated to the 1,125 experienced home
exchangers who participated in the authors' several
international vacation home exchange surveys—undertaken
with the cooperation of
Karl Costabel of Vacation Exchange Club,
Key West, Florida;
and Heather Anderson, of HomeLink International (GB),
Virginia Water, Surrey, England.*

*The wealth of information and up-to-date data gleaned from
these surveys represents the very fabric of this book and the
fiber that binds its chapters together.*

Contents

Preface

WHAT'LL WE DO FOR A VACATION THIS YEAR?" This was the question we'd asked ourselves every year for decades, and the same question is being asked by millions of vacationers the world over. Skiing in New England . . . a cottage on the seashore . . . visiting Washington, Williamsburg, or Boston . . . a cruise to anywhere . . . Paris in the spring . . . New Hampshire in the fall . . . a car trip to Florida's Gulf Coast. Yes, conventional vacations. We had tried all these and a parade of others.

At the time of our retirement in 1983 from forty years in book publishing, we first heard of home exchanging—vacationers exchanging their homes with other vacationers. The idea intrigued us!

Learning more about this totally different holiday concept convinced us to try home exchanging. The questions about where to go still came up, but now there was the added question: With whom could we exchange homes? We found that home exchange opportunities were as wide as the United States and even went far, far beyond.

There were opportunities to live in an apartment high above Kowloon and Hong Kong Island . . . to find ancestral homes in Germany, Greece, Ireland, Rhode Island . . . to tour off the beaten track in England's Lake District . . . to shop for arts and crafts in Santa Fe, New Mexico . . . to watch kangaroos just outside the door in Australia's outback . . . to enjoy daily swims in a private pool overlooking a fishing village tucked away on Spain's Costa Brava . . . to ski from a chalet in Canada's Laurentians or Utah's Sun Valley. All of these fabulous vacation spots became available to use through home exchanging.

Our first home exchange vacation was in Portugal, a villa overlooking the Mediterranean, the second home of a New Jersey tax attorney. This exchange partner and his wife had a memorable vacation at our Sanibel Island condominium in Florida. Over the years that followed, we totally enjoyed more than eighty home exchange vacation arrangements: many visits to London, the Far East, South Africa, Scandinavia and nearly all of Continental Europe, England, Scotland, Wales, and seashores near and far in the States.

Those people truly committed to home exchanging—some might call it an addiction—often have half a dozen or more exchanges each year. A lot of traveling? Yes, but during our professional years, domestic and foreign travel had become a way of life for us.

Home exchangers are quite correct when they say, The key to your home opens the door to unique and adventure-filled vacations, worldwide. Other catch phrases include: Just your airfare, and you're there . . . Exchanging is like walking in the shoes of another culture . . . Twice the vacation for half the price . . . It has completely changed our lives! Today, countless thousands of vacationers are experiencing "new-look" holidays. Their secret? The home exchange concept.

The thirty-two chapters that follow trace in depth the philosophy of the "live-in" vacation, the best ways for home exchangers to contact each other, tested new holiday destinations for the twentieth and twenty-first centuries, and how everyone can experience fully this new approach to total vacation enjoyment. It's all here: Different types of home exchanges, "step-parenting" pets, swapping cars (75 percent of home exchangers do), how to prepare your home for exchange partners and how to live in theirs, taking along your children or your grandchildren, do's and don'ts in exchanging, the upside and the downside of home exchanging, insurance and home exchanging, an entire chapter on the inevitable question, and much, much more.

Some very special features of this book can be found in the first-person stories of seventeen experienced, noteworthy home exchangers. The eye-catching drawings by Al Hartley, well-known illustrator of the "Archie" comics, depict various aspects of home exchanging. The reference section includes a directory of professional services available to home exchangers, guide letters and forms for use in home exchange communications, and a valuable checklist to make home exchanging easy and enjoyable.

More than one thousand experienced vacation exchangers from the United States and forty countries responded to an international vacation home exchange survey. This book arose from the wealth of information and data provided by these survey participants—exchangers who over the years have experienced more than four thousand worldwide exchanges, making this one of the most authoritative books available on home exchanging.

Our first home exchange-related book, *Trading Places* (1991), went through three printings in four years. This book adds ten new chapters with home exchanging accounts from every continent, half again as many exchange hints and helps, and provides an in-depth, up-to-date preview of what might very well develop into your best-ever vacation.

Two years in the writing, we have designed this book for vacationers everywhere, in particular (1) to bring the global home exchange concept into sharper focus for those seeking something different from the conventional vacations of yesteryear and (2) to challenge those currently home exchanging to enhance their experiences with more exciting, more fun-filled, more adventure-packed exchange opportunities.

We would like to express our special gratitude to Larry Stone and the entire staff of Rutledge Hill Press, to editor-writer Toni Sortor, to research editor Anne Bellew, and to Shirley Francess Secretariat.

CHAPTER 1

The Vacation Home Exchange Concept

HOME EXCHANGING MAKES FOR THE BEST VACA-tions my wife and I have ever had. Living among the 'natives,' local shopping, and meeting people not part of the tourist service industry are the best parts of all," writes a Brooklyn, New York, physician who has exchanged in Italy and France.

"The concept is phenomenal. . . . We believe exchanging homes brings an otherwise suspicious, avoidance-oriented world closer together," noted an exchanging financial planner and his R.N. wife in Hancock, New Hampshire.

Each year up to two hundred thousand people in the United States, Canada, Great Britain, Europe, South Africa, Australia, New Zealand, and elsewhere in the world are actively engaging in vacation home exchanging. Furthermore, the surveys show the home exchange universe has been growing at the rate of 20 percent annually. Such large numbers seem to confirm the fact that vacation home exchanging (or "house swapping," as the British say) is becoming a here-and-now, worldwide vacation concept worthy of vacationers' earnest consideration.

> In principle, home exchange is simple: two families from different parts of the country—or different corners of the world—schedule their vacations in such a way as to arrange to swap their houses, apartments, or condominiums. The exchange can be as short as a weekend or as long as a few months or more. (*AAA World*)

Certainly there is nothing really new about exchanging. Prehistoric man traded crudely made weapons for food, animal skins, firewood, and other basics to living in that age. Down through the centuries, exchanging became a way of life. Although it has to a large extent been replaced by the use of currency, exchanging remains a viable means for people everywhere to obtain perceived needs and desired items.

There is little recorded history of the home exchange concept. However, *Signature* magazine (the periodical of Diner's Club, International) claims that in the sixteenth century, "Ambassadors to the French court had a housing problem. They couldn't stay in hotels; hotels as we know them today didn't exist. Neither did rented accommodations. So they hit on an ingenious solution. They swapped residences with their ambassadorial counterparts from the French court." The idea has caught on today.

> If you want all the creature comforts and conveniences of home when you're on holiday, then swapping your house, hairdryer (and even the cat!) with someone, somewhere else in the world can be the perfect solution. (*The Women's Journal,* London, England)

The development of modern-day home exchanging in the United States, Europe, and elsewhere dates back to the 1950s and 1960s, when several organizations—vacation home exchange clubs—published annual directories that included, for a modest fee, complete information with names and addresses about those desiring to exchange their homes. As the years passed and thousands of vacationers learned of the great advantages of home exchanging, each of those long-established organizations publishing listing directories sensed the need for more than a single directory each year. Now these larger clubs issue up to five directories annually, some with up to six thousand listings per issue worldwide.

> Here's the basic idea: You make arrangements with another family, leave the keys, and travel to each other's houses. There you stay rent-free, taking care of plants and cats, enjoying meals and other comforts just as you would at home, but surrounded by the sights and experiences of an entirely new town, region or country. (*Investors Business Daily*)

With these pacesetter clubs successfully enabling vacation home exchangers to contact other exchangers, a number of other home exchange clubs were established during the 1970s, 1980s, and early 1990s. Some of these clubs offer more regional listings, and others are worldwide in their scope of home exchange offerings. Collectively, all of these various exchange directories now provide countless vacation

home exchange opportunities, and exchangers today have at their fingertips resources that can put them in touch with unlimited numbers of other potential exchangers worldwide. These resources have served as the springboard for the quite astonishing growth of the vacation home exchange concept, especially during the past decade.

> As long as the potential home exchanger is flexible and patient while making the arrangements, vacation home exchanging can prove an enjoyable and an economical alternative to hotels. (*Fort Myers [Fla.] News-Press*)

What is it about vacation home exchanging that attracts large numbers of families who have never previously exchanged homes and motivates even larger numbers of experienced home exchanging families to engage in vacation home exchanges time after time, year after year?

Well, the surveys reveal that two basic elements of home exchanging seem to motivate most vacationers: the relatively low cost and living in a *home* away from home. Regarding the matter of cost, a mechanical engineer from Istanbul, Turkey, writes: "If you vacation in hotels, it's so expensive to sleep and to eat. But when you have a home exchange, you pay only the airfare and the regular expenses of living at home." A television person in Nunawading, Australia, recommends: "Home exchange is a great way for the fixed-income, retired person to travel anywhere in the world."

> Savings on lodging alone add up to as much as $3,000 a couple for a two-week vacation in Europe. (*Money* magazine)

Three-time exchangers in Europe, a Churchville, Pennsylvania, couple—college professors who travel with their two children—write, "Vacation home exchanging has been a great opportunity for us, one allowing us to enjoy vacations with our whole family that we could not have afforded otherwise." In this same vein, a Manchester, Connecticut, family, having exchanged twice in England, arranged to have their older children (and their spouses) travel with them, providing inexpensive family reunions that were enjoyed by all.

A manufacturer's representative and three-time exchanger living in Minneapolis, Minnesota, puts it more succinctly: "In home exchange, you get more bang for your vacation buck!"

> Many first-time home exchangers worry about leaving behind their china, silver, and other expensive items, but theft in home exchanging is rarely a problem. Most exchangers feel their possessions are much safer than they would be if their houses weren't occupied. (*Modern Maturity*)

Along with the relatively low cost, home exchangers are of one voice in preferring home living over vacationing in hotels, motels, or rented cottages. For example, the deputy headmaster of a school in Scotland (who has exchanged in Spain and the United States) writes, "Holiday home exchanging is a wonderful way of truly getting the 'feel' of a country, which, as a two-week tourist, one could never achieve." A Seattle, Washington, screenwriter, who has exchanged in Hawaii, England, and Scotland, writes: "Vacation home exchanging gives one a chance to stretch out and to truly relax and feel *at home* in the home of one's exchange partner." Finally, after three exchanges in England and one in

Switzerland ("Florida is next on our exchange list"), a civil engineer in Seville, Spain, writes: "I think home exchanging is the best way to visit and to know a country. The best hotel in town is 'nothing' compared to living in a regular home."

All members of a given family may not necessarily be equally enthusiastic about taking that first "giant" vacation home exchange step. A woman in Lima, Peru, writes, "Our two teenagers and I were excited about the possibility of home exchanging; my main problem was getting my husband, a physician, to participate. But we did finally home exchange in a small city, Kempton, Germany. I felt like we were a part of the place. It will always be special. I hate going from hotel to hotel; it may be interesting at the start of a vacation trip, but after 'hotel-ing' for three weeks or so, I just can't take it anymore! Yes, vacation home exchanging is the *only* way to go."

> Thousands of Americans are enthusiastic about exchanging homes while traveling within the United States or abroad. First, it sharply reduces travel expenses, because accommodations are free. Second, instead of having to dine out, you can prepare whatever meals you wish in your own kitchen. Third, exchanges often include use of the family car. (*New York Times*)

And talk about unusual, stimulating vacations! How about the family from Big Sky, Montana, whose Caribbean exchange "home" turned out to be a forty-two-foot sloop, which came fully equipped with a captain and first mate? Then there's the retired New York City couple who arranged a fifteen-week chain of vacation home exchanges in six different European countries. A retired book publisher and his wife languished for a week in a million-dollar, twenty-eighth-floor penthouse—a veritable museum of priceless art—overlooking Florida's luxury resort of Turnberry Isle. The director of a nursery school in Orleans, Massachusetts, along with her husband and two sons used home exchanging in various ways, that is, to Florida, the gathering place for their in-laws' fiftieth wedding anniversary (with lovely trays and lace tablecloths courtesy of their exchange hostess); to be with their son—a student at Tanglewood in Massachusetts; to visit Disneyland in California; and to visit Civil War sites and do genealogical research in western Maryland. New Jersey exchangers spent six weeks high in the hills of Hong Kong Island, with a panoramic view of that busy harbor and the shopping mecca of Kowloon. This was their first exchange with a prepaid live-in maid, who not only did the cooking and the house cleaning but all the shopping and laundry as well.

There are many benefits to house swapping. For one, it's a good way to save money. You pay nothing for the house, and you can prepare meals at home if you choose. Another plus: Some exchangers like the security of having guests in their home while they're away. (*Horizons,* by American Express)

Webster's Ninth New Collegiate Dictionary defines *serendipity* as "the faculty of finding valuable or agreeable things not sought after." An English widow of six years experienced a vacation home exchange serendipity some years ago. The listing of her Buckinghamshire home in a home exchange directory put this woman in touch with exchangers living in New Zealand. There is nothing unusual about home exchangers contacting other exchangers who live halfway around the world, but as this woman writes, "This story has an especially happy ending: I sold my home in England and moved to New Zealand, where I married one of my home exchange partners!"

From Cos Cob, Connecticut, a book manufacturer writes: "Our Hawaiian home exchange a few years ago resulted in a business opportunity for my wife, who is now North American representative for a ladies fashion house owned by our Hawaiian home exchange partner."

If you can't live without a sauna and a pool (although some exchange homes have one or both), then vacation home exchanging may not be for you. If you're reasonably flexible and like more than just traveling superficially, a home exchange provides a great deal of satisfaction. (*Denver Post*)

An Oklahoma City registered nurse, on returning from a month of home exchanging in the Dominican Republic, reported: "I was completely spoiled with a maid who had my breakfast ready when I wanted it and was willing to prepare for our guests with only a few hours' notice. But the best part of this exchange was we could swim every morning in our exchange partner's pool. I shall never forget that trip!"

Thousands of people vacation home exchange every year. They find each other in various of the home exchange directories. They report that their houses are returned to them clean, with laundry done, and the plants watered; that they were much more comfortable than they would have been in a hotel; that they saved a good deal of money; and that they saw much more of local life than they could have as conventional tourists. (*Christian Science Monitor*)

"Wanting to vacation on the other side of the world, we wrote to exchangers in New Zealand, who had actually moved to Australia, where they eventually received our letter. The result: a memorable Australian vacation, among the highlights of which was being invited to a New Year's Eve party along with ten neighboring couples." So writes a news reporter in Silver Springs, Maryland, who, with his wife and children, have enjoyed fifteen different vacation home exchange experiences.

> Whether you prefer the excitement of Manhattan, the loveliness of Paris, or a Colorado Rocky Mountain high, you can vacation in all of them for less than you ever imagined, if you catch the home exchange fever. (*Good Morning America*)

Having exchanged in four U.S. states, the Virgin Islands, Mexico, France, and Italy, an East Falmouth, Massachusetts, teacher exclaims: "The vacation home exchange experience heralded a new dimension in my travel life."

A London, England, family of five writes, "We've had eight home exchanges—from Denmark and Norway to Wyoming and Saskatchewan (and other places in between). The most amazing offers drop through the letterbox from February through June. In vacation home exchange, 'the world is your oyster'; you can go anywhere!"

> Exchanging homes lets one enjoy being a tourist while living like a native. (*New Choices*)

An engineer in Honolulu, with more than thirty years of home exchanging experience says, "We are into our second generation of exchangees—the adult children of families with whom we traded homes years ago are coming to visit us now."

While many happy endings (and very few unhappy ones) result from vacation home exchanging, the facts are that low cost, flexibility in planning, new friendships made while living in a home away from home, and the downright fun and adventure of it all are among the more important reasons why, with each passing year, more and more families and single travelers are becoming a part of the worldwide vacation home exchanging community.

CHAPTER 2

People Who Tried It . . . and Liked It

The Hales family—Tony and Julia—now live in Great Britain, West Wales. Tony, who was managing director of a London advertising agency, retired early. When not working on his house, he likes to spend his spare time fishing, sailing, and home exchanging. Julia, a former journalist and medical secretary, now a homemaker, is a great home exchange fan and loves to travel. The Hales have two married daughters and three grandchildren.

Chalk up one "first" for the Hales: they included two home-exchanging months in their recent round-the-world trip. Globe-encircling home exchangers, indeed.

The Hales write:

Tony retired from the world of advertising at the age of forty-nine. At last we had freedom. Our elder daughter had her own apartment near London and was working as a secretary for an insurance company. Our younger one was away at university.

Of course, we had traveled in the past, but due to the pressure of business, only for a couple of weeks in the summer and a couple in winter.

Package holidays were never really satisfactory. We had tried cruises. We had traveled up the coast of Norway on a small cargo boat. We had even gotten as far as western Australia, but always time was too short. Now we had all the time in the world.

We bought a modern three-bedroom house in a small Cornish fishing village. It was delightful in the summer, but the cold, wet, windy winters were depressing, so we decided we would go away each winter for two, three, or even four months.

Then we realized what it would cost to rent apartments and houses and cars for such a long period. It was time to think again.

Home exchange could be the answer, said Julia. There was an advertisement in the newspaper for a directory published by HomeLink, Great Britain. We sent for it, and a new and exciting world was opened up for us.

Home exchange would give us the opportunity to travel to other countries and become temporary residents, not tourists or holiday makers. We would get to know the locals and understand their ways of life and customs.

We adopted a relaxed attitude toward the idea of exchanging. We weren't worried about people staying in our house or using our car. If they damaged something, no doubt they would replace it or pay for it. If not, too bad.

Our first exchangers were a delightful couple from Florida. They were experienced exchangers and must have been rather surprised by the speed with which we welcomed them to Cornwall and rather abruptly departed. We were so anxious not to intrude on their privacy that we spent the night in a hotel in the next village before leaving for a holiday in Wales. Later that year, we all met again at their second home in Florida and have since become very good friends.

By the time we exchanged again, we had moved to Wales. While on holiday, we had discovered a delightful little village on the West Coast. Situated on the banks of the Teifi estuary, it was near the ruins of an abbey founded in 1115, had an old water mill producing traditional stone-ground flour, three inns, and a vast, sandy beach just one and a half miles away. It was ideal.

But would any exchangers want to come to Wales? People didn't seem to know enough about it. On one occasion, we were asked if it was near London!

Taking advantage of Tony's advertising experience, we put together a package. Photos of the inside and outside of the house, the garden, and the surrounding countryside were included, together with leaflets and brochures about the village, local beaches, castles, sporting activities, etc., and of course about Wales itself.

Perhaps we overdid it slightly, but if you have a proposition you might as well make it as attractive as possible. A letter of two or three paragraphs is not enough. Having said that, it might well be enough if your house is on the beach in California or Hawaii . . . but in Wales, on the banks of the Teifi?

Our efforts to arrange Florida exchanges were successful, and for the next few years we had holidays in Key West, Marathon, Naples,

Sanibel Island, Anna Maria Island, St. Petersburg, and Orlando. All were successful, and each had its own excitement. Traveling from Orlando to Fort Myers on a Greyhound bus was one. Our hosts thought it rather an odd thing to do. To us, it was romantic—at least it was until the bus's air conditioning broke down.

We were taken sailing on a magnificent thirty-four-foot Westerly. A superb day. Tony was taken fishing in our exchanger's motor launch. That was exciting, too, particularly when they became lost in the maze of waterways crisscrossing a large mangrove area. The tide was falling, and they had visions of spending the night there and being eaten alive by mosquitoes. They went aground several times, and each time the owner heroically leaped into the water and pushed the boat off the mud. Tony rather nervously stayed on board, looking out for snakes and alligators. Then, motoring slowly up a narrow, twisty channel that seemed to lead nowhere, the boat came round a bend and into the main channel. More by luck than judgment, our captain and his mate had made it.

Guard dogs made our exchange on the Florida Keys rather different. The property shared a garden area with the house next door. This meant that whenever we went in or out, we had to get past two enormous Doberman dogs. We were introduced to them, and they sniffed all round us. We were assured they would know us in the future. We would creep in and out, hoping they wouldn't notice us, but we never managed it. They were too smart. We never made friends, but at least they accepted us.

We always exchange cars, and in Florida we have had everything from enormous Cadillacs down to subcompacts. One of the problems is that everyone drives everywhere and sometimes it's difficult to get enough exercise. On Anna Maria Island, we were delighted to have two bicycles on which to explore the island. We also found an ice rink in a nearby town and thoroughly enjoyed gliding around in the coolness of the rink while the temperature outside was more than ninety degrees. We made a friend of the proprietor, who was amazed to have people from Wales turn up. He insisted on giving us coffee and cakes in his office whenever we went there.

At Naples, we rented a small motor launch and spent many happy hours fishing, picnicking, and just lazing around on the water. Very relaxing.

Key West was so different. Very lively in the evenings and full of unusual characters who seemed to appear only at night. Daytime was peaceful and pleasant, and we were able to explore some of the fascinating old houses. Harry S Truman, Ernest Hemingway, famous sailboat skippers, and even wreckers all had opulent homes in Key West.

Orlando was another success. We thought it might be just for children, but we were wrong and thoroughly enjoyed it. In fact, we have been back on two later occasions. Epcot—Experimental Prototype Community of Tomorrow—was a fascinating look at new technology. Universal Studios and Disney-MGM were of particular interest to Tony, who had been involved in producing films during his advertising days.

In fact, all of our Florida trips were great successes. We soon settled in and found our way about. The people were friendly and welcoming, the homes and apartments were luxurious, and the weather was nearly always perfect.

Driving was no problem. With wide roads, low speed limits, cars with automatic transmissions and power steering, it was really quite easy.

Home exchanging had given us some marvelous holidays in Florida, but we felt we were getting in a rut. It was time to go farther afield.

Our ambition was to do a round-the-world trip, and finally we made it. We flew from London to San Francisco, to Hawaii, to Auckland, to Sydney, to Adelaide, to Singapore, and back to London. In between we managed two lengthy exchanges: a month on the Hawaiian island of Oahu and a month in Australia at Mount Compass, a small village south of Adelaide on the Fleurieu Peninsula.

Hawaii was magnificent. Everything we hoped it would be. We were delighted to find our exchange home was on the unspoiled Northern Coast, well away from the skyscrapers and multilane highways of Honolulu. The beaches, the dark and misty mountains, and the crashing surf meant that our stock of film soon needed replenishing. The tourist attractions of Polynesian feasts, dances, recreations of old lifestyles, and so on were very enjoyable, but the most memorable occasion was a visit to Pearl Harbor. We were both very moved by the experience, and it is one we shall always remember.

At Adelaide airport we were met by our Australian exchangers, who drove us to their magnificent home just outside the village of Mount Compass. It was secluded and reached by a narrow road leading up through the woods. After showing us how to pump water from the well into the supply tanks and how to operate the irrigation system for the garden, our exchange partners gave us a few words of advice about snakes and spiders that might be found lurking in the under-growth. When they were satisfied we could cope, they hitched their trailer to their second car and went off to spend the month in a resort farther north.

Left to ourselves, we decided to explore the whole of the Fleurieu Peninsula. We loved it. The roads were almost empty, and the scenery was so varied: one moment rugged hills and parched plains, then thick forests, and then a bend in the road would bring us to lush, green farm-land. The towns and villages were small, and the people friendly and helpful, particularly when they discovered we were English. The area is not geared up for overseas tourists, which means it is delightfully unspoiled. The magnificent beaches were often quite empty.

We couldn't leave Australia without spending a few days in Ade-laide. We drove to the city center, found a hotel (unusual for home exchangers), and parked the car. We didn't need it again until we left. Our timing could have been better, since there was a heat wave and the temperature was in the upper nineties—almost unbearable for exploring. However, we managed a very interesting tour of the city by tram, visited several museums, went on the river, and were lucky enough to get two tickets for the theater. Tony achieved an ambition when he spent a day at Adelaide Oval watching South Australia play cricket.

All too soon it was time to return to the United Kingdom, where we would be kept busy preparing for our exchangers' arrival. When they arrive, we move out of our house and into a small self-contained annex. This enables us to collect them from the station and show them over the house and around the village. From then on, it depends on what kind of holiday they want. Some prefer complete privacy and want to do their own thing. This is fine. All we do is perhaps meet for an occasional meal together. Others are more gregarious and ask us to accompany them on their trips around Wales and spend more time together. Whatever they choose, we feel we should do everything we can to make sure our exchangers enjoy the time they spend in our home.

It's been said that home exchanging introduces a new dimension into one's life. Absolutely correct. For the cost of transportation only, we have (literally) traveled the world and have truly "lived" the cul-tures of each of our home exchange destinations. We view home exchanging as something more than a holiday concept: It's an adven-turous lifestyle!

Maggie and Bob Hanusa moved to Maui, Hawaii, in 1973 from Iowa, where Bob had grown up and was a partner in the family plumbing and hardware business. Maggie hailed from northern California and was the homemaker for the growing family.

She was thrilled to be chosen as one of the one hundred finalists eligible to go to Honolulu for the 1971 Pillsbury Bake-Off. This was their first trip to Hawaii, and after seventy-two hours on the island of Maui, they decided to make this their new home. The next year they made the move with four of their five children, ages seven to seventeen. The oldest had graduated from high school and was continuing in college on the mainland. Two of their three daughters still live on Maui, as do two of their six grandchildren.

Hanusa Plumbing Service was established soon after the move, and the demand for Bob's services (mainly repair and remodeling jobs) kept him extremely busy. He worked by himself with Maggie serving as company secretary-bookkeeper. Her pay was dinner out once a week.

Vacations were few and far between during the first twelve years when the children were growing up and the business going full blast. Trips to the mainland about once a year were mostly to visit family but usually included some fun things such as hiking, white-water rafting, and sightseeing.

Maggie Hanusa writes:

When our youngest child left home ten years ago, we vowed that we weren't going to sit around and get old—that, as our means, opportunities, and health permitted, we would travel to the "ends of the earth." Adventure and independent travel are more appealing to us than traveling with tour groups and staying in large, fancy hotels. Thus, the concept of exchanging homes and cars sounded like the perfect way to go. In 1984 we began our "career" in home exchanging. It has infinitely broadened our lives to a new world of travel, adventures, challenges, and many new friends.

Our first time out was to the New England states in the fall, when the leaves were ablaze with color. Our comfortable exchange home was in a town with a population of two thousand—definitely not a big city and no big-city traffic. We met local people by going to craft fairs and fall dinners. Our hosts offered us the use of their vacation home on Cape Cod, and we stayed there a few days, too.

To date we've made twenty-two home-car exchanges and have had no disasters, only many different experiences—some funny, some odd, almost all good, and some great. Arrangements have been made through directories, newspaper ads, and church bulletins. Newspaper ads could be risky, but we felt pretty confident placing them in New Zealand, Iceland, and small-town South Dakota papers. However, when placing an ad, be sure you ask the price of the ad! Bob placed a one-column-one-inch ad in the Reykjavik, Iceland, paper to run seven times. What was charged to our Visa account? $840!

Correspondence, phone calls, and faxes are used as means of communication, and I feel I have pretty good judgment about people. So far, we've had some very fine people in our home and continue to keep in touch with some of them. If at all possible, we try to meet our exchangers—at our home, their home, or wherever. We almost always wish these get-togethers could be longer (or sooner—we met one couple a year after our exchange with them).

Exchanging homes is a matter of mutual trust. Housekeeping standards may differ (I don't expect to find everything in place in the kitchen when we return). Over the years I've made up a loose-leaf binder of notes on various things about our home and its appliances, the location of the fuse box and water shut-off, who to call for what, etc. Our blender base unscrews for cleaning, for example; all of them don't, we discovered on one trip. I suggest that people work with food on the garbage-disposer side of the sink. If they plug up the drain on the other side with food scraps, I advise them that this is their responsibility.

On a New Zealand exchange, in addition to the car, we also had a small camper van at our disposal, and in Iceland we had the use of a four-wheel-drive vehicle for out-of-town use. (I am so grateful Bob has that special ability to get in any car and drive it as if he's driven it for ages—no matter what side of the road it's driven on or where the driver sits.) We've had everything from Cadillacs to Metros. One Cadillac was a 1972—a veritable tank—but it got us where we needed to go. Another time we had someone's new car well broken in by the time they got home. Someone else broke in a new car for us some years ago: when we left home it had six hundred miles on it; when we returned, it had two thousand. Quite a feat in a three-week period, since Maui has only six hundred miles of roads!

In Czechoslovakia we were in a home on the very outskirts of Prague and looked out across miles of wheat fields. (This was a hospitality exchange, but our host family has yet to make it to our home after four years.) The public transportation system made a car unnecessary on this trip. Prices were very reasonable in Prague, but communism had left most store clerks with a very surly, I-don't-care attitude. It did not seem to matter to them whether they sold anything or not. They were very suspicious, and in a small store where tourists don't normally go, we were watched like hawks. At the time, communism had been gone for less than eight months, which made our visit to Czechoslovakia most interesting. We learned much about their ways and what was going on from our hosts and consider the hospitality exchange a real bonus in a country so different from ours.

Since our home is no longer childproof, we'd rather not open it to small children. As nonsmokers, we prefer nonsmokers. One time I was working with a couple in their seventies on a possible exchange. After several letters and phone conversations, we agreed to go ahead—both being very adamant about no children on either side. About a month before the exchange, a letter came from them with an outline of the things we had agreed to. I was shocked when they said eight people would be coming to Maui, but I was flabbergasted to read that three of the eight would be their very young grandchildren. I canceled. Pet care is definitely not for us, and I so state. Nevertheless, on two occasions we've found we had a cat to care for and wound up buying cat food both times—once even having to buy a can opener to open it. That particular cat threw up all over the living room carpet and then wouldn't eat for days. I now attempt to double- and triple-check to make absolutely sure there are no animals to deal with on an exchange.

In the introductory letter I send out, I describe our home, the area, and ourselves. Since television seems to be such an essential part of almost everyone's life, I do put in the letter that a television does not fit into our lifestyle and there is none in our house. I also state that we certainly don't object to our guests renting one, and in my loose-leaf binder is the name of a friend who rents televisions and has brought many through our door.

A couple of times we've done an exchange so that I could make a wedding cake. When our older son announced he was marrying a gal from a small South Dakota town, I got the idea that we might be able to arrange a home exchange for the wedding so I could make the wedding cake. The Midwest couple who responded to our newspaper ad never dreamed they would ever have a Hawaiian vacation for essentially the price of their airfare. They went by themselves (that is, no children) to our home but consented to thirteen of our family staying in their house—including four small children aged one month to four years.

On another such "cake trip"—for my niece's wedding this time—I discovered during preliminary correspondence that the lady of the house also decorated cakes. She offered me the use of all her pans, equipment, and cake stand, which eliminated at least two extra pieces of luggage from the massive pile that came off the baggage conveyor in the airport.

People have asked us, "Why would you want to go to Iceland? What on earth is there to see there?" We loved its stark beauty. There were few trees, but waterfalls came from every nook and cranny. We got to try puffin (a local bird sold in supermarkets), but I don't think we'd like it for a daily diet. During our stay, we took a one-day trip to a small village in Greenland and got in on the excitement of a whale hunt. Our hosts' relatives served us an Icelandic Christmas dinner in August, and friends of ours on Maui served our exchangers one of our typical Christmas dinners.

Our love of hiking has brought us many "mountaintop" experiences. One of our favorite places is New Zealand, and one of our more famous hikes was tramping the Milford Track there. Our five-week exchange in Nelson was one we simply did not want to leave. The location was lovely, the hiking was great, the home we were in was beautiful—albeit having a "different" kitchen. The lady of the house must have spent little time there. Salt and pepper were the full extent of the herb-spice assortment, and we had to buy a can opener and a paring knife. (I now bring some of my own basic things—knife, peeler, can opener, etc.) The neighbors on either side were just great and would regularly bring us fresh-caught fish and wild pig chops.

The unexpected can always turn up at the last minute—or almost the last minute—as it has for us on several occasions. Arrangements were complete for an exchange in Scotland when our hosts had something come up less than a month before our scheduled departure. I just got busy, went through the directories, and made phone calls until I found a couple who just jumped at the chance for a Hawaiian holiday. The location wasn't our first choice, but it worked out fine. The original couple gave us a lot of help with arrangements and even had us stay with them for a few days.

Just this past year I was in the hospital battling an infection at the time we were scheduled to take off once more for New Zealand. Our guests-hosts had left home almost a week before and were out of touch. They found out when they arrived on Maui that they would have to share our house with us and we would not be going to theirs. Fortunately (at least to all appearances) they didn't seem to mind. We had them use our phone to call home and make arrangements about their now-empty house—plant watering, etc. We gave them our car, and basically, they just did their own thing. Our guest room is large, downstairs by itself, and away from our quarters, so they even had some privacy.

It's my feeling that it is foolhardy to try to make provision in the beginning for remote eventualities—to try to cover the possibility that one party can't make it. Life is an adventure, travel is an adventure, home exchanging is an adventure: One never knows for sure exactly what is going to happen or what the circumstances will be, and it seems a waste of energy to try to deal with exigencies before one has to. If something does happen to foul things up, it can usually be worked out. (Admittedly, Hawaii is a prime exchange area, so we have fewer problems with rearranging things.)

Why do we like home exchanging? We don't like hotels and the feeling that we have to go somewhere so the maid can clean the room. We greatly prefer the relaxed style of living in a home and meeting the neighbors, friends, and family. Almost always we have instant contact with friends or relatives. Many times there have been great neighbors who have told us about the places we should see and the neat things we should do—nontouristy things. We drive a local car and feel as though we're part of the community, doing the things locals do. If we want to stay at home one day with our feet up, we can. We can do our own cooking, try all sorts of "foreign" foods, and shop in what to us are often "exotic" neighborhood markets. It's fun and occasionally even challenging (cats, cat food, can openers, etc.) to go into someone else's home and live there for an extended period of time . . . and I haven't even mentioned the enormous savings in vacation expenses.

Hosting and exchanging have brought many interesting people from around the world into our home and taken us into theirs. After ten-plus years of doing this, we have contacts and friends almost anywhere we would want to go and are always looking forward to the next adventure—the next mountaintop.

CHAPTER 3

Meet Mr. and Mrs. Homer Exchanger

EARLY ON IN THIS BOOK IT WOULD SEEM APPROPRIate to focus on the vacation home exchanger. Who are these home exchange people? Are they young people, middle-agers, or older folks? Where do they live? How many are retired? What about their occupations and professions? What is their vacation home exchange experience? When did they start exchanging? How many times have they exchanged?

The data developed from the surveys, in which more than one thousand experienced vacation home exchangers participated, provides a definitive answer to each of these questions and serves as an authoritative resource for exploring other aspects of the vacation home exchange experience.

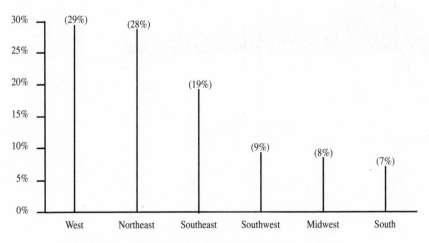

Chart A-1—Where U.S. vacation home exchangers reside

Rather than combining in this chapter the profile data covering U.S. exchangers and their counterparts elsewhere, the survey makes a distinction between these two groups. Not only are the facts and figures derived from the surveys of keen interest, but especially interesting are the differences between the U.S. and non-U.S. vacation home exchangers.

Where do these exchangers live? Specifically, in what sections of the United States do they live and where outside of the United States?

While there are home exchangers in all fifty states, Chart A-1 underscores the fact that three-quarters of the U.S. exchangers reside in the western, southeastern, and northeastern parts of the country. The Big Three states are California, Florida, and New York.

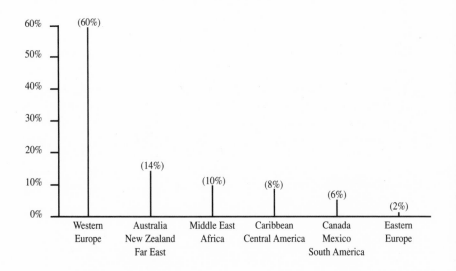

Chart A-2—Where non-U.S. vacation home exchangers reside

And where do the non-U.S. exchangers live? Chart A-2 shows, perhaps not surprisingly, that well over half of the exchangers outside the United States live in Western Europe. The largest number of Western European exchangers live in Great Britain. Germany and France are also high on this list.

Some have said that the vast majority of vacation home exchangers are retired, that the "golden oldies" have lots of time on their hands and, because of their fixed incomes, seek out "bargain" vacations. This is not

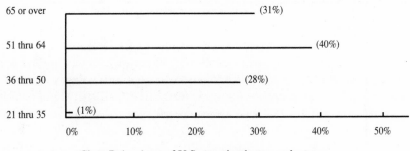

Chart B-1—Ages of U.S. vacation home exchangers

necessarily so. Indeed, Chart B-1 shows that nearly three-quarters of the U.S. home exchangers are in the fifty-one and over-sixty-five age groups, while just 28 percent of the non-U.S. exchangers are between the ages of thirty-six and fifty. Further, it is clear that non-U.S. exchangers start their vacation home exchanging at an earlier age than those in the U.S.: 10 percent of them start while they are between the ages of twenty-one and thirty-five, while only 1 percent of the U.S. exchangers start that young. Note too the percentage comparisons between the U.S. and non-U.S. exchangers in the fifty-one and over-sixty-five age groups, showing considerably higher percentages of U.S. exchangers in the latter category.

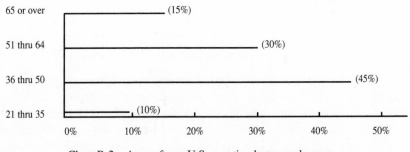

Chart B-2—Ages of non-U.S. vacation home exchangers

While some single persons do vacation home exchange with friends—widowed women who had home exchange experiences prior to their husbands' passing and others traveling alone—85 percent of home exchangers worldwide are married and travel as couples.

What about the occupations and professions of these vacation home exchangers? The forerunners of modern-day exchangers were the teachers of the 1960s. Why? Teachers have always had ten to twelve weeks of summer vacation and weeklong vacations at other times during the school year. A particularly economical way to travel, home exchanging has afforded teachers the opportunity to extend their vacations over longer periods of time, especially during the summer months. Finally, with more available vacation time, teachers also have more flexibility in their vacation planning. (Later chapters will underscore the key role flexibility plays in home exchanging.)

Increasingly, during the 1970s and the 1980s, couples and families in occupations and professions other than teaching latched onto the vacation home exchange concept. Currently, business executives and middle-management businesspeople top the worldwide list of exchangers' occupations and professions. Charts C-1 and C-2 project other interesting insights into the occupations of U.S. and non-U.S. exchangers.

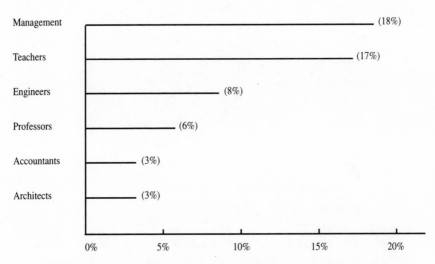

Chart C-1—Top six occupations/professions of U.S. vacation home exchangers

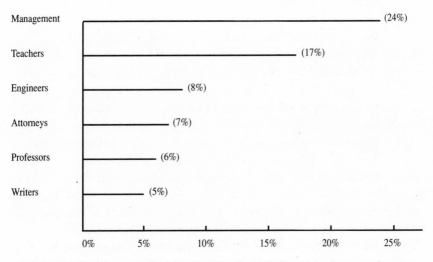

Chart C-2—Top six occupations/professions of non-U.S. vacation home exchangers

Not included in these charts are many other occupations and professions in which national and international home exchangers have been in, or are now engaged in, including:

railroad workers	veterinarians
insurance agents	fashion consultants
nurses	funeral directors
police officers	artists
dentists	flight attendants
auto mechanics	optometrists
secretaries	civil servants
farmers	ministers
social workers	lumberjacks
ballet teachers	bank managers
factory foremen	bus drivers
builders	

From this data, one can be reasonably sure that the vacation home exchange community includes men and women in nearly every conceivable occupation and profession, including owners of a fruit farm (apples, pears, and plums) in Staplehurst, an hour from London, England, who exchanged in Florida, and the Vacation Home Exchanging International Three U's: an *U*ndertaker in Whakatane, New Zealand; an *U*nemployed person in New York City; and an *U*nderground miner in Green River, Wyoming.

Some say that bed-and-breakfast travel first became popular in Great Britain long before the advent of the London Hilton and motel row near Heathrow Airport. Now this may well be true, but Chart D clearly shows today's Americans were active in home exchanging prior to non-U.S. exchangers. In fact, nearly two-fifths of today's U.S. exchangers had started vacationing home exchange style before 1980, as compared with only 10 percent of those exchangers living elsewhere in the world. Further, only one out of four U.S. exchangers has been exchanging only since 1990, while nearly half of the non-U.S. exchanges have been exchanging during the nineties.

The final element in profiling the experienced vacation home exchanger according to the survey is the number of actual "swaps" these people have had. In other words, just how experienced is the "experienced" vacation home exchanger? Chart E shows that one-third of U.S. exchangers have had either one or two exchanges, compared with

	U. S. exchangers	Non-U. S. exchangers
before 1980	16%	10%
1981 thru '85	26%	13%
1986 thru '90	30%	30%
since 1990	28%	47%

Chart D—Dates of first home exchanges

approximately one-half of their non-U.S. counterparts. Of interest, too, is the fact that 22 percent of U.S. exchangers have had ten or more different exchanges, while only 17 percent of non-U.S. exchangers have reached that milestone.

	U. S. exchangers	Non-U. S. exchangers
1 or 2 exchanges	32%	52%
3 thru 6 exchanges	33%	20%
7 thru 9 exchanges	13%	11%
10 or more exchanges	22%	17%

Chart E—Number of home exchanges completed

What's the most active home exchange nation in the world? The Netherlands holds this honor. This small nation (15.1 million) has the world's greatest number of home exchangers in proportion to its population.

This overview of vacation home exchangers projects a very clear picture of Mr., Mrs., and Ms. Vacation Home Exchanger, worldwide: (1) most U.S. exchangers live in California, Florida, and New York, while most of those living outside the U.S. reside in Great Britain, Germany, and France; (2) the greatest number are middle-aged (thirty-six to sixty-five years old); (3) their occupations and professions range as wide as the world itself; (4) 20 to 25 percent are retired persons; and (5) with an average of almost six exchanges each, most have been vacation home exchanging for more than ten years.

Of the more than one thousand exchangers participating in the surveys, many have second homes. Most of these prefer to exchange their second homes, while others exchange both their homes.

How do home exchangers "profile" each other? A ten-time exchanger (who moved to Sanibel Island, Florida, after a home exchange there) puts it this way: "We have always felt that vacation home exchangers are found only in a selected segment of society; that is, they are relatively well educated, stable, and interested in expanding their horizons."

The assumption can safely be made that home exchangers throughout the world have enjoyed participating in the vacation home exchange concept and are looking forward to home exchange as an important part of their future vacation plans.

CHAPTER 4

Unlimited Vacations—The Home Exchange Way

OVER THE YEARS, THE VACATION "HABITS" OF people have changed. A decade ago, for example, most vacations were two or three weeks in length and nearly always took place during the summer months.

In these "think leisure" 1990s, most working people are blessed with an increasing number of vacation weeks (three, four, or more) during any given year. Some people spread their vacation time over long weekends—short-notice family visits, ski trips, or just getting stuff done around the house. Others enjoy getting away for longer periods of time.

Families with school-age children and teachers still stick to vacationing in the summertime and/or enjoying shorter trips keyed around other school holidays. But retired persons, some professional men and women, and others are fortunate in being able to set their own vacation dates—winter, spring, fall, traditional holiday periods, or whenever they and their home exchange partners choose.

Regardless of how and when you plan your vacation, and whether you travel as a family, a couple, or an individual, the home exchange concept may well be just the ticket for your vacation enjoyment.

More than likely, spending your vacation living in someone else's home will be a new vacation experience for you and your family. But this is still a vacation, and for any vacation (home exchange or otherwise) a certain amount of advance planning is necessary.

Remember, if you home exchange, your vacation plans have to be dovetailed into those of your home exchange partners. For this reason, the earlier you begin your vacation planning, the better. Experienced home exchangers feel the amount of enjoyment received from a problem-free vacation is in direct proportion to the amount of advance planning that goes into home exchange vacation arrangements.

Before you actually start contacting potential home exchange partners, it is important to give a lot of thought to what you would consider your dream vacation. Do not waste time and energy initially on considering with whom you will be exchanging homes until you have put together—in detail and in writing for your own reference—when you would like to go, where you would like to go, how long you would like to stay, and so on. You do this realizing that in all likelihood you will be able to retain, through a proper home exchange arrangement, many (if not most) of the elements you consider important for your best-ever vacation.

Among the different aspects of vacationing home exchange style is the fact that, as has been previously emphasized, you will be paying nothing for the roof over your head. This cash saving can either be put in the bank, go toward a new jet ski, be spent on a twenty-fifth anniversary diamond, or be used to upgrade your dream vacation—from Boca Raton to Bermuda to Barbados or perhaps even to Barcelona.

So what are the most important elements of your dream vacation? Many of these are the same kinds of things you considered in planning previous vacations.

- When to go and how long to stay
- Where to go
- Facilities required
- Destination transportation
- Cost

When to Go and How Long to Stay

Summer . . . Christmas . . . Easter . . . the High Holidays . . . winter . . . a week . . . two weeks . . . a month or more. Perhaps you want to spend a week or two at the shore and then another week sightseeing in Washington, D.C. or Southern California. Maybe you'd prefer two weeks each in London and Paris, for instance, splitting your time between two (or more) vacation destinations.

Nearly half of American home exchangers vacation for three to four weeks at a time. Some 24 percent vacation for two weeks, 14 percent for one week, and another 14 percent for more than four weeks. (This latter category includes a large number of home exchangers in the

teaching profession and those who are retired.) Fifty-eight percent of non-U.S. exchangers vacation for three to four weeks, 16 percent for more than four weeks, 21 percent for two weeks, and only 3 percent for one week.

A Honolulu newspaper publisher with ten vacation home exchanges in Europe and the United States often coordinates his exchange dates with events he and his wife look forward to attending: Paris during the two hundredth anniversary of Bastille Day and London during the championships at Wimbledon (he stayed at the home of a banker whose home was directly across the road from the tennis club).

"I scheduled my vacation with home exchangers to coincide with a get-together with my daughter, who was attending boarding school," writes a Chevy Chase, Maryland, professor.

Where to Go

Where you go, of course, depends on what you want to get out of this dream vacation. What is your vacation concept: the mountains, the seashore, a quiet lakeside, nearness to family and/or children's activities, skiing, fishing, golf, tennis, or just plain relaxing—*any place?*

A botanist from Stockholm, Sweden, his wife, and their young child had an August home exchange in Greece. He writes: "The weather was catastrophically hot in Athens (107°F). My wife got sick—so sick that we went back to Stockholm after one week of a planned month-long vacation. Fortunately, we were able to stay with my parents-in-law, so our Greek exchange partners spent the full four weeks at our home." Do not let this happen to you. Before firming up vacation arrangements, check out the weather with your exchange partners, the local chamber of commerce, or the national tourist bureau serving your proposed destination.

People whose work involves travel have opportunities to tie a vacation home exchange into their business trips. New Yorkers, after attending a business convention in Minneapolis, might spend ten days or so fishing for walleye pike in the northern Minnesota lake district. A business trip to London, Paris, or Frankfurt affords an opportunity to vacation elsewhere in Europe.

Back to your dream vacation plans. Perhaps you are thinking of spending time in New Orleans . . . or western Canada . . . or Rome . . . or San Francisco . . . or Hong Kong . . . or Acapulco. Maybe you want to visit relatives in Peoria or Brooklyn. In your dream vacation planning, if you name a place, the chances are that someone living there (or near there) would consider your home and your locality in their dream vacation planning.

If your sights are set on a known vacation resort area, such as spring skiing at Vail, Colorado, basking in the winter sunshine at Boynton Beach, Florida, or visiting New England in the fall when the leaves are changing color, you may well find yourself confronted with a rental situation. Home exchanging condo owners often rent their condos during a given resort's high season. This is quite understandable from the owner's point of view but disappointing to vacation home exchanging purists.

Facilities Required

This is easy. How many adults and how many children are in your vacation party? Two adults and two teenagers? Okay, you will require three bedrooms and will hope to get two full bathrooms. On this matter of bedrooms, a printer from Kingsport, Tennessee, writes: "My wife and I prefer to sleep in separate bedrooms. When traveling on business, we of course cannot always afford a two-bedroom hotel or motel suite. But while vacation home exchanging, we always endeavor to get at least two bedrooms—and have yet to be disappointed."

Other basic elements may (or may not) be important to you: an elevator (if someone in your family has a bad knee), clothes washer and dryer, a wet bar, television, radio, VCR, air conditioning (a must in certain locations), necessary facilities for the handicapped, microwave oven, dishwasher, garage, nearby shopping, and public transportation.

"If it comes to flipping a coin," suggests a book salesman in Hillsdale, New Jersey, "between a home or second-home condo exchange, if one is talking about a two-week vacation, take the home. A home always comes fully equipped with all the basics: more living space, ample bedding, and all of the kitchen supplies, plus 'built-in' neighbors. Such is not always the case with a seldom-used condo."

Before you entered the wonderful world of vacation home exchanging, for your $1,500 (or more) a week at the shore you received a barebones, cramped cottage (no screens attached), very tired beds, a small refrigerator (with the freezer not working), a television (for an extra two bucks a day), and electricity, featuring an outdoor meter ticking away your precious vacation dollars. A home exchange vacation puts you in a lovely home or condominium with all the conveniences of your own home, and it is all yours to enjoy—for free.

Destination Transportation

If your vacation destination is, say, eight hundred to one thousand miles from your own home, you probably will want to take your own car. If, on the other hand, your sights are set on Hawaii, South America, or the Swiss Alps, there is a very good chance that car swapping with your home exchange partner could be a part of your exchange arrangement. Why pay hundreds of dollars a week for a rental car when you can drive your exchange partner's Volvo station wagon throughout your three-week home exchange vacation in Stockholm?

This exercise in mapping out your dream vacation will take more than a little thought, more than a little time. As a result, however, you will have established the most important guidelines for a successful vacation home exchange.

Cost

Exchangers from Jacksonville, Florida, enjoyed their vacation at Whitby Island in Washington. Later, their "host couple went into the bed-and-breakfast business. The house we stayed in for three weeks at no cost is now $125 per night!" As vacation home exchangers, you need not budget for hotels, motels, or cottages by the sea. If you drive, you will have gas and tolls to consider, and if you fly or go by train or bus, these fares must also be figured in.

Along with that of transportation, the cost of food is a major element in your vacation budget. Home exchangers always have breakfast and nearly always have lunch at home. And dinners? Well, this depends entirely on your vacation lifestyle. Part of the fun of vacationing is dining out, and those who usually prepare the meals will be the first to vote for trying out the local restaurants at least a couple of times a week. After all, this is a vacation. And a vacation indeed it was for a Washington, D.C., journalist and his wife. During a recent fourteen-day London, England, home exchange, these folks attended eleven different performances in West End theaters and dined out every night. This is not typical, however. In a given week, more than half of all U.S. vacation home exchangers have three to four meals in restaurants. For non-U.S. exchangers, this percentage is slightly lower, about 40 percent.

You can come up with an estimate of the costs of your meals out. Figure that the costs of supermarket purchases and necessary household supplies will be about the same as at home. Incidentally, these food and household supplies are not really vacation expenses, since you would be spending approximately the same amount of money on food and supplies if you were living at home.

Add to that the cost of golf-related fees if you are golfers, chartering fishing boats if you fish, the use of courts if you are tennis players, boat rental if you are boaters, and other sports- or hobby-related expenses. A Cologne, Germany, family of four writes: "We always try to exchange with Americans who offer an apartment in a condominium community. Then we have most outdoor facilities at our doorstep—tennis, swimming pool, barbecue, and sometimes golf, too." As some of these complexes are "adult" communities, not welcoming children, it's important for those exchangers traveling with children to make this fact known early on to their potential exchange partners.

No matter how much time and effort you spend in advance estimating the costs of vacations, after returning home—suntanned and rested (?)—when all the bills are in, you inevitably find you have exceeded your expected costs. In estimating vacation costs, it is always a good idea to add 5 to 10 percent for those inevitable vacation contingencies.

Remember, in vacation home exchanging, there are two parties involved: you and your home exchange partner. For this reason a home exchange vacation (unlike a weekend with friends in the country) necessitates extensive and detailed planning.

At this point, it would be appropriate to make a comparison between the costs of home exchange vacations and regular (or more conventional) vacations.

This first cost comparison is between a two-week home-exchange vacation and a conventional vacation of the same length. It is based on the budget for summer 1996 travel prepared by the Johnsons, a retired couple who own a townhouse in Arlington, Virginia, and their thirteen-year-old granddaughter. The Johnsons' home exchange partners are a working couple who own a large condominium in Pasadena, California.

While in California, the Johnsons will be using their exchange partner's car. They will be driving around greater Los Angeles and also to San Diego, Santa Barbara, Lake Arrowhead, and elsewhere in Southern California. They will be doing a lot of sightseeing and expect to drive about fourteen hundred miles during the two weeks.

Here is the Johnsons' budget for this home exchange vacation:

Airfare (3 round-trip tickets @ $800)	$2,400
Meals out (3 persons; 6 evening meals; 6 noon meals)	426
Meals at home and household supplies	225
Sightseeing and sporting events	500
Personal items, gifts, and souvenirs	275
Gasoline	78
	3,904
plus 10 percent contingencies	390
total	$4,294

As vacation home exchangers, the Johnsons estimate the cost of their two-week Southern California vacation will be about $4,300. If the Johnsons' party of three were to make this same two-week trip as conventional vacationers, their budget would look like this:

Airfare (3 round-trip tickets @ $800)	$2,400
Hotels/motels (14 nights @ $80)	1,120
Meals for three persons in hotel/motel dining rooms or in restaurants (13 days)	1,400
Sightseeing and sporting events	500
Personal items, gifts, and souvenirs	275
	$5,695
plus 10 percent contingencies	570
total	$6,265

As home exchangers, this vacation for three will cost about $4,300—nearly $2,000 less than the cost of this party of three taking the same vacation as nonhome-exchangers.

The second cost comparison is also prepared around a two-week home exchange vacation and a conventional vacation. It is based on the budget for summer 1996 travel for the Turners and their teenage son. These exchangers own a home with a swimming pool near Sarasota, Florida. For their two-week exchange vacation, the Turners have selected London—a two-floor apartment in De Vere Gardens (just a stone's throw from Kensington Palace). The Turners' home-exchange partners and their sixteen-year-old son will be staying at the Turners' Florida home. Car exchanging will not be a part of this arrangement.

The Turners' budget for their first home exchange vacation abroad looks like this:

Airfare (3 round-trip tickets @ $750)	$2,250
Meals out (3 persons; 6 evening meals; 6 noon meals)	860
Meals at home and household supplies	300
Sightseeing and theater	750
Personal items, gifts, and souvenirs	425
Public transportation and taxis	250
	4,835
plus 10 percent contingencies	480
total	$5,315

The Turners estimate the cost of their two-week home-exchange vacation in England will be about $5,300. As a comparison, if the Turners were to spend two weeks in England on a conventional vacation, here is what their budget would look like:

Airfare (3 round-trip tickets @ $750)	$2,250
Hotels (14 nights @ $175)	2,450
Meals (14 days)	1,600
Sightseeing and theater	760
Personal items, gifts, and souvenirs	450
Public transportation and taxis	250
	$7,760
plus 10 percent contingencies	770
total	$8,530

The cost of a two-week conventional vacation in England during summer 1996 would be about $8,500. That is $3,200 more than a home-exchange style vacation. Why the big difference? Home exchangers do not pay hotel bills, and they have most of their meals at home.

There is a real estate broker in North Wales, United Kingdom, who had his heart set on a Florida holiday for his family of four. "I could swing the airfare, but I was stopped cold when it came to the high costs of condo rental and month-long car rental, as well. Year after year, it was the same familiar story: maybe next year!"

Happily, everything came into focus when this family learned of home "swapping," as they say. Father, mother, infant daughter, and mother-in-law had a glorious month on Florida's Gulf Coast. The following year they were in Orlando for a month plus another four weeks near Miami. Their first goal—do Florida—had become a reality.

Now experienced exchangers, what's this family's next goal? South Africa—two-week exchanges in four different cities.

The "miracle" of home exchanging—and some vacationers call it just that—has opened up every corner of the world to those families establishing home exchange vacations as important goals in their family life experiences.

CHAPTER 5

Different Strokes for Different Folks

MOST VACATION HOME EXCHANGES ARE DIRECT, or simultaneous, exchanges, arrangements under which each party in the exchange occupies the other's home during the same period of time. It is interesting, yet perhaps not surprising, to observe that experienced vacation home exchangers (and sometimes first-time exchangers as well) are adding creative new twists to the overall vacation home exchange arrangement. Some of these different types of exchanges take place between persons who own second homes. Most often, however, this new approach to home exchanging takes place between one-home couples and/or families with children.

Among these new-look home exchange arrangements are the following:

1. Alternate Date Exchange. Two couples are involved. Couple A stays at the home of B, while B perhaps vacations elsewhere. Then, at a later date, couple B stays at the home of A, while A vacations elsewhere. This arrangement is ideal for teachers, retired persons, and others who are in a position to take two or more annual vacations.

2. Substitute Exchange. Two or three couples are involved. Couple A stays at the home of B. Couple B vacations elsewhere, while a member of couple B's family or a friend of couple B stays at A's home, thus substituting for B. This type of exchange can be a part of the arrangements from the start or can be used if one of the couples has to abort the original arrangement, thus sidestepping, so to speak, the type of "ultimate disaster" discussed in chapter 31.

3. Three-way Exchange. Three couples are involved. Couple A stays at the home of B; B at the home of C; and C at the home of A. Because all three of these exchanges take place during the same time frame, the vacation schedule of all couples involved must coincide. If two couples have difficulty with the exchange dates, an additional couple tends to compound the problem. But if the three couples making this type of exchange are family members or close friends and each is willing to be flexible about dates, a three-way exchange can often be arranged successfully.

From experienced exchangers in Maryville, Tennessee: "Our three-way exchange was both interesting and fun. We were offered the exchange by a Maryland couple, whose second home is in the Caribbean. Not wishing to be so far away at that point, we arranged with a friend who has a place at Kiawah Island, South Carolina, to go to the Caribbean. We went to Kiawah, and the folks from Maryland stayed at our place."

4. Time-share Exchange. Two couples are involved. When a couple owns a condominium for one particular week (or more) in a given year, this is known as time-share, or interval, ownership. Those who own time-share properties sometimes prefer not to return to the same vacation spot every year. Exchanging their time-share properties enables them to enjoy a variety of vacation destinations within or outside of their time-share plan.

5. Hospitality or Friendship Exchange. Either two couples, two single persons, or a single person and a couple are involved. Partners A and B stay together at the home of A. At a later date, both partners stay together at the home of B. This arrangement is becoming increasingly popular, especially among single persons and "golden oldies" who enjoy making new friends and seeing new places and who have an inclination and the time to get up and go for a weekend or a week or more, anytime, anyplace. (See chapter 25.)

6. Car-for-House Exchange. A husband-wife real estate team in Evansville, Indiana, writes: "We exchanged our second home for the use of a car for three weeks in England. We picked up the car at the airport and drove it to the home of the exchangers staying at our main home; the car owners, you see, stayed at our second home. A complicated arrangement, for sure. But to get use of a free car for three weeks in England, you have to stretch a little."

7. Recreation Vehicle Exchange. Many conventional holiday seekers do "wheels-up" vacations—taking off in air buses for Club Meds in Acapulco, Marbella, or wherever. But home exchangers prefer to hit the road in wheels-down holidays in motor homes or campers known as RVs. A couple (both teachers) in Maitland, Florida, exchanged homes *and* motor homes with a couple in Germany. "A great time," they write. Having had a successful home exchange in the United States, an English airline captain and his wife are readying their six-berth camper for an exchange. They have offered to exchange "all of the United Kingdom and perhaps some of the Continent, as well" in return for a lengthy camper exchange in the States.

"During the winter," writes a Portsmouth, Rhode Island, exchanger, "we live on our boat at a Florida marina. We would consider a boat-house, a house-house, or a motor home-house (or boat) exchange." A retired marketing executive and his wife sold their home in Livingston, Texas, and live full time in a motor home. "In no way does this limit our exchange opportunities," they say, "because there is a great deal of interest in exchanging motor homes, houses, and apartments in Europe for a motor-home vacation in the United States. We have received ten responses from a recent listing in one of the key home exchange directories."

8. *Pulpit Exchange.* Summer (a month or two) is the time some churches exchange pastors with churches elsewhere in the United States or in Europe—England, mostly. Their respective churches pay the transportation charges, and the pastors and their families enjoy some vacation time as they are not expected to assume all the pastoral responsibilities of the church, generally just the sermon on Sunday mornings. Of course, while on this type of exchange, the pastors live in each others' homes and may or may not exchange cars. For example, a pastor in Bournemouth, England, has just such a pulpit exchange in Georgia. Afterward, he and his wife and their three children enjoy a five-week, regular home exchange vacation in Florida.

9. *(Strictly) Business Exchange.* Over the past thirteen years, a Billings, Montana, couple has exchanged homes in California, New Mexico, and Mexico. These folks have also exchanged in New York City more than twenty times! They like New York that much? Could be . . . but in actual fact, business meetings take this husband to New York twice annually. Rather than staying in a Manhattan hotel ($200 or more per night), he and his wife swap their second home every six months for ten fourteen-day home exchanges in New York. How often do they dine out? Seven nights per week! What aspirations do they have for future home exchanges? Paris, France, and—yes— New York City.

From Cambridgeshire, England: "My husband makes twelve to fourteen business trips to the United States each year. Occasionally, we manage to combine one or more of these with an exchange; for example, last year we based ourselves at a Florida exchange whilst he made trips to New York and South Carolina—a few days each. Thus, we were able to spend more time together as a family instead of his being away from home for long periods of time."

10. Sports Exchange. The year 1992 was a memorable one for Barcelona, Spain, exchangers. The Olympic Games attracted exchangers from every part of the globe. The same is true for the Olympics in Atlanta, Georgia, in 1996.

"We were anxious to attend the big Auburn-Alabama football game last fall . . . and couldn't get a motel anywhere within a fifty-mile radius," wrote an Orlando, Florida, exchanger, "so I said, 'Let's check out the home exchange directory.' 'No way will you find a home exchange in Auburn, Alabama,' exclaimed my learned spouse. I accepted the challenge. Result: we had an absolutely marvelous week in Auburn featuring the Big Game!"

It was off to Seattle, Washington, for a university art professor and his school-librarian wife, who arranged for a weekend exchange, enabling both to attend the Arizona State University-University of Washington football game.

A New York attorney—totally addicted to Major League Baseball's annual spring training—and his real-estate-broker wife arranged to stay at a Bonita Bay, Florida, exchange condominium. "I traveled to nearby Fort Myers, spending the days at ball games, while my wife loved the shelling on the beaches of Sanibel and Captiva Islands. Because we went in two different directions, we used our generous exchange host's *two* Cadillacs!"

11. Wedding Bells Exchange. In Phoenix, Arizona, an environmental-electrical engineer writes, "When our niece was recently married in Windsor, Ontario, an army of family members prepared to descend on Windsor. To our astonishment, we were able to arrange for the entire family group to stay in two different homes not far from Windsor while those homeowners stayed in our Phoenix home."

Another exchanger writes, "Our partners came all the way from Ireland to the States—just to get married! They had a wonderful honeymoon in our home, replete with reception and several dinner parties thrown in their honor by our friends and neighbors while we were enjoying their home in Ireland."

12. Stork Exchange. "An unusual reason for an exchange, we figured," writes a Long Beach, California, exchanger. "When our daughter had her first baby in Virginia last year, we exchanged for a month in a nearby home. It was just perfect: we stayed out of the new parents' hair, we saved lots and lots of money, and we got in some quality grandparent-bonding time!"

13. Student Exchange. When one hears about international student exchanges, one thinks of high school or university young people of about the same age, spending a term with a family in a different country and attending a school or university in that country. The following term, the guest student becomes a host student in his/her country. There is a great deal of student exchanging in Europe, where distances from one country to the other are short. Since World War II, various international organizations have been very successful in promoting and sponsoring overseas student exchanges, mostly between the United States and England and the United States and France. Among the advantages of student exchanges: these fortunate young people have the advantages of "living" a different culture, learning a language, and often making lifelong friendships, not only between the students, but between their parents as well.

Perhaps because of the growth and success of international student exchanging, vacation home exchange directories increasingly list young people who are seeking host families. Their families, in turn, will become host families during either the next vacation or school session. Indeed, the two directories with the largest numbers of vacation home exchange listings and others as well now have special youth exchange sections. A fourteen-year-old English student seeks an August exchange in France or Switzerland: "I want to improve my French." A German student says: "I am looking for a family with a girl of my own age (fourteen) for exchange next summer in America." A listing from Brazil reads: "Fifteen-year-old boy wants to holiday-exchange in Europe or United States."

In some instances, home exchange families are exchanging their young people during school vacations; others are hosting them during the school or college terms. For example, a Valparaiso, Indiana, registered nurse hosted a student from Vitre, France, during a five-week school vacation. "He was fun," she writes, "and interesting, and I enjoyed his stay and corresponding with his parents." The next year she consented to host a youth for the entire school year, a student from Cologne, Germany. "First I hesitated, but then, since I live alone and he sounded like a nice boy, I agreed. Then I thought, 'What if he's a problem? Why am I doing this crazy thing when my own sons are now grown and gone? Extra washing, PTA, homework, adolescence, ugh!'"

But this student exchange arrangement worked out wonderfully well, and later this R.N. host visited the families of these young men in France and Germany. Indeed, recently this student exchange hostess enjoyed six weeks in Germany and later on the French Riviera as a guest of the German student's parents. "You can see," she writes, "how exchanging has expanded and enriched my life—far beyond my wildest dreams!"

14. Services Rendered Exchange. Probably the most unusual exchange of this nature mentioned in the survey was that of a plastic surgeon who provided his professional services at no charge in return for two weeks of skiing at a patient's ski lodge in Colorado.

But services offered certainly don't require the training and professional expertise of a physician. In fact, one hears most often about house-sitting services provided while a host is on vacation or away from home for other reasons and prefers not to leave it unoccupied. One of the home exchange directories even lists home-sitting opportunities—240 of them in seven countries, to be exact.

A New York City school guidance counselor—a seven-time exchanger—occupied the St. Croix, Virgin Islands, home of someone who was hospitalized and then in a rehabilitation facility for an extended period following surgery. "We enjoyed our midwinter vacation," she writes, "in a home surrounded by wonderful, blooming gardens and the most beautiful vistas I've ever seen of land, ocean, and neighboring islands."

Two teachers, a married couple in Universal City, Texas, have traveled many miles as vacation home exchangers—Paris, London, Germany, and Hawaii. In more recent years, however, they have enjoyed house-sitting for others. "I take better care," this woman writes, "of other people's homes than I would of my own. I'm very careful, considerate, particular, neat, tidy, and clean. I do not smoke, drink, or (heaven forbid!) use drugs. When we leave a home, it's the same (or better) than when we arrived."

An exchanger who owns a hotel in Aspen, Colorado, offers his vacation exchange partners one of his lodge's two- or three-bedroom apartments. Of course, in this instance, the hotelier receives no rent for these accommodations, but he and his wife and their youngster "have had vacations in Florida, Hawaii, Jamaica, and Spain. On our first exchange in Florida, we bought the condo next door (which we still own) and, in Jamaica, our 'cottage' came with a private pool and beach, a cook and butler (who wouldn't let us lift a finger!), a gardener, and a car!"

Another slant on exchanging for services: With the cost of commercial dog and cat kennels skyrocketing, travelers often are on the lookout for pet sitters. On rather short notice, a London home exchanger decided to spend two weeks around Christmas with relatives in the United States. What to do with her two full-grown German shepherds? A kennel wasn't an option because these particular animals are people-dogs—they need "family." Why not, she thought, try to find a pet-sitting exchange? From an exchange directory, she selected thirty-five potential last-minute pet-sitters and out went the letters. In no time, she received eighteen responses—eight were not interested; the remaining ten were. A few letters and phone calls later, the dogs' owner had arranged for her worry-free visit with family in the United States; "a lovely, independent and utterly reliable woman from Montreal" enjoyed Christmas in London, and for two weeks the dogs had a caring "step-mum" to play with and take them on their walks.

A San Francisco "service" exchanger wrote, "I'll go anywhere, anytime, if someone will just come and take loving care of my four cats!"

There's also the home repair exchange—just what it sounds like and a natural for families who own second homes in desirable resort areas. If the place needs painting or wallpapering, electrical work, plumbing, or whatever, arrangements can be made with skilled men and women to move into the house, do the necessary work, then stay on for a week or two of vacation. The cost? Sometimes nothing more than materials because the worker, on completion of the work, has enjoyed a free vacation. On other occasions, the homeowners pay modest fees, but certainly not as much as locally hired tradespeople would charge.

There are now a goodly number of couples around the world who might be said to engage in "armchair" exchanges. They have had enough exchanges to be able to sit in their respective armchairs, do essentially nothing, and have an exchange just happen. "We have become good friends with two of our exchange families and have been in their homes often," writes a Massachusetts couple. "It's not unusual for them to phone—to tell us they'll be away during a certain period, and ask us if we'd like to use their home at that time."

A Florida exchanger offers, "After six years of vacation home exchanging in New England, New Jersey, and Florida, and various cities in England, Germany, Spain, and Switzerland—with repeat exchanges in almost every instance—my wife and I have reached what we believe is a unique position in home exchanging. It is a position that can be attained easily by other multitime exchangers if they are interested. Over the years we have developed close friendships with a half-dozen exchangers in the United States and Europe. These people know our latchstring's out to them; they can spend a couple or three weeks at our condo any time it's not occupied, and we feel quite comfortable picking up the phone and saying, 'We'd like to come to Cape Cod (or London,

Cannes, Nuremberg, or wherever) in the spring, say, for three weeks. How does your exchange schedule look for May?' We usually connect on choice number one; if not, we're a sure bet for choice number two.

"There are, however, two catches—givens, if you will—to this system: (1) you have to like repeat exchanges, and (2) you have to plan at least a year ahead. But we're retired, and the one thing we've got is lots of time!"

Armchair exchanging (or whatever name you think fits), these exchangers go out of their way to accommodate each others' schedules on call, so to speak, and are ready to host the exchange friends they have made over the years.

As one can easily tell, there are many, many ways—through exchanges or otherwise—in which one's home (or second home) can play a very significant role in the vacation or travel plans of people around the world.

CHAPTER 6

Pemaquid Harbor, Lobsters, and the Leaning Tower of Pisa

Born in Seattle, Washington, Howard S. Brower grew up in Newton, Massachusetts, did his undergraduate studies at New York's Bard College, and earned his law degree at Suffolk University; he then did postlaw work in the taxation program at Boston University. He now specializes in business law, finance, and real estate development.

Howard's number-one hobby is traveling, especially home exchange traveling. Other interests and hobbies include all water sports, hiking, and music—baroque, chamber, and early music.

Andrea C. Brower was raised in New York City and later in Englewood, New Jersey. A graduate of the University of Pennsylvania, she worked in the teaching field and later in real estate. Her "occupation" today is the Browers' daughter, eight-year-old Amanda. Her hobbies are home exchanging ("which I love"), reading, and traveling anywhere.

Howard Brower writes:

Italy was the first destination in what's become our family's love affair with vacation home exchanging.

Did it all begin in the pages of a home exchange directory? No. Word of mouth? No. It began in the unlikely location of a parking lot at Shaw's Restaurant, near our second home in Pemaquid Harbor, Maine, where we had the pleasure of meeting a fine Italian family.

My wife, Andrea, and our daughter Amanda had entered Shaw's, but I was sidetracked by observing an Italian family that had just disembarked from three rented vans. An older gentleman in the group spoke English. He was translating an in-depth dissertation on the wonderful world of lobsters and lobstering being given by several of the locals. At first, I was on the sideline, but later I began conversing with this multi-lingual gentleman, who turned out to be an official of the Pisa, Italy, airport. He was friendly, warm, and very engaging.

Much later, seated in the restaurant, I told Andrea about this encounter, and she said, half in jest, "I wonder if he'd like to trade his home in Italy for our home here in Maine." We had bantered with the idea of home exchanging for some time. We'd read about it in several travel magazines but had never taken that first courageous step—sometimes referred to as the strangers-in-my-bed step. The concept of trading had always intrigued us for some undefined day in the future. But the perfect opportunity could just have presented itself.

I raced back down the stairs to find the group getting into their vans. Supervising this operation was my newfound friend. Just before he boarded his van, I inquired impulsively, "Would you ever consider exchanging homes with us? Your place in Pisa for our home, which is five minutes from here? Maybe for a month?" I was astonished when he immediately said yes. He loved Maine and had traveled there twice previously. He liked it so much he'd brought his entire family on this trip. We were almost finished with our lunch, and I invited him and his family for a visit to our home.

Our house is unpretentious and small (although it does manage to sleep twelve) but is right on the harbor. Having arrived at our home, all twelve of his family piled out of their vans and rushed in, very excited. They were an intelligent and well-dressed group, thrilled about being invited into an American home. After being shown about the house, they talked about Maine, Pisa, and home exchanging. A few minutes later, we traded addresses and telephone numbers and bade each other farewell. Several international telephone conversations later, arrangements were firmed up; the next summer we'd actually be home exchanging in Italy. We were very, very excited.

To our surprise, our Italian friend came to Boston on business during the winter and invited us for dinner at his hotel. He presented us with an excellent bottle of wine from the Tuscany region, and we spent the rest of the evening becoming acquainted. This is an amazing man, a true intellectual who speaks five languages, has traveled extensively around the world, and exhibits unlimited curiosity about new ideas.

When summer arrived, we were off to Tuscany—our inaugural home exchange. We were all quite excited and a little apprehensive about the forthcoming, totally new travel experience, actually living in an unfamiliar part of the world.

Our Tuscany home turned out to be in Palaia, near Pisa, and our experiences there were absolutely joyous. It was a sixty-acre estate, a working gentleman's farm that produced a considerable quantity of dates, figs, grapes, and olives. In fact, our host pressed his own olive oil and produced his own wine. There was an incredible wine cellar with bottles dating back one hundred years. We went out each morning to gather fresh eggs and produce (what an adventure for our then six-year-old daughter!).

There was a full-time caretaker who explained all the ongoing activities of the farm. He couldn't speak a word of English, and we couldn't understand a word of Italian, but we communicated through sign language and charades. With a twinkle in his eye, he'd lie down on the ground, put his hand deep into a rabbit hole, and produce a tiny baby rabbit for our daughter. He'd also catch baby chicks for her to cuddle and love. In addition, we had all the food we wanted fresh from the farm. It was a rural delight to be able to gather fresh peaches, bright red plum tomatoes, figs, dates, pears, and many vegetables.

Our host also raised many game birds—pigeons, pheasants, ducks, and geese. He had a huge net spread over the trees and posts, making a large enclosed area for the wildlife. One day I was helping the caretaker in the barn that many of the pigeons called home. I was just gesturing and commenting on the number of birds and, inadvertently, pointed to some on a low beam. The caretaker interpreted that gesture as a request for the ingredients of pigeon pie. Before I realized what he was doing, he reached up, grabbed a pigeon, twisted its neck, and flung it to the ground. I was dumbfounded and pointed again, shaking my head and saying, "No. No more . . ."

Again he misunderstood the message and reached for another bird—a second death in the pigeon family! He bent down, picked up the two birds by their necks, and handed them to me with an extremely proud look on his face: He had just provided us with our dinner.

Somehow, I communicated my hesitation in handing my sophisticated wife two pigeon carcasses complete with feathers to prepare for our evening meal. He offered to bring them home to his wife to prepare for roasting. The next morning he returned, still beaming with pride, carrying two dressed birds on a beautiful pottery plate covered with a fine linen cloth. I looked beneath the cloth and winced; there was very little meat left, and what remained seemed to have a strange odor and color. I imagine pigeon is a staple of the diet in many countries and, when prepared properly, could be quite good (as we later discovered in Morocco), but this did not look the least bit appetizing. I baked them with garlic, butter, and olive oil and attempted to dine, but simply could not finish. Neither my wife nor daughter would join me. Most of the pigeon remained.

This presented another problem. We usually placed our trash in a bag and hung it on a tree. Each day, the caretaker would then collect and dispose of it. Of course, we didn't want him, an extremely proud Tuscan and a man of the soil, to discover we hadn't consumed all the pigeon. We, therefore, took the carcasses with us on the next day's outing; we carried them a full day in our cooler and then disposed of them eighty miles away in a trash container. We felt confident our indiscretion would not be discovered.

The house, a 250-year-old brick farmhouse that our host had restored, was in a beautiful rural setting of rolling hills sprinkled with farms and estates. It had large rooms and many piazzas. When we arrived, the area was in the throes of the worst heat wave of the century. It was extremely hot, and although it cooled down somewhat at night, the average daytime temperature was 105 to 110°F. Electricity is extremely expensive in Europe, and it is rare for even the finest home to have air conditioning. Americans live a very pampered lifestyle and assume their standards will be duplicated when traveling. But we learned to accept the heat as part of the Mediterranean experience. We even learned to tolerate the occasional hungry mosquito who came to dine, the bat who made his home in our living room rafters, and the friendly mouse who scampered across my wife's bare toes while she was preparing a meal. This was all part of the exchange experience!

During our first few days in Italy, our host and his wife would come by to offer assistance while we adjusted to our new surroundings. On one such visit, our host was reading on the piazza, and I was washing the car. Every few days I would clean the Scorpio, as the countryside was extremely dusty. It was a way to show our host we were caring for his property. This time he glanced up from his book and there I was— 110°F in the shade—hosing, sudsing, and rinsing. He looked up and said, "Is this an American custom? Must I do this in Maine? Am I obligated to wash and clean your car every day? I'm not sure I want to go."

I assured him it was not an American custom, and it was not even a rule of home exchanging. It was just a personal eccentricity of mine to wash other people's cars but never my own.

In the years since Tuscany, we've home exchanged in Provence, France; in St. Maarten in the Caribbean; in Mediterranean Spain; and most recently in Playa del Carmen, Mexico. In the years ahead we have our sights (and our hearts) set on Australia, New Zealand, Hawaii, Greece, Great Britain, and Scandinavia.

Yes, home exchanging has introduced us to a vacation concept with unlimited opportunities. We've heard amazing stories of how travelers have stumbled into home exchanging, fallen backward into home exchanging, or even been dragged into it—protesting all the way—by adventurous spouses. But only the Brower family accidentally began the addictive tumble into home exchanging on that lobstering pier in Pemaquid Harbor, Maine.

CHAPTER 7

Arranging Your Dream Vacation, Part 1

THERE ARE TWO WAYS TO GET INTO THE VACATION home exchange game. One way is for you to take the initiative by seeking out home exchange–minded people who are offering to exchange homes you feel would meet your vacation needs. The other way is for others to take the initiative in seeking you out because they feel the home you are offering for exchange would meet their vacation needs. Either way, both parties stand to win.

Okay, but where can you find these potential home exchange partners? What resources are available to put potential home exchange partners in touch with each other? The directories, newsletters, and other types of listings prepared and released by various regional, national, and international vacation home exchange clubs constitute by far the best available resources. Most are not clubs in the true sense of the word; there are no initiation fees, no annual dues, and no memberships as such. They simply charge a fee for a listing in their respective directories or newsletters. Complete information about these home exchange resources appears in the reference section at the back of this book.

For experienced home exchangers as well as those new to this vacation concept, perhaps the best resources are the clubs offering the largest numbers of listings. These larger clubs regularly list vacation exchange homes throughout the United States, including Alaska and Hawaii. Most also list international resources, featuring vacation home exchange opportunities in more than fifty countries.

If you have not yet arranged for your home to be included in the listing of a vacation home exchange organization (and this procedure is discussed in chapter 8), taking the initiative would be your first step.

But when does one take the initiative? The survey shows that 60 percent of exchangers start their home exchange arrangements four to six months in advance of their vacation dates. Another 25 percent make their initial contacts seven to twelve months ahead. Now and then successful home exchange arrangements are firmed up at the drop of a hat (or a coin in the pay phone), but these cases are few and far between. It is an axiom that the more home exchange experience people have had, the more time they allow for their exchange arrangements. Conversely, those aspiring exchangers who endeavor to put together a successful exchange in a few weeks or a month or two in advance of the desired date are generally disappointed. A New Jersey businessman writes: "We now always allow a year or more to plan our European exchanges, and it's getting to a point where we have to allow more than six months planning time for an exchange right here in the States. The early [home exchange] bird gets the [home exchange] worm."

First, you will need to secure current listing directories from several of the vacation home exchange listing organizations. (See the reference section at the back of the book.) There is usually a modest charge for these directories. With these resources in hand, you will be amazed at the in-depth nature of the listings included. With a few appropriate identification changes, here is the information given in a typical listing appearing in one of the recent home exchange directories:

ORLANDO, FL, U.S.A.

Mr. and Mrs. Homer Exchanger are offering for exchange their one-floor home in a suburban community eight miles north of Orlando, FL; with three bedrooms and two baths, five persons can be accommodated; young/older children okay; Walt Disney World nearby.

Six years old, this centrally air-conditioned home features a fully equipped kitchen (including microwave oven and dishwasher), clothes washer-dryer, television/VCR/radio, sauna, large sun deck with barbecue, and a pool with a flagstone patio; weekly pool and yard care provided.

The house is in a secluded neighborhood with a large yard. No pets please; shopping, tennis, golf nearby; car exchange preferred.

In his midsixties, Mr. Exchanger is a retired business executive and an experienced home exchanger. Nonsmokers, he and Mrs. Exchanger desire a one-floor exchange home (or condominium) in/near Williamsburg, VA, or in/near Boston, MA. Exchange dates desired: two or three weeks between June 1 and August 31 or in October; might consider other dates. Write/phone: Homer Exchanger, 18 Wilburn Place, Orlando, FL 33855; (555-123-4567).

The above is the information this home exchange listing gives you. The organizations compiling and producing these listings often use classified-ad type abbreviations and listing codes (e.g., ac—air conditioning; sk—skiing nearby; fn—friendly neighbors, etc.). This coding of vacation home exchange listings certainly makes the directories more manageable, although some users feel that deciphering the codes takes an inordinate amount of effort and time. Thus abbreviated and coded, twenty to thirty different listings can appear on an 8½" x 11" page. Some directories include photos of homes, but there is usually an additional charge to the lister. The other advantage of coding is that a coded listing lends itself to use in foreign-language listings; that is, while the coding remains unchanged, the code explanation can be in French, Spanish, German, and many other languages.

Now back to your dream vacation. If your family has its sights set on a three-week Florida vacation in July and you own a home in Duxbury, Massachusetts (south of Boston), you might well find that your family and the exchangers listed above could become home exchange partners. You could enjoy staying in their home, seeing Walt Disney World and the other wonders of Orlando and Central Florida. The exchangers, in turn, would find your Duxbury home perfect for sightseeing in and around Boston, visiting relatives on Cape Cod, seeing Plymouth Rock, or just plain relaxing in "their" New England home.

While the exchangers' listing indicates their interest in a car exchange, your family of four would probably be driving your car to Florida, so the exchangers would either have to take their own car north or make rental car arrangements.

Finally, note that the exchangers are retired and are experienced home exchangers. The former is important because retired persons usually can be more flexible in the important date-setting aspect of the home exchange arrangement. The latter is important because experience in home exchanging can be as helpful as it can be in butchering, baking, and candlestick making.

In perusing the home exchange listings, also watch for those that carry two addresses, a clue that the listing exchanger owns two homes. Why watch for such listings? Most second homes are in or near resort areas (ski resorts, oceanside or lake resorts, or condominium communities featuring tennis, golf, private swimming pools, and/or a variety of social activities). Perhaps one of these vacation-centered areas will be just right for you and your family. Those fortunate enough to own two homes can be quite flexible in their home exchange scheduling, and this could be important to you as you endeavor to work out a mutually convenient time frame with a potential exchanger.

A word of warning about the selection of exchange dates: A real estate agent in Falmouth, England, writes, "We were well along in our exchange arrangements with our potential U.S. exchange partner when we realized there was something terribly wrong with our date fixing. We thought we were going to Grand Rapids, Michigan, in November, or '4-11-96' by our style, and he thought he was coming to Falmouth in April, '4-11-96' by the American style. Fortunately a disaster was averted when we were reminded that in England (and in many countries, except the United States), when using numbers for the dates, the day comes first and the month comes next."

In the case of the Orlando, Florida, listing, it is the exchangers' home (not yours) that is listed for home exchange, so you must take the initiative and contact them, provided you feel your home would meet their needs as these have been detailed in their listing.

The exchangers have given specific information as to where they would like to vacation: in or near Williamsburg or in or near Boston. In many cases, however, those listing their homes for exchange are not specific as to where they would like to vacation, so you will frequently see "northeastern U.S." or "any seashore" or even "anywhere." As you read through the various listings, watch for these more general destination indications because, here again, very likely these exchangers will be more flexible in their home exchange arrangements.

On this matter of flexibility in planning, a lawyer from West Palm Beach, Florida, who has exchanged in London and Ireland, writes: "We have had our home listed in two different directories each year, but have lost several vacation home exchange opportunities, because we have decided exactly where and when we want to go. We have just not been flexible enough in our planning."

Among home exchangers, there is a difference of opinion as to whether the initial contact of one exchanger by another should be by telephone. One exchange school of thought warns in only rare instances should the phone be the first contact.

Why not phone? First, they say, you must realize that there is a good chance other potential home exchangers may well be contacting the same people you are contacting, so you want those you contact to remember you and the home you are offering. More than likely, they will not remember the details of your telephone call. They will not recall whether you said June or July, and you will not recall whether they said two or three weeks, and they will not recall . . . , and so on.

There is another reason for not telephoning initially. Remember, you have seen their listing in the home exchange directory, so you know something about them and a lot about the home they are offering to exchange. They, on the other hand, know nothing about you and nothing about the home you are offering to exchange. This information cannot be communicated in a brief telephone conversation, possibly a call that catches them during mealtime or happy hour or while the baby is being changed.

Of course, there are those exchangers who feel it's far better to make the initial contact by phone. They contend: (1) people can communicate better and more promptly by phone, (2) a phone conversation speeds up the all-important "friendship" factor in the exchange relationship, and (3) one can get fast answers to home exchange–related questions by phone.

Certainly, the phone is a must if for some reason a developing exchange correspondence has gone wrong—a misunderstanding, an illness, or simply a delay in communication. If time is short, a phone call to a potential exchanger might just save the day, or the phone could just put you on a fast track to firming up a last-minute vacation home exchange arrangement.

Home exchangers around the world concur that the fax machine is God's great gift to the home exchange community! With a fax, one can instantly reach others with information, typed or printed. Of course, faxes are transmitted over regular telephone lines; hence, the cost of sending a fax would be at least the same as the standard telephone rate. However, communicating a given message by fax requires less phone time than the same message given verbally over the phone. Fax and e-mail communications also result in a written document—important for future reference.

A fifteen-time exchanger in Plymouth, England, writes, "Last week I used my new fax machine to button down all elements of a month-long simultaneous exchange holiday in Cape Town, South Africa. Four different faxes, back and forth, with our exchange partner did the trick—in as few as three days." To have accomplished these same arrangements by letter and phone would have taken a month or more.

An increasing number of homes have fax machines. Frequently, exchangers arrange to use the fax machines in their offices. Even in the smallest towns, businesses will often make their fax machines available for a modest charge to the public, in particular, law or real estate offices.

Unlike conventional vacation planning with travel agents, elaborate tour brochures, advance deposits, and so on, vacation home exchanging is decidedly personal in nature. After all, your eventual exchange partners are going to be living in your home, sleeping in your beds, and you in theirs, so home exchange communication must be on a personal, friendly basis.

The initial contact should definitely be made in a personal (or faxed) letter, typewritten if possible. The suggested initial contact letter (see the reference section at the back of the book) need not be lengthy but should include the following:

1. The name of the directory in which you saw their listing.

2. An indication of your possible interest in home exchanging with them.

3. Any questions you might have about their home.

4. Any suggestions you wish to make about exchange dates in light of the exchange-date information given in their listing.

5. An interior and exterior photograph of your home and possibly a photograph of those in your exchange group. (Some exchangers provide regular-sized color prints, while others have discovered the color photocopy machine, available at many photocopy service centers. While color copies tend to be expensive, one can often reproduce four, six, or more color prints on one 8½" x 11" sheet. This makes the per-print price oftentimes less than regular color photos.)

6. Reference to the fact sheet attached to your covering letter.

Objectivity and honesty are of prime importance, not only in the preparation of your fact sheet, but in all areas of your vacation home exchange communications. Exchangers from Eugene, Oregon, had been assured by their California host that the home had a swimming pool. "Right," they wrote, "but the pool was only half full, and the water was covered with moss and slime—unusable."

Five-time exchangers from Barbados write: "It is important one knows how many people the exchange entails. We had stayed in our English host's second home in Marbella, Spain. Later, before he was due at our Barbados home, our exchange partner asked us to arrange a cradle for his one-year-old son; then he arrived also with a twelve-year-old daughter." Teachers from Pacific Palisades, California, were "misled into believing we were getting a single family home in Great Britain, when actually it was a duplex." Then there was the family from England, exchanging in Phoenix, Arizona: originally, they were to have five in their party—five from England, that is. Their teenagers had friends in various states across the country who came to stay for a day or two or for a long weekend. These visitors brought the exchange body count up to eight or ten people occupying the condo designed for a maximum of six.

The fact sheet should give some information about you and those who will be traveling with you in addition to information about your home and the community in which you live. This is a very important document. A potential home exchanger will read it to decide whether your home meets his family's vacation needs and whether his family would feel comfortable having your family occupy their home. If this potential home exchange partner has a positive response to your fact sheet and has a good feeling about the possibility of exchanging with you, he will answer your letter. If he has a negative reaction to your fact sheet or does not wish to exchange with you at a particular point in time, then either you will get back a putting-aside-your-communication-for-future-reference letter or no response at all.

View your fact sheet as a sales tool—the vehicle that encourages and motivates a potential home exchanger to be in further communication with you. Your fact sheet should be objective and must project an honest overview of your home and your family. At the same time, however, you need not mention that occasionally in humid weather your back door sticks or that your pool man sometimes misses a pool cleaning date.

This fact sheet can easily run to a couple of pages and should most definitely be typed, as you will be using photocopies of it in your contacts with other potential home exchangers. Remember: Always send a personally typed or handwritten cover letter with your fact sheet and photographs.

A Geneva, Switzerland, home exchange couple received eighty-seven home exchange inquiries during a forty-five day period following their first listing in a vacation home exchange directory. Of these, only six were personally written. Since these exchangers—a busy working couple—could not possibly answer the eighty-one form letters, all of these were dumped into the trash. Responses were mailed to the six persons who had taken the time to write personal letters. Following a series of letters back and forth—and several international phone conversations—this Geneva couple enjoyed a successful four-week exchange in Florida, and their Florida friends visited them the following year.

To how many different persons should you write? This depends entirely on the number of home exchangers who list homes where you would like to vacation and whose home exchange directory listings lead you to believe they might also be interested in vacationing at your home. If you carefully examine the listings, chances are you will want to write half a dozen or more initial letters, each of which would be accompanied by your fact sheet and photographs.

"Using a vacation home directory, I had written only three families who listed exchange homes in ski areas," writes the wife of an attorney whose main home is in New London, Connecticut. "One of these contacts telephoned and said they had never seen New England in the fall and wanted to use our Sherbourne, Vermont, vacation home the next October, which they did. The following March we occupied their large ski lodge in Breckenridge, Colorado, and this was a dream vacation come true: our family of nine having a skiing vacation together."

In making a determination as to whom to write, your dream vacation guidelines are most helpful. But perhaps you hope to go to Virginia Beach in early September, mostly because you like the ocean and your family wants to vacation in the Southeast. More than likely, Myrtle Beach or Hilton Head in South Carolina would suit you just as well as Virginia Beach. If so, write to those listed in all three of these southeastern Atlantic coastline resort areas if you feel from their listing information that these people might be interested in exchanging with you. Maybe someone in Virginia Beach is offering just the right place for your family, but there is no way you are going to get these Virginia Beach home exchangers to vacation in your Cleveland, Ohio, home when their listing clearly shows that their vacation sights are set on Llandudno, North Wales. The point is that within the general framework of their vacation aspirations, home exchangers should be as flexible as is possible, especially in where and when they want to go. From a financial consultant in Chevy Chase, Maryland, an apropos comment, "Our philosophy is—if you don't get the exchange arrangement you want, you should want the one you get."

Never underestimate the importance of first impressions. If you were going for a job interview, you would be dressed appropriately. If you were selling your home, you would have it clean and looking at its best. If you were going to meet your future in-laws, you certainly would not take along an old girl or boy friend.

There is a story going around New York that one of the top women's fashion magazines had advertised for a particular type of model for an upcoming issue: five-seven in height, slim, age twenty-one to twenty-four, blonde hair, blue eyes. At the appropriate hour, a dozen models gathered for the all-important interview. Yes, they all looked alike, including one who brought along a monkey on a green leash. Any one of those women would have been perfect for this assignment, but the job went to the model with the monkey. The interviewer just could not forget that monkey.

The point is that the potential home exchanger to whom you write will undoubtedly be hearing from several other people. While cramming a green-leashed monkey into an envelope would be a bit difficult, you do want your initial communication to stand out from the others. You can do this. Put your best foot forward with a well-written personal letter, a fact sheet, and photographs.

To strengthen the positive first impression you want to make on this potential home exchanger, you might want to send a map and indicate the location of your home (an architect in Tel-Aviv, Israel, provides potential exchangers with three-color plans—interior and exterior—of the home he offers for exchange); the names, addresses, and telephone numbers of several persons with whom you have exchanged or a fan letter from one or more of these persons. Another up-to-date touch was introduced by an Aalter, Belgium, couple who included a short video of their home and their family, information about places of historical significance in the area (the survey underscored the fact that American home exchangers rate places of historic significance over seashore, lakes, mountains, ski resorts, and other vacation destinations), or some other enclosures that will have a positive influence on your potential home exchangers and make them exclaim, "Hey, this is one exchange opportunity we should follow up on right now!"

CHAPTER 8

Arranging Your Dream Vacation, Part 2

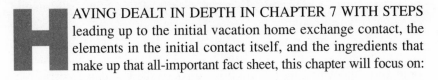AVING DEALT IN DEPTH IN CHAPTER 7 WITH STEPS leading up to the initial vacation home exchange contact, the elements in the initial contact itself, and the ingredients that make up that all-important fact sheet, this chapter will focus on:

Trials, tragedies, and triumphs in the correspondence following up the initial contact.

"Marketing" your home and community as a viable vacation home exchange destination.

The actual vacation home exchange arrangement.

Hopefully, you will get some positive responses from your initial contacts. You should then promptly acknowledge these with appropriate follow-up communications. As you move through this getting-to-know-each-other-and-our-homes stage of the correspondence, there are a few matters you will want to bear in mind.

First, to maintain continuity in these correspondence exchanges, one person in your family (or vacation group) should handle all correspondence, and copies of all correspondence (photocopies or carbon copies) should be kept in chronological order for future reference. Very likely, one person will handle all communications at the other end, too. As you move toward firming up a home exchange arrangement, you and your potential exchange partner will find yourselves becoming friends, writing and answering letters on a first-name basis.

Depending on how extensive their home exchange correspondence becomes, exchangers generally develop quick-reference filing systems tailored to their particular needs. It is surprising how often personal letters are undated. Be sure to date your letters and memos. If you file chronologically, it is maddening to have an undated letter pop up in your file; if you do receive such a letter, simply mark it with the date it was received and file it accordingly.

Before you go from the vacation planning stage to the correspondence stage, it is important that everyone in your vacation home exchange group is familiar with your vacation planning and plays an active role in putting together the vacation plan. After all, it is their vacation, too.

Further, as mentioned previously, you and your potential home exchange partner must be totally honest and open with each other every step of the way as the planning unfolds. Also, all matters related to the exchange must be in writing. Even the details of telephone calls should be noted in writing and dated.

By having one person at each end handling the correspondence, by having each correspondent involve his or her family in the developing arrangements, by having both sides of the exchange correspondence honest and open in their correspondence, and by putting into writing all matters related to the exchange, you will be taking a giant step toward avoiding possible serious misunderstandings as the exchange unfolds.

"An elderly handicapped woman exchanging with us," writes a retired Corpus Christi, Texas, engineer, "didn't tell us until a week before the departure that she would not be able to drive while here. Our nearest shopping center is two miles away. A last-minute scramble to find neighbors and friends who would take her shopping saved the day. Now, we include 'car necessary' in our exchange directory listings."

"People should not be afraid to address the 'accessibility' issue," says an exchanging teacher in Saint Croix, Virgin Islands. "If a person requires a wheelchair, this fact must be stated early on in the correspondence, along with door widths and the number of steps into and inside of the home. The whole house need not be accessible—just a bedroom, a bathroom, and a place to eat. (In our case, my wheelchaired partner has little interest in going into the kitchen—only what comes out of it!)"

One serious misunderstanding concerns smoking. No smoking is now a recognized fact of life in almost all modes of public transportation, public buildings, offices, restaurants, hotels, and even car rentals. Today, some home exchangers include "no smokers, please" in their exchange directory listings. An increasing number of people do not permit smoking—especially cigar and pipe smoking—in their homes or cars. Many nonsmokers are also uncomfortable when using the homes and cars of smokers. So this subject must be addressed during the earliest stages of vacation home exchange correspondence.

"A bed full of water? Be serious." Yes, in the 1960s the manufacturers of waterbeds had to overcome a mighty obstacle: water in your bed? But their perseverance was rewarded, and to this day in many homes (especially in the United States) the beds of choice indeed are waterbeds. "There was a waterbed in every damn bedroom, and I didn't get a decent night's sleep until we got back to our home—and bed!" writes a particularly irate home exchanger. From a school psychologist-elementary teacher couple in Charlevoix, Michigan: "When we exchanged with a family near Washington, D.C., we slept on their waterbed and liked it so much we went home and bought one for ourselves!" If waterbeds are a part of the scene in your bedroom, it would be a good idea to mention this fact early on in your correspondence with potential vacation home exchangers.

When the preliminary correspondence reaches the point of the home exchange beginning to come together, you will find the remaining big obstacle is the selection of mutually convenient vacation dates. Perhaps you and your home exchange partner both want to exchange during the first three weeks in August. No problem; you have a deal. More often than not, however, the date you want will not be the same date your home exchange partner has in mind. If both parties to a potential exchange are firmly locked into the different dates, you probably won't be able to work it out this time, but there is always the possibility of an exchange at some point in the future.

This matter of date selection may well challenge the understanding, patience, and flexibility of both parties to a potential exchange. However, if both parties are genuinely interested in vacationing in each other's homes, chances are this particular home exchange will eventually materialize. Home exchangers from Florida had three years of communication with a family in the Far East before they agreed upon a firm date. All this effort finally developed into these people spending a month in Hong Kong and side trips to Bali and China, and their Hong Kong exchange partners spending a month in Florida.

Another way to circumvent a date conflict: some experienced exchangers, particularly those with second homes, have developed a system of "banking" exchange time. Reports a nurse in Kansas City,

Missouri: "We have two homes. When we find exchange partners who are just 'right' for us, but we can't seem to get together on the exchange dates, we arrange for them to use our second home (most of our exchange partners stay there anyway) for the length of the exchange—two or three weeks. But we don't go to their place at that same time. So, in effect, we have a 'credit' with them for two or three weeks at their place at some future date convenient to them and to us. This year we will pick up this credit and spend two weeks at a ski lodge in Aspen, Colorado, and they were at our home last summer." Some exchangers will thus build up credit (or "banked" exchange time) with two or more different partners for future vacations. It is recommended, however, that the dates of banked vacations not be extended over too long a period of time. Experienced exchangers like to get on with their scheduling, keeping things fairly current; thus they prefer not to bank too many exchange weeks.

Understanding, patience, and flexibility are key elements in playing the vacation home exchange planning game and in the handling of the followup and follow-through correspondence. A retired accountant living in Jackson, Tennessee, writes: "I sent nearly a hundred initial letters requesting exchanges; 90 percent of my letters were ignored." But she persevered and was successful in arranging several exchanges, including one in Tucson, Arizona—house-sitting.

"In my exchange directory listing, I gave 'California' as my destination choice," writes a London exchanger, "and I got a flood of letters from lovely homes in San Francisco with pools (and one with a Mercedes!) to a man living in the desert in a car trailer. I should have stated in my listing that I wanted to go to Los Angeles."

A "professional volunteer" from Nanuet, New York, felt she had been misinformed when told her initial home exchange letters should be photocopies: "I handwrote my fifty-one letters. When I asked my eventual exchangers why they chose me, they said it was because my letters were handwritten." Aspiring vacation home exchangers, take heed: if you send your initial letters handwritten (or place handwritten notes on your fact sheet), you will turn heads at the other end of the correspondence exchange.

From her first listing in an exchange directory, a home exchanger in Majorca, Spain, received "more than fifty replies"—proof-positive her initial approach rang the bell or that Majorca is a hot spot in the world of home exchanging.

From Bracebridge, Ontario, Canada, a medical doctor says: "I don't answer form letters. I find I must write ten letters to get one that may

lead to an exchange." A lot of writing, yes. But by following this for-
mula, this doctor and his wife have enjoyed twenty-two vacation home
exchanges in ten years—four homes in France, three in Australia, and
the others in Germany, the United States, Italy, Portugal, Holland, and
elsewhere.

A husband and wife (accountant and teacher) in Moss Point, Mississippi, write: "Our biggest complaint is that so many people simply do not
respond at all. We always answer every inquiry we get, but when we send
our fifty to seventy-five letters, we only get responses from fifteen to
twenty." Nevertheless, this couple has had five successful home exchanges
in Illinois, Louisiana, Pennsylvania, New Hampshire, and Colorado.

"Vacation home exchanging is becoming very popular *and* competitive. Therefore, it's important for the exchange correspondent to move fast and intelligently in the initial contact and in all follow-up communications," says a former marketing executive now living at Hilton Head Island, South Carolina.

A retired teacher in Corpus Christi, Texas, writes, "Right after the annual exchange directory is delivered, we get busy scrambling for exchanges. The competition is fierce, but we Texans are finally gaining on California and Florida as Europeans find out there's a whole country in between! In just a few days we leave for a month each in the Netherlands and Germany and two different exchanges in England."

From a husband-wife team (apartment owners-managers) in Santa Barbara, California, who have had seven home exchanges in the United States and in Europe: "When we were arranging an exchange in Germany, we had twenty replies to our initial letters. Of these, three families were very anxious to come to our home. During the correspondence that followed, we had to keep three families 'on the string' until our decision was made, then the other two were really disappointed."

From a working mother and caterer for corporate directors' luncheons living within a stone's throw of London's Hyde Park: "Last year I received fifty-six replies and could not cope, so I went to stay with a friend in Providence, Rhode Island. Now I'm corresponding with a couple in California for an exchange next summer."

"The vacation home exchange correspondence is basically satisfactory," writes a civil servant from Gasteiz, Spain, "but obstacles must be overcome. For example, some offers must be excluded because of the size of family, others due to date conflicts, and still others due to the types and qualities of accommodations offered. So the number of real 'possibilities' may turn out to be very limited. It does work, though, as long as you and your corresponding partners are realistic about what you are offering and what you can reasonably expect to get." Exchangers from Sequim, Washington, write, "It's a big home-exchanging world out there."

A school principal in Kimberley, Ontario, addresses the positive-negative feelings that are important elements in the getting-to-know-you communication stage: "You get a feeling about those with whom you are corresponding, learning about their homes, their cars, their families, jobs, interests, hobbies, and so on. Photos and phone calls complete the picture. It's difficult to describe . . . but certain feelings develop (nearly always positive; occasionally negative). One exchange prospect, for example, assured us a relative would be available to assist us if necessary—he lived, in fact, right beside their home in a travel trailer with six dogs!"

The preceding potpourri of comments from experienced vacation home exchangers in the Far East, the United States, Europe, and Canada make clear that vacation home exchange correspondence is no Sunday school picnic. On the contrary, it is a veritable obstacle course, with exchangers endeavoring to put together the best possible vacations for their families. Once again, success depends on all parties to the potential exchange having full measures of understanding, patience, flexibility, and truthfulness.

It is more than likely that you and your home exchange correspondents will be in communication with more than one potential partner at the same time—perhaps two or more. Within the United States, this is not much of a problem, as first-class letters from one state to another usually will be delivered in two or three days. Nevertheless, all parties to the correspondence should answer letters promptly. This is especially true when you go international in your vacation home exchange aspirations. When you can fly from anywhere in the United States to London in less than twelve hours, why it takes an airmail letter seven to ten days to make the same trip has to be one of the great mysteries of the age. Nevertheless, there you are—seven to ten days over, a few days for the letter to be answered, and seven to ten days back. You wind up waiting two to three weeks to get a simple question answered, such as How about making car exchange a part of our arrangement?

Up to now in the negotiations, using the telephone has been left to good judgment. But when a quick decision is necessary, that is the time to use the telephone (or a fax machine) to get last-minute details squared away for the home exchange arrangement.

With the passing of several months, exchanges of letters and photographs, plus a phone call or two and much discussion and differences of opinion among your family members ("This is the place to stay; it's got a pool." "No, this one's right on a golf course!" "Wow! A week in Copenhagen." "Hey, look here, a half-mile from Disneyland." "Ooohhh, Barbados—let's go there."), you will finally make a decision as to where to go, when to go, and with whom you will exchange homes. At this point you can start packing.

Heretofore, emphasis has been placed on the home exchange efforts that have come about because you took the initiative, because you sought out appropriate partners through the use of the available home exchange directories, newsletters, and listings. Why did people not seek you out? Very simple: your home has not yet been listed in any of the vacation home exchange resources. You have been playing Vacation Home Exchange with only one foot in the game. Get both feet in by arranging for your home to be listed in several of the existing resources. Then as new directories with your home listed are released, others will take the initiative by contacting you.

If your home is in a popular vacation area—and there are far too many of these to attempt to list at this point—do not be surprised if you receive fifty, seventy-five, or more exchange communications within two or three months of your initial listings. If your home is in an area not known as a vacation destination, you will receive fewer communications. But remember, vacation home exchanging is like real estate: it just takes one right person to make a deal.

To get into the home exchange marketplace, write to the clubs requesting application forms and complete publication information, including insertion fees, deadlines for completed applications, publication dates, and whether or not photographs with the listings are acceptable. Check the reference section at the back of the book for club addresses.

When you receive a listing application, make a couple of photocopies, then study the listing instructions. If the instructions are not clear to you, telephone the club for clarification. We believe you will find that the data on the fact sheet describing your home will provide you with all the information you will need for the application. Use a photocopy of the application as your worksheet so as to not mess up the original that will be submitted to the club. Type or print this application form carefully, following the instructions. If a form calls for a twenty-five-word description of your home, give them about twenty-five words, not forty or fifty. If you decide to incorporate a photo with your listing, be sure you select a photo with high color contrast (dark and light). Otherwise, when your photo is reproduced with your listing, it will lack definition. It will look something like a smudge, and no one wants to vacation in a smudge.

When you have completed the application, photocopy the original for your files and send the original to the club—with or without a photograph—and with a check for the listing fee. Generally these fees are minimal when you realize that one listing brings your home to the attention of hundreds—more likely, thousands—of persons, nearly all of

whom are interested in the vacation home exchange concept. Along New York's Madison Avenue, this is a textbook case of targeting the market.

There are other resources available, as a London medical doctor discovered. While enjoying an August vacation at a rented home in a Florida resort area, this doctor and his wife thought it would be great to return there for the Christmas holidays. So off the good doctor went to the weekly newspaper serving the area. He was putting together the ad: "English family desires to exchange home in London's fashionable Kensington district for private home with pool during upcoming Christmas holidays." The woman taking his ad at the desk said, "Okay, you can stop right there. My husband and I have just the right home here, with a large pool, for you and your family. And we would love to have a Christmas holiday in London." There were three nice things about this experience—four, actually. First, it is a bonus to a home exchange arrangement when both parties can meet before the exchange date. Second, there was clearly no date-selection problem. Third, all concerned enjoyed their Christmas holidays and are now convinced that home exchange is a viable vacation concept. The fourth? Well, this London doctor was able to make a contact without having to pay the newspaper's classified ad fee.

To attain maximum exposure for their home exchange aspirations, some exchangers run classified ads in newspapers serving the areas in which they would like to find a home exchange partner, plus similar ads in their high school or college alumni bulletins and newsletters. These are certainly worth a try. Such ads should include some information about the individuals in your exchange group and should emphasize details about the home you are offering for exchange, the number of persons in your group, your date preferences, and the area or areas in which you would like to vacation. One sure way to increase the number of responses for these ads is not to use a box number for responses, as many classified advertisers do. Rather, include your name and address but no telephone number. You may attract a few crackpot letters, but you also stand a good chance of doubling the number of responses to your ads.

Important too is not being shy about mentioning your vacation home exchange plans. Tell your relatives, friends, pastor, fellow church members, doctors, Rotary, and other service club friends. Tell anyone who will listen that you are offering your home in exchange for a vacation home in Richmond, Virginia—Richmond, Indiana—Richmond, England—Richmond, California—or Richmond, wherever. By so doing, some home exchangers have had vacation home exchange opportunities come out of nowhere. Initially, you will find some of those with whom you speak are just a bit nervous about the idea of actually living in someone else's home. They will have questions, which you will easily answer. Very likely they will be interested in hearing about your vacation home exchange experiences.

"In Norway, we were interviewed by the local newspaper. We invited the young reporter to 'our' home for lunch. He, in turn, wrote a delightful article about vacation home exchanging, which ran with our picture in the paper." So writes a Falls Church, Virginia, retired couple. A teacher in North Andover, Massachusetts, writes: "The kids and I appeared on Boston television to be interviewed about vacation home exchanging." Media exposure helps promote the exchanger's own home and, in general, showcases home exchange as a viable vacation concept to many others.

A young couple in England wrote to a friend in Tasmania and told her they were toying with the idea of arranging a hospitality home exchange in Toronto, Canada. Back from Tasmania came, "Oh, you should write to my friend living in Toronto." A few letters ensued, and some months later this couple's hopes became a reality. A New Hampshire realtor makes this suggestion: "We mail videotapes of various homes to potential buyers not living in our area. Home exchangers also could easily videotape their homes inside and out, mailing the tapes to potential home exchange partners."

Eleven-time (from Hawaii to Denmark) San Francisco exchangers network their way into home exchanging: "For instance, we traded with a couple living in a New York City apartment. While there, we talked to others in the same building and now have exchanged with some of them as well. At home and on the road we establish our home exchanging 'reputation' and thus have had many home exchange doors opened to us."

A Hilton Head, South Carolina, multitime exchanger met with home exchange friends, a young couple in Kent, England. In the discussion, the couple mentioned that they would love to spend a couple of weeks skiing in France the following winter. The South Carolinian had an exchange friend in the south of France who had a ski lodge in the French Pyrenees. He wrote his friend, asking if he would like to arrange a three-way exchange: The English couple to the ski lodge in France, the French family to Hilton Head, and the family from South Carolina to Kent. By return mail came the letter from France: "Exchange folks are a great, happy family. Yes, of course, I will write your English friends. We can accommodate them, and we will enjoy the sun and fun next summer at Hilton Head." A few letters between France and England and Hilton Head and England set this three-way international exchange plan in motion.

A retired educator living in Denver, Colorado, a seven-time exchanger, writes: "We have never initiated a request for a home exchange because our second home is in the middle of six Colorado ski areas. As a result, we get vacation home exchange requests from all over the world." Retired after thirty-one years with General Motors, a six-time national and international home exchanger now living near Los Angeles, California, writes: "Although we still list our home in a home exchange directory and we do send out some letters, our most successful exchanges are those with people who have contacted us."

There is another side to making contact. What if your home is in an area or country not frequented by large numbers of vacationers? A Danish lawyer who has exchanged in France, England, and Wales writes, "Especially in Denmark, as well as other Scandinavian countries, it is very uncommon to swap homes. Perhaps because of this, other European families' attention to Denmark is low. We have sometimes found it quite difficult to find a European family interested in exchanging. We are very enthusiastic about this way of spending holidays and certainly hope exchanging homes will become more popular here in the years to come."

From Middleton, Wisconsin: "Despite the fact that I listed our home in a home exchange directory a year ago, we have thus far had no requests for an exchange."

From Brown's Bay, New Zealand: "I hope you have more success with your book than I have had with home exchanging!"

From Turun, Poland: "I did place an announcement in a home exchange book, but till now I have only four inquiries and one exchange—in Germany. Maybe Poland or my city is not attractive."

If you happen to live off the beaten track it behooves you to be a little aggressive. Do not simply list your home in one or two directories; list it in four or five. Rather than sitting back and waiting for the mail each day, decide where and when you would like to go and prepare an interesting fact sheet. From the directories pick out a hundred or two hundred listings in places you would like to vacation. Then make a massive mailing of your fact sheets. Try to personalize your mailing by placing a brief handwritten memo on each fact sheet. Make a commitment to yourself: I will vacation home exchange someplace next summer! Accept this commitment as a challenge and work hard toward attaining your goal.

Alpharetta, Georgia—Fontana, Wisconsin—Port Ludlow, Washington—Manchester, Connecticut—Johnson City, Tennessee—Kenilworth, Illinois—Yadkinville, North Carolina, to say nothing of Norway, Turkey, Yugoslavia, Zimbabwe, Liechtenstein, and the Dominican Republic. There is vacation home exchange activity in thousands of cities and towns in the United States and across the world. To make successful contacts, however, some aspiring exchangers just have to work harder, a lot harder, than others. Contacting interested vacationers is like fishing. The people who are out there fishing regularly—really working at it—are the ones who catch the fish.

Now about the home exchange arrangement—*arrangement* may sound a bit forbidding. It need not be. In fact, as the home exchange letters go back and forth, many elements of the arrangement will have been agreed upon by both you and your home exchange partners (the dates, facilities available, acceptability of young children, pets or no pets, car exchange, and so on).

Here are a few additional elements of the home exchange arrangement to consider:

1. *Use of telephone:* See chapter 13.

2. *Use of utilities:* water, gas, electric bills (the host partner covers these charges).

3. *Liability insurance:* check this out with your insurance agent, but chances are your policies will cover your partner and his family, just as they would cover any guest in your home (see chapter 16 for more information on insurance).

4. *Overnight guests:* home exchange partners should share with each other if and when they are to have overnight guests. After all, it is your home, and you want to know who is staying in it.

5. *Pets:* Dogs and cats. Acceptable or not? For obvious reasons, many home exchangers do not wish pets to be a part of the arrangements, but there are exceptions and these exceptions should, of course, be acceptable to both parties to the exchange.

6. *House problems:* plumbing, roof leaks, electric, appliances, etc. The host partner covers the cost of necessary repairs.

7. *House cleaning:* The host partner should provide a thoroughly cleaned home. It is the guest partner's responsibility to keep the home clean and neat during the exchange period and to clean it thoroughly on departure, unless other arrangements have been agreed upon by the two partners.

8. *Damage:* To appliances, to items provided by the host partner, and to the home itself. Generally the guest partner accepts responsibility for such damage.

9. *Cooking utensils, dishes, flatware, linens:* All are supplied by the host partner.

In preparing for a home exchange, some exchangers feel more comfortable if they prepare a document that summarizes the more important elements of the home exchange arrangement. This could be put together in the form of a contract or a less formal letter of agreement, the terms of which would be acceptable to both partners. A document like this can easily be prepared. See the reference section at the back of the book. At the same time, many, if not most, exchangers do not feel it is necessary to enter into a formal arrangement with their home exchange partners. After all, even if you have not yet met them, your home exchange partners are friends, welcome guests in your home, just as you are welcome guests in their homes.

Nevertheless, items such as those listed above—and others that may occur to you or your partner—should be dealt with in the correspondence prior to the exchange date. Remember: a contract is only as good as the signatures it bears. Many, if not most, exchangers go without formal contracts because they feel reasonable people can solve reasonable problems. Certainly the vast majority of home exchanges are reasonable in every sense of the word.

CHAPTER 9

More People Who Tried It . . . and Liked It

Although Gina Sartor's life career has been that of a language professor at various universities in Italy, for fifteen years her number-one hobby has been holiday home exchanging.

Ms. Sartor's main apartment is in the city of Milan, Italy. Her other apartment is in Belluno, high in the Italian Alps, just eighty miles from the Brenner Pass, the border between Austria to the north and Italy to the south.

Ms. Sartor's exchange partners occupy either one of her two apartments.

Gina Sartor writes:

It was from a television talk show that I first learned of holiday home exchanging; that was in 1980.

The sharing-homes concept sounded interesting to me. But looking back, I (as with most of my home-exchanging friends) was just a little bit concerned about turning either of my apartments over to people I really did not know. Well, the funny thing is, during the arrangement part of a home exchange—writing letters, sharing photos, telephone conversations, and sometimes actually meeting each other—the stranger syndrome vanishes. It took me three years to realize that by the time the exchanges take place, my exchange partners and I are no longer strangers. Actually, after just a few exchanges, I came to the point where I was very glad to give other people the opportunity to stay in one of my apartments, see my country and Milan (or Belluno, as the case might be), and get to know my neighbors. But the process of turning my concerns into confidence took some time—about three years in fact. Part of this change in my attitude was the fact that, when occupied by exchange partners, my apartments are more secure when I am away, sometimes for periods of a month or more.

My first exchange was in London. Sixteen exchanges followed: Sydney, Australia; Quebec in eastern Canada and Vancouver in Canada's far west; the United States—Boston, Los Angeles, Chicago, New York City, and San Francisco; and, finally, Amsterdam in Holland. I very much enjoy going to new places, but I also like to return to previous exchange locations to renew friendships with former partners and their neighbors and to feel, once again, very much "at home" in these different but familiar surroundings.

Having been there five times, I feel very much at home in Canada, especially in Vancouver, where I became a member of the local seniors club. I was happy to share in this club's various activities—painting lessons, tennis matches, short trips, and a wonderful cruise, too. I have visited each of the five U.S. cities twice. In the years just ahead, I hope to once again holiday exchange in Canada, America, and Australia. Perhaps I'll have repeat exchanges in these cities—exchanging with the same families—or perhaps I'll find new exchange partners. I must underline the fact that I have always met very friendly people doing these exchanges. In Australia, through reading and the encouragement of exchange neighbors, I learned how to become a vegetarian . . . and these same friends taught me how to have a healthier lifestyle, making various plants and herbs a part of my diet. My dilemma is that I like to return to see my previous exchange friends, and yet I always look forward to meeting new ones!

Because I travel alone, I like to stay in exchange homes with lots of nearby neighbors or apartments with people everywhere. In Australia, I was in the middle of a heavily wooded area; however, in the company of my exchange partners' daughter and her husband, I visited some of the rain forests, saw many kangaroos and other animals, and observed different ways of living in villages occupied by the aborigine people. All of Australia is so wonderful, I plan on exchanging there again.

I always try to make my arrangements at least six to eight months before the actual exchange date. As to the length of these exchanges, I have some friends who prefer to devote only two or three weeks to each of their exchanges. I prefer to spend a month or two (or more) at each home or apartment. Last year I spent one month in each of two cities in Australia—Sydney and Batmans Bay. Then it was Canada—four different exchanges, one month in each. Next year and the year following, I hope to spend at least six months home exchanging in various parts of the world. Yes, I do love home exchanging!

My skeptical friends say, "So what's so great about holiday home exchanging?" I tell them it is the many friendships that develop. Sometimes my exchange partners have two homes, and I see them often when I stay in one of their homes. Some meet me at the airport on arrival and stay over in separate homes or nearby hotels for several days. I always like this, because my exchange host helps me get acquainted with the home (especially its appliances).

I have friends in Holland. I went to their apartment two times, but they have not yet come to Italy. You would never meet kinder, more friendly people than home exchangers. In Vancouver, a man loaned me his apartment twice. One time, instead of going to one of my places in Italy, he went to Mexico, so I offered to pay him rent. He refused, telling me, "I am happy you like my place; I do not want any money." Then there was a jeweler in New York. On arrival at my exchange apartment there, I came upon a drawer full of jewels. I immediately telephoned my partners. They said, "No problem, we have a very safe alarm device. Don't worry." It never seemed to occur to them that I (a stranger) might help myself to some of their jewels. It's this kind of reciprocal esteem, as I call it, this trust in one's home exchange partners, that sets home exchangers apart from other travelers. I guess it is a sort of fellowship that develops between people who have respect for each other and are willing to share with other exchangers their most valuable material possessions—their homes and sometimes their cars, as well.

Also, I feel home exchanging offers people, young and old alike, the great opportunity of visiting other countries inexpensively and observing and being involved with new and different traditions.

(Another home exchange plus: I know of a couple whose home exchanging experience developed into a love affair!)

I always tell those new to home exchanging to be specific in the information about their homes that appears in the home exchange directories. Equally important: before contacting a potential exchanger, one should carefully study the description of this exchanger's home. For example, as I mentioned, I travel alone and offer either one of my two relatively small apartments, and in the listings I state my desire for a small apartment in a city. So, it's a waste of communication time and/or telephone expense for an exchanger whose home has four bedrooms and two bathrooms to contact me. And yet, recently, I was obliged to turn down ten or more exchangers offering me their huge houses in exchange for one of my apartments—far too small to meet their needs. So, exchangers should be accurate and realistic in their listing information and in interpreting for their own use those listings of potential exchange partners.

Among the things I do not like about regular travel is that somehow I always seem to end up in a smoker's room or car. With home exchanging, you can occupy nonsmokers' homes and cars, assuming you make such a specification in your arrangements. Also, I love cleanliness and find most exchangers' apartments are very clean—not always the case with hotels, rented cottages, or whatever. Consequently, I expect my home exchange partners to take good care of my apartment and possessions . . . and they do!

Finally, during the communication stages, in addition to the details regarding my apartments, I send photographs, maps, and other material that I think would be of interest to potential exchangers. The more information exchangers share with each other, the better. I view home exchanging like a beautiful flower that needs nourishment, sun, and a friendly heart.

I just wish I'd learned about home exchanging decades before 1980!

After twenty-five years—the last few as director of management systems in NASA's Washington, D.C., headquarters—Dick Mulligan retired eight years ago. His wife, Phyllis, is a retired Maryland social worker. Retired *is not quite accurate. Dick does some management consulting in Florida, and Phyllis does school volunteer work and takes both computer and aerobics courses.*

They had lived in Upper Marlboro, Maryland, for thirty years, raised two boys and a girl—all three now grown with their own careers in marketing. The Mulligans have been home exchanging since 1972. Now living in Centreville, Virginia, near Washington, D.C., they have made thirty-five exchanges in Europe and the United States, most have also included side trips. As they readily testify, the possibilities are endless. Phyllis says, "Exchangers are fascinating. We've traded homes with all kinds of people: retired military, teachers, computer programmers, engineers, and owners of all kinds of businesses. Sharing experiences with them over coffee or 'spirits' is usually the highlight of our exchanges."

Dick Mulligan writes:

Home exchanging is and has been a significant part of our lives. It has provided wonderful opportunities, experiences, and adventures, not only for us but especially for our children as they were growing up, greatly broadening their horizons. It also adds a whole new dimension to retirement—new places, foods, customs, faces, interests. It keeps us alive! Last summer, for example, while exchanging in Holland, we visited friends made on previous exchanges in both Bonn and Paris. Both families have visited us in our winter home in Palm Coast, Florida, and we keep up with each other's families, children, and neighbors through annual letters and occasionally overnight visits.

Ninety-five percent of the people we've exchanged with during twenty-plus years have been very fine people with nice comfortable homes. They take care of our house just as we take care of theirs—a mutual commitment. If we have doubts, we ask for references and call them to explore a third party's view of the prospective house, area, and other factors.

We have listed solely with the Vacation Exchange Club, U.S.A. for quite some time. We make a list of the states or countries we're looking at for a particular trip, then send twenty-five to thirty personalized inquiries to listings in those locations, stating that we would be interested in up to thirty days sometime during a specified three-month period—for example, three to four weeks during June, July, or August. Then we sit back for a while to see what happens. Obviously, from our history, it usually works out.

We really love foreign exchanges. In another country, not only do you meet new people and make new friends (as exchangers do, apparently, everywhere they go), but you become immersed in a different life—the history, customs, and politics of a whole new culture. Parties with our neighbors are usually great fun. These new friends are very interested in the United States, and the talk is often very candid. There are new kinds of foods, different kinds of buildings, crafts, and trades you've never been exposed to before. There are museums that you thought existed only in art appreciation courses.

There are other differences, too. You need to have some familiarity with the language. A phrase book helps with everyday communication. Hopefully, there will be directions for everything from the car to the can opener because, believe me, foreign equipment, appliances, and cars are different from what we're used to. By the same token, ours are different to foreign exchangers, and even more specific instructions should be left for them than for American exchangers. The most helpful direction is probably a good friend or neighbor who is familiar with how things work in your house, is willing to help, and whose phone number is posted conspicuously on the refrigerator or bulletin board.

We exchange both our Maryland and Florida homes, but primarily the Maryland one because we like to "vacate" during the summer and that's when we're in Maryland. But often Europeans prefer the sun and beach aspects of the house in Palm Coast (not to mention Walt Disney World), even during the hottest time of the year (July and August). One couple from the Netherlands came in August because they said they loved the heat and humidity.

Having two possible exchange locations allows for more flexibility and opportunities, but it can be difficult having two homes clean, properly equipped, and ready for occupancy all the time.

It is vitally important to us to have a reliable car during an exchange, because we always plan extensive side trips. When one looks at some of the places we have wandered off to while basing ourselves somewhere else, it is easy to see why: Russia, Morocco, Austria, Scotland, Yugoslavia, Wales, Luxembourg, and Finland among others. We've really only had one bad car, and that was in Europe. We paid a total of three hundred dollars to get it fixed twice and our hosts refused to pay us back their half—sort of adding insult to injury.

In 1989 we traded with an Italian screenwriter and his actress wife. Their home was a villa about thirty miles southwest of Rome in the town of San Felipe Circeo. There was a luxurious pool, a garden complete with Roman sculpture, and great neighbors. We enjoyed delicious sidewalk café dinners in Rome, roving opera singers, accordionists, and, of course, great wines and endless varieties of pasta. Rome is absolutely spectacular—you feel wrapped in history—the churches, palaces, monuments, fountains, and elegant shops are almost overwhelming. Particularly impressive were Vatican City and the Sistine Chapel, Trevi Fountain, the Colosseum, and the Pantheon, with the sun streaming through the opening in its magnificent dome.

We had the use of our host's Mercedes and took a side trip to Naples, where Mount Vesuvius rises over the bay and towers above Pompeii, the town it buried in A.D. 79. We were on our way to a museum and were stopped in traffic when one of those ubiquitous motor scooters pulled alongside and a young man reached into the car and grabbed Phyllis's purse. Fortunately, she had had the wisdom to wrap the straps securely around the gearshift, so he didn't get it as easily as he had planned. He and I had quite a tug of war while Phyllis proceeded to bite him on the shoulder. He finally took off. He and his accomplice were caught within two hundred yards by the police. Later, at the police station, the two young thieves stood by and watched as Phyllis emptied her purse of tissues, lipstick, maps, phrase book, etc. She keeps her money in a belt around her waist.

Trading with a school principal and his family in 1992, we visited Avignon, Provence, in the south of France. It was a lovely home with a pool, right on the Rhone River. Avignon, home to the popes from 1309 to 1377, is a walled city and is famous for (in addition to its bridge— remember *Sur Le Pont D'Avignon?*) its many impressive monasteries, chapels, aqueducts, and papal courts dating back to that era.

From there we visited the French Riviera, just a few hours away. The beaches (topless!) of Cannes and Nice are magnificent, and the seafood—mussels, shrimp, and lobster—and wines are superb. We also drove south to Barcelona for a five-day side trip—about a day's drive from Avignon. Our jaunt came about three weeks after the closing ceremonies of the Olympics, and we enjoyed visiting for ourselves, instead of through a television camera, all the Olympic venues (they were still selling T-shirts and other memorabilia).

Barcelona is a beautiful city, well laid-out, right on the Mediterranean Sea, with a bustling modern business district. There are tree-lined boulevards, gardens, parks, fountains, great shopping areas, and super nightlife. The Templo de la Sagrada Familia—designed by the great architect Antonio Gaudi in 1891—was amazing. Montjuic, a mountain just to the south, overlooks the area, offering panoramic views of both the Mediterranean and the city, particularly the Palacio Nacional and the Barcelona Fountains' spectacular water-and-light show. *Un problema, Menor en Barcelona:* We had a flat tire late one night. The Spanish equivalent of AAA did come, and they did fix it—for ninety dollars! "You are very unlucky, Señor," I was told. "If you had flat in daytime, only fifty dollars." Obviously, you have to be on your toes in any large city, anywhere.

In 1993 we were off to Woodinville, Washington, on the outskirts of Seattle. Our house on a lake (with catchable bass) was replete with a large hot tub and a superb nearby winery. St. Michelle is now our vineyard of choice whenever we buy wine.

Seattle is stunning, still a pretty well-kept secret but emerging lately from overexposure on *Frasier.* Surrounded by mountains and emerald blue waters, stretched out beside sparkling eighteen-mile long Lake Washington, overlooked by majestic Mount Rainier in the distance, and home to the Space Needle and the incomparable Pike Place Market—

Seattle offers one spectacular sight after another. The salmon cooked Indian-style is absolutely sensational!

Our Seattle exchanger also had a cabin on Orcas Island (one of the San Juans) on a hundred-foot bluff overlooking Puget Sound. It was about a three-hour car-ferry ride from our Woodinville home, and we spent a week there with a side trip to Vancouver, British Columbia—perhaps the prettiest, most exciting city we've ever seen. Although unusual words to use about a city, *happy* and *carefree* come to mind—with striking views and a terrific elevated public transportation system.

Vancouver has a magnificent harbor, great beaches, outstanding parks (Stanley Park is very special), beautiful gardens (Sun Yat-Sen is unique), stately forests, a gleaming modern business district with gorgeous hotels, magnificent bridges, and an exotic Chinatown plus the Robsonstrasse for gourmet dining. In case we haven't made ourselves clear, Vancouver is fantastic—a special blend of Canadian, British, U.S., and Asian cultures. Not to be missed if one is anywhere close.

The year 1993 also saw us in the Netherlands, staying near Den Bosch, about a forty-minute drive south of Amsterdam. Holland looks just like the illustrations in *Hans Brinker and the Silver Skates* with its many dikes, canals, windmills, huge cows, and field after field of tulips and daffodils. There are lovely small towns (we visited Brooklyn and took pictures of the original Brooklyn Bridge) with Delft pottery shops everywhere, including but not limited to the town of Delft—all with a neatly scrubbed, freshly turned-out look. The whole country sparkles. Amsterdam is something else. Talk about vitality and variety! This city by the Zuiderzee offers grand canals, old palaces, and the stately merchants' homes (one of them the hiding place for Anne Frank) pictured on those five-thousand-piece jigsaw puzzles. The Rijkmuseum showcasing the work of Rembrandt and Vermeer is in Amsterdam, as is another gallery just for Van Gogh. Rembrandt's home and studio for about twenty years around 1650 is here. So are the Zeedijk (the Sailors' Quarter—wow!) and an amazing (certainly to us) red-light district just behind the cathedral. There are American hippies (still) everywhere and cafés that sell marijuana openly. The Heineken and Amstel breweries are here (lots of free samples on tours), and many of the world's finest diamond cutters work here (no free samples).

And, last but perhaps most fascinating of all, The Dam—Amsterdam's Times Square—is a true window on the world where, sipping your Heineken and nibbling your raw herring, you can watch a unique and ever-changing parade of world travelers. Only an hour's drive from our exchange home was Rotterdam, the busiest port in Europe.

On some of our exchange trips, I've been able to combine a little business with pleasure—giving management presentations in London, Paris, Rome, Madrid, and elsewhere. Occasionally, we hear of other home exchangers—people in real estate, finance, data processing, and other specific business areas—who also have seminar or lecturing opportunities while on home exchanges. This type of activity broadens one's scope of influence and interests . . . and can have beneficial tax consequences.

We hope our home exchange travels in the years just ahead will include Ireland, Texas, some of the great U.S. western states, and incomparable Athens.

As Phyllis and I reflect on the most enjoyable experiences we've had over the years, home exchanging is very high on the list. Truly, for us, exchanging has been much more than a vacation concept. It has given us a window on the wonders of the world, especially its people. It's amazing how we share so many interests, anxieties, and pleasures and how open we can be in discussing them with our new world friends.

Bertie and Nina Sugarman live in Kingston-on-Thames, Surrey, England. After serving four and a half wartime years in the Royal Air Force, Bertie began his career with the multinational firm Unilever PLC. In 1985, when he retired, Bertie was responsible for the company's real estate department in Great Britain. Bertie is an active retiree—with tennis, bridge, and painting high on his hobby list.

Bertie and Nina have two daughters and a son: Peter is a merchant banker, Caroline has her degree in dance, and Helen is marketing manager for an Australian wine company.

Having studied in France, Spain, and Germany, Nina Sugarman is an accomplished linguist.

The Sugarmans first learned of the holiday home exchange concept in a 1987 issue of the London Daily Telegraph. *More recently, Nina wrote, "I'm all for home exchanging, as each trip presents a challenge. Initially, I was nervous about the idea, but now feel that home exchanging is a first-class way of traveling."*

Bertie Sugarman writes:

L ike most first-time home exchangers, we thought long and hard about this holiday concept before finally plucking up our courage and agreeing to exchange both homes and cars with a couple in Vancouver, Canada. He is a purchasing agent, she a school principal. We were delighted with this first exchange home, with mountains and pine forests at the rear and views across Howe Sound to the Pacific beyond. Happily, our exchange home partners were equally enthusiastic about their stay in our home in Kingston, a very old town where English kings were crowned in Saxon times.

We were happy to use our partners' car, but they found the combination of heavy London traffic and driving on the "wrong" side of the road as something of a worry, so they tended to use our public transport, which they found very good.

Our arrival in Vancouver was scheduled for the day before our partners' departure for London. Unfortunately, our flight was delayed, and we had a journey of twenty hours, including an unscheduled stopover in Winnipeg. We arrived exhausted at what was, for us, 7:00 A.M., at which point we had to take in the details of their home and car, there and then, shortly before they left for London. Quite a daunting prospect!

When they arrived back in Canada at the end of their five weeks' stay, we still had three more days to go, and they insisted that we stay right in their home while they stayed with a relative. To say thank you, on our last night we took them to dinner in Queen Elizabeth Park, which gave us the opportunity to review our respective home exchange experiences.

We had arranged for various neighbors and friends to entertain our partners—either for tea, drinks, or dinner—and our partners found this to be one of the highlights of their trip, giving them an insight into the local community.

In Vancouver, I managed to get temporary membership at a prestigious country club where I played tennis, and Nina and I had several games of bridge with Canadian neighbors. We visited Vancouver Island and had a pleasant trip back through the San Juan Islands, staying overnight in Anacortes. There we put up in a delightful bed and breakfast, where the innkeeper (as her granddaughters referred to her), a charming Jamaican woman, went by the beautiful name of Creamy Wilkins. Her granddaughters, Mahogany and Lushandra, entertained us in July with Christmas hymns played on an organ.

We so enjoyed Canadian hospitality that our next trip was to Burlington on Lake Ontario. Our exchange home there was a comfortable bungalow on the seventeenth tee of the Burlington golf course. Our host, a company director, and his wife, an accomplished sculptor, were lovely people, and we enjoyed their company for twenty-four hours before they left for our home in England.

From Burlington we explored Niagara Falls and motored up to Montreal and the Laurentian Mountains. We much enjoyed the French atmosphere and the meals, but our trip to Niagara nearly had disastrous consequences. We were out for several hours; only when we were almost back at the house, did we remember that a neighbor's cat, who was a frequent visitor, had been left locked in the house in our absence. We had switched on the security alarm when leaving and expected to find the local police surrounding the house but, much to our relief, all was well. Pussy was still slumbering in the kitchen by a radiator, right where we had left him, and had obviously not moved a muscle since our departure!

The following summer found us in Quebec City, in the home of a professor and his partner, a town planner. This couple had two delightful boys, Samuel and Sebastian, aged ten and eight, raised by their French grandmother. We were assured that the two youngsters were well behaved, and this assessment proved entirely accurate. On our return, our home was spotless. Huguette, the grandmother, even after thirty years in Canada, spoke not a word of English. She was a delightful character who had had a variety of jobs, ranging from cook in an Alaskan lumber camp to counseling a young Frenchman living in New York who had psychiatric problems. After six weeks she had apparently knocked him into excellent shape, just as she had her two grandsons.

And so to California, where we exchanged with a vice president of Merrill Lynch and his wife. We spent three days in San Francisco, being shown around by a university professor and his opera-singer wife. We had hosted his stay in London the previous year, and they really brought San Francisco to life, showing us its many undiscovered sights. We then motored along the Pacific Highway to Capistrano, taking in Carmel, Monterey, Santa Barbara, and the Hearst Castle on the way. What an eclectic collector Mr. Hearst was: everything, including the kitchen sink!

Friends joined us for a week's visit, and we drove to the Grand Canyon and Las Vegas. It's difficult to decide which was the more amazing.

Another year passed, and back we went to Canada. With our elder daughter, Caroline, now married to a Canadian and living in Montreal, we stayed near them in Westmount at the charming exchange home of a translator and his librarian wife.

Here we were joined by Nina's parents, who made a first-time trip to Canada from their home in Spain at the ages of eighty-eight and ninety-one. They were delighted to have the opportunity to see how their favorite granddaughter was adapting to her new life and to meet for the first time their fifth great-grandchild, born just three months earlier.

What else on the home exchange front? During a recent trip to Portugal for a wedding, we had an American couple stay in our home, and we hope to visit their condo in Florida next year during the depressing English winter. They have a beautiful apartment twelve stories up, on the Gulf, overlooking the mangroves in Naples, all black leather and white marble, just like Hollywood.

What are our criteria for a successful exchange?

1. Detailed homework. Several letters, photographs, and phone calls to establish rapport with the people you hope to exchange with.

2. An acceptance that different countries have different customs and that everything will not necessarily be just like home.

3. Ensuring, if possible, that our family and friends welcome our exchange visitors and invite them for a drink or a meal soon after their arrival.

4. Meeting your exchange partners, either in their home or yours.

Home exchange is great, and we can't speak highly enough of the concept. We will certainly return to Montreal, where our daughter lives, and would also very much like to visit New Zealand, Australia, and South America, but apart from these places we are always open to interesting offers.

All our exchange guests have enjoyed their experiences in Great Britain—at least, that's what they tell us—and say that our home is very well situated, being only twelve miles southwest of London in a very pleasant area. The large royal park on our doorstep, Richmond Park, is a great draw, and the River Thames and Hampton Court Palace are only just down the road—not to mention Wimbledon and its wonderful museum. We've lived here more than thirty years, and we love it.

Every home everywhere has unique aspects about it—elements that probably would be of keen interest to one or more potential exchangers. It's just a question of making the contact. For the exchange contacts we've made over the years, we say thank you to HomeLink International.

CHAPTER 10

Putting Out Your Welcome Mat

N MOST CASES A VACATION HOME EXCHANGE WILL PUT your family and your home exchange partner's family in totally new and unfamiliar surroundings. Therefore, you and your partner should make every effort to acclimate each other to your respective homes and communities. This chapter focuses on two very important elements of home exchanging: (1) the preparation of your home for those with whom you are exchanging and (2) the information you make available to your guests about your home (both inside and outside) and the services available to them in your community.

Some exchangers view getting their homes ready for an exchange as an onerous task—the only disadvantage to home exchanging. It need not be such if you think of it as sort of a nonseasonal spring cleaning, if you involve everyone in the family, and if you bear in mind that your exchange partners are preparing their home for you. A Connecticut exchanger reports that one of the exchange services recommends that you try to look at your home through the eyes of a stranger. Another suggests that you have a friend—one who doesn't spend a lot of time in your home—do a walk-through with a pad of Post-its, placing one wherever he or she thinks a little "attention" might be needed.

There's a lot to be learned from experienced exchangers. Never assume that the workmen you hired to do something will actually do it if you're not there to supervise and approve the work, even though that may have been the agreement prior to your departure. A Hancock, New Hampshire, couple had built their own home over several years. "However, as our professional work demanded more time and our two young children required more and more tending, some finishing touches were delayed—the doors inside the house, for example. Thus, we had no doors to the bedrooms and also, more importantly, none to the bathrooms. The unspoken rule in our family was 'If the bathroom light is on, go in another direction!' Although we had hired someone to install doors during our four-day overlap with our partners at their home in Europe, when they arrived here there were still no interior doors in our home. Initially distressing—especially to their two teenage daughters—they finally fell into dealing with it navy-style: yelling out who was using what bathroom as they entered and shouting an 'all clear' when they left."

A retired naval officer and his wife, who live in Hawaii and have exchanged all over the world, advise hosts to leave at least two large drawers and about two feet of closet space for each exchange guest. Another exchanger suggests indicating the guest-use drawers by leaving them slightly open. There should also be some closet-shelf space available and plenty of hangers.

It is also recommended that personal items be removed from dressers, tables, and other places that contain items not necessary to the functioning of the home. Cleaning the medicine chest provides a great opportunity to dispose of outdated, half-full bottles of old medicines, colognes, and the like. Other personal medicine-chest items should be placed in your "locked room" or wherever you are storing items you do not want used. However, providing a basket with a couple of in-the-package toothbrushes, a bar of soap, unopened bottles of alcohol, peroxide, aspirin or ibuprofen, sample-size shampoo, conditioner, toothpaste, and a note saying "For You" is a thoughtful touch. So is leaving a hand mirror and perhaps a hair dryer on the bathroom counter. Having clean towels and washcloths on the towel bars also lets your exchange guests know they are expected and that your home is their home during the weeks ahead.

Household staples—toilet paper, extra soap, tissues, paper towels, detergents, dishwashing soap, cleaning materials, and so on—should be easily accessible. As these are depleted, they are generally replaced by your guests. A spot-remover kit with half-a-dozen different types of stain removers and complete instructions is another useful item.

Help your guests keep your house as shipshape as possible by having available a vacuum cleaner (with replacement bags and instructions) and a suitable assortment of brooms, mops, and dust cloths. The refrigerator should be clean and empty, with the possible exception of a note, a welcoming meal, and maybe a bottle of wine, a carton of eggs, a loaf of bread, and milk. It is fine to leave frozen food in the freezer—even invite your guests to use some—but there should also be freezer space available for them. Some people place their refrigerator-freezer contents into a separate freezer and lock it. The stove and other appliances should be clean and ready to use. Business owners in Brownsville, Texas, point out, "If you have decorative burner covers for your range, be sure to remove them. We've had guests who have turned on the stove without realizing the covers should first be removed. End of decorated burner covers!"

While honesty and truthfulness seem to be inbred characteristics of vacation home exchangers, it just makes good sense to put away jewelry, silver, heirlooms, and other items of monetary or sentimental value. "One exchanger left his entire coin collection out all over the house," reports a chemical engineer in Baytown, Texas. "There were people besides us going in and out of the house—cleaning, tending the plants, etc.—which concerned me greatly. No coins were missing, but I worried that we would get blamed if some were." Exchangers from Kaneohe, Hawaii, no longer put their sterling away after finding a beautiful tea service proudly displayed on their first exchange in England. They have, on the other hand, videotaped the contents of their home for insurance purposes, "but we've never had any kind of problem." Perhaps your furniture includes some look-but-don't-sit side chairs. Put these away while you're away.

Special attention should be given to expensive electronic equipment—word processors, computers, fax machines, and exceptionally valuable stereo systems. Presumably, by the time your exchangers arrive, you will know whether or not they are computer literate—even what make they use—and can base a to-store-or-not-to-store decision on what you know. It's possible you may have conducted some of your correspondence via e-mail or via the Internet. If you have communicated by fax and choose to store your machine, be sure your guests know how to find the nearest fax-sending facility. Bulky as these systems are to store, especially since you may be storing some other things, you may need to put them in cartons and ask a family member or neighbor to hold them until you return, or make it very clear which equipment is off-limits and not to be used by your guests. Do, however, leave a television set or two and perhaps a VCR, with instructions and a local channel directory, and one or more radios. If your area has occasional power failures, a portable radio, flashlights, and candles will be most appreciated.

Some homes have a closet that can be locked—perfect for storing things you do not want used. In his second home in Majorca, one exchanger had two such closets—one for items not to be used by guests, the other containing such things as the ironing board, beach chairs, towels, raincoats and ponchos for afternoon showers, and extra linens. A closet key was left for his exchange guests, but it was the wrong key. The guests had access to a closet full of their host's personal items and valuables but no way of getting to the things he intended for their use.

Of course, an adequate supply of everyday china, flatware, glassware, and cooking utensils for the number of guests in the exchange party should be readily available in your kitchen and/or dining room. One exchanger warns about swapping with a confirmed bachelor "who may not have even a clue as to what's needed for a family of three or four, even though the accommodations may be more than adequate."

Food staples (salt, sugar, flour, condiments, and the like) should be left in kitchen cabinets, the pantry, or other appropriate places. Let your guests know they are welcome to use these basic kitchen items. Generally exchange guests replace what staples they use.

If you have alcoholic beverages in your home, you will need to decide whether or not you want to make these available to your guests. Many hosts prefer to put their wines and liquors away during exchanges; others store only the most costly and select. In any case, a bottle opener and a corkscrew should be provided with your other kitchen utensils.

A Dundalk, Ireland, exchanger writes, "We always tell our exchangers that they have the run of our property and anything on or in it for the length of the exchange—including anything they like from our bar. Once, however, sometime prior to leaving on an exchange, I had purchased two bottles of vintage port—much sought-after, very expensive—put them in the bar, and then not given them another thought. Some months later, long after the exchange, when it came time to toast a child venturing off to graduate school, I decided to open a bottle of the port. Neither bottle was anywhere to be found. At Christmas, we received a lovely letter from our exchange partners thanking us again for the wonderful time they had at our home and complimenting us on our taste in port of which they had enjoyed a glass each night after dinner."

Sometimes incoming mail can be a problem. One exchange host in Finland told his local post office to hold his mail during his four-week home exchange. So the post office dutifully held all mail, including that of the New York fashion designer staying at his home. "I just knew I had letters coming from my office, letters that had to be tied up by the P.O. with my host's hold-for-his-return mail. So I pleaded with the postal counter clerk, with the supervisor. Finally, the postmaster himself picked through my exchange host's mail and produced just the letters I was expecting."

Something similar confronted an exchanger in New York City. All her host's mail was addressed to a post office box, along with hers. She had no key to the box and, therefore, no access to her mail. Several phone calls rectified this situation. The best way to avoid mail problems is to invest in an inexpensive laundry basket or a milk crate, have the mail delivered as usual, and ask your guests to put yours in the laundry basket or crate.

Then there is the matter of home delivery services (there are still places where more than just the morning paper and pizza are delivered to one's home). Regular delivery of everything other than the paper should probably be suspended for the length of the exchange. Life does go on, however, during an exchange—fuel oil must be delivered, utility meters must be read, the world's noisiest garbage truck will roll through the neighborhood or dump your condo building's Dumpster at 5 A.M. But your guests should not necessarily be expected to need milk every other day, eggs every Friday, or the car washed every Wednesday when the boy who does it for you gets out of school—all of which one Georgia family discovered came with their exchange in England.

Several responders to the survey said that they had had bad experiences with exchangers taking on their pool or lawn care. Exchangers with pools should probably continue their pool service while gone, and those who employ a lawn service should consider maintaining the regular schedule.

In addition to having a house cleaned and ready, the survey revealed that high on the home exchanger's want list is detailed information about the use of the home, both inside and out. There are things you know, things you are used to, things that are obvious to you that a stranger coming into your home for the first time, much less living there for two weeks or more, would have no clue about. How to dispense all this information? Well, posters and signs that say, Don't Touch! Don't Shower Too Long! Don't Sit on This Chair! Don't Use Too Much Electricity! are not the way to go. "We really needed to enhance our sense of the ridiculous to enjoy our vacation that year," comments a teacher from Milan, Italy, whose exchange apartment in Spain was so decorated.

Occasionally, travel schedules permit a meeting of partners in advance of the exchange, perhaps at one of the homes or at the airport. This is a great opportunity because, after all that correspondence, it is fun and nearly always reassuring to meet those who will be living in your home. If the meeting is at one of the homes, the host has an opportunity to give his guests a tour of the home and property. These pre-

exchange meetings, however, in no way substitute for in-depth, written information about your home. Indeed, "a rapid-fire oral blitz of home-related information is wasted on a jet-lagged or car-weary traveler," writes a retired Ridgewood, New Jersey, educator.

How do you go about it, then? For starters, once you're committed to exchanging and are working out details, you might want to post a legal pad in a conspicuous place on which family members should jot down the known, the used-to, and the obvious things as they think of them, as well as any little quirks or idiosyncrasies about anything in or around the house.

All of this and all of the how-to information you wish to pass on to your guests can be placed in a home information kit. The material in this kit should be typewritten or printed so that it can be read and reread during the early days of the exchange and referred to by your guests throughout their stay. This kit can be in the form of an alphabetized or indexed ring binder or on 3"x5" cards in an indexed file (an advantage to the latter would be the ease in adding, deleting, and/or revising sections from time to time). An optometric assistant in Ashland, Oregon, who with her husband has had more than thirty exchanges since 1974 recommends typing the pages and placing each in a plastic sleeve. "This will last for years," she says. A Bethesda, Maryland, college counselor keeps her notebook information in a computer file—"easy to amend, if necessary, easy to print for each new exchanger, and my guests can take what they like for souvenirs."

Your exchange guests will be using the appliances in your home— refrigerator, stove, disposal, clothes washer and dryer, dishwasher, microwave oven, trash masher, and so on. Some families keep the owner's manuals for their appliances. If you have these available, they certainly should be an integral part of your home information kit, along with such 1-2-3 instructions (preferably in your guests' language) for their use as seems appropriate. Because one host in France left absolutely no instructions, a Connecticut family found the washing machine to be a "continuous source of amazement. The first six days of our vacation were spent trying to get our clothes out of the washer!" A Vero Beach, Florida, exchanger writes, "During an exchange in Sweden, we couldn't flush the toilet until a neighbor came to the rescue." Eccentric appliances are not restricted to Europe. All across the United States, appliances do not do what they are supposed to do when they are supposed to do it. The vacation home exchangers' solutions to dilemmas such as these should be found in the home information kit that their hosts have carefully prepared.

The operation of heating and air-conditioning units can be absolutely baffling. A California host's guests had nothing but problems with his home's unit until he included the following information in his information kit under "Heat and air conditioning, thermostat":

> The thermostat is on the wall in the hall. If cold air is desired, place "Fan" switch on "Auto" and "System" switch on "Cool." If warm air is desired, place "Fan" switch on "Auto" and "System" switch on "Heat." In either case move the thermostat lever (at bottom of unit) to desired temperature and be sure doors and windows are

tightly closed. Frequently, at times other than summer, you will be quite comfortable with "Fan" switch on "On" and "System" switch on "Off." Then screened doors and windows may be opened.

While this may seem like overkill, with the thermostat in front of them and these operating instructions in hand, guests in this California home should have no problems whatsoever regulating either heating or air conditioning.

A home exchanger vacationing in England noticed some discolored water seeping through the ceiling of the linen closet of his exchange home. Not just any plumber out of the phone book, but the plumber who was familiar with this home was needed—and fast. Fortunately, the host had left his plumber's name and telephone number in the home information kit. In an hour, on Good Friday, no less, this plumber was there and the problem—a toilet leaking two floors above—was solved, with the repair bill going to the exchange host and the plumber staying for lunch. After returning home, the exchange host laughingly wrote that somehow this particular plumber always scheduled his work just before the noon hour and always stayed for lunch.

By all means include the names of your plumber, your electrician, and the people who service your appliances and your garage door opener, if you have one. List the locations of your home's master electric switch and fuse or circuit-breaker box, and don't forget to indicate where the gas and water shutoffs are.

"Hel-l-l-lp!" exclaimed a Seattle, Washington, couple when a faucet in their exchange home fell apart. "We couldn't find the main water shutoff valve anywhere. It turned out to be halfway down the property, encircled by some tropical foliage." When water leaks occur, it is imperative to know the location of the main valve. If you don't know where yours is, find out and include this information (perhaps with a drawing if it's not obvious) in your home information kit.

Additional information might include entries such as:

> *Garbage:* Where are the plastic garbage or trash compactor bags? When is garbage pickup? Where is the garbage put for pickup? Do you have curbside recycling? When?
>
> *Supermarkets:* Locations? Best prices? Best selection? Best bakery? Best deli?
>
> *Parking:* In the garage? Driveway? Street? (If so, which side?)

Plants: Watered? Fed? How often?

Pets: In or out? How often fed? Vet's name and address? (See chapter 18.)

Public transportation: Schedules? Locations of stops?

Restaurants: Indicate those that you're fond of, the ones you'd be taking your guests to if you were there to take them.

Services & shops: Dry cleaner, laundromat, specialty shops?

Television: Best channels for news and weather and times. VCR tapes available? Best price for blank tapes?

And where is the pencil sharpener, the potato masher, or anything else possibly essential that may be tucked away in some obscure place? Hammer? Screwdriver? Pliers? Scotch tape?

A teaching couple lists, "Things we get used to that are strange to newcomers—hot tub or Jacuzzi procedures, which way our VCR and television are hooked up, light switches in odd places, the weird 'bang' our refrigerator makes every once in a while, how you get the !@#?! door to the microwave open when the food's done and you can't get it out." An exchanger in Spain adds, "What will be ripe and when in the garden and whether it's promised to anyone or available to our exchange guests."

Americans exchanging in suburban Nuremberg, Germany, were glad their hosts left them complete information about the city's subway system. They were in and out of downtown by subway several times a day—convenient, safe, inexpensive travel. Only twice were taxis used— from and to the airport.

These days an increasing number of homes seem to be equipped with burglar alarm systems. Alarm systems can be very temperamental, some- times making a terrible racket during thunderstorms, if you're a fraction of a second late disarming them after entering the house, or for no perceptible reason at all. In learning how to live with your security system, your guests will need to know how to operate and care for it, along with the name and phone number of the firm that services it. A night-light placed close to where one deactivates the system would be a great help to your arriving guests, as would the code posted on the wall, unless this makes you uncom- fortable (with instructions, of course, to remove and file).

Filed-away instructions wouldn't have helped this Minnesota con- sultant, however: "In Boston, as we returned from a day of sightseeing, we entered the house with not a one of us remembering the proper code to disarm the security system. A contingent of Boston's finest arrived in very short order but must have realized when they saw our six children that we probably were not burglarizing the place."

Or this couple: "While exchanging with friends in Orlando, Florida, we were staying in their vacation condo. After having had a number of burglaries, they had installed burglar alarms, smoke alarms, and light timer switches. Great was our alarm when we set off all of these hidden devices by accident! Although our host did warn us about the existence of these horns, bells, whistles, and buzzers, coming from the very peaceful, rural farm life of South Africa, we had never previously encountered them, much less had any use for them."

Exchangers staying in your home will also want guidance from you in case of an emergency—addresses and phone numbers for fire and police departments (in addition to 911, if your area has this or a similar service), doctors, emergency rooms, walk-in clinics, dentists, and your insurance agent. (See chapter 16.) Also include information about the use of elevators or fire exits if you live in an apartment building or multifloor condominium complex.

A London exchanger "once drove around for two hours with an abnormally high temperature visiting doctors who wouldn't see me without a prior appointment. Eventually, I found a walk-in clinic which was first-rate." New Jersey exchangers learned that tick-bite fever was prevalent in their exchange location of Transvaal, South Africa. Their doctor host had provided the appropriate medication just in case. A Dorset, England, exchanger goes even further to meet the emergency needs of his exchangers, "Use my clothes if you find yours are not suitable." Which brings up the point that it is wise to inform your exchange partners in advance about your weather extremes so they will bring along the right clothing.

If your community has a private or municipal swimming pool, tennis or racquetball court, or a golf course (or you belong to a country club) and arrangements can be made for your guests to use these facilities, they will need complete information. A Colorado couple wrote that their hosts thought of everything. "They arranged for tennis partners, golf partners, and a sightseeing boat trip. It was an utterly delightful vacation—much better than we could ever have arranged for ourselves."

"The doctor we exchanged with in Holland left a large table overloaded with relevant books, maps, and brochures. We hadn't mentioned our interest in bird watching, so the fact that he left a book on identifying the area's birds just must have been ESP!" was the glowing report from Stoney Creek, Ontario, exchangers.

A trip to the local chamber of commerce will likely produce all kinds of visitor-oriented information about your exchange corner of the world. (See reference section.)

Are your exchangers history buffs? What does the local community college have scheduled during their stay? Or the historical society? What historic buildings are in the area?

Are they bird watchers? What are the best close-by places for them to add to their Life Lists?

Are they music enthusiasts? What will be available in your town or the surrounding towns while they will be there?

Include information as to your whereabouts should your home exchange guests wish to reach you for some reason. Remember, home exchanges are not always simultaneous. While someone is occupying your home, it is quite possible you might be visiting an elderly aunt in Chicago or snorkeling in Key West or skiing in Aspen. Your guests will want to advise their family members and friends how they can be reached while vacationing at your home. If they are staying in your permanent residence, they will, of course, know your address and phone and fax number from their communications with you. On the other hand, if you have a second home and your guests will be staying at this location, you will need to give them this information in advance.

Home exchangers worldwide agree that their hosts' neighbors, relatives, and friends often add a great dimension to their vacation experiences. Underscoring this, a businessman from Des Moines, Iowa, writes that, in addition to entertaining them and taking them sightseeing, the neighbors they have met "have become true friends. We exchange notes and Christmas cards sometimes for years after meeting each other. And the neighbors have been of inestimable help at times when we've had so-called crises—the power outage in Banbury, England, for example, in a house that, so far as we could tell, had no breaker box. Our next-door neighbor came over and fixed us up."

An attorney and his wife from Tampa, Florida, shared this experience from Austria: "We were met at the train by our partner's brother, who took us to his home for a delightful welcome lunch. During our stay, he and his family took us on several outings in the surrounding countryside and to visit some of the local vineyards. The father of both these men was the mayor of the town, so we had tea with him and a tour of the town hall."

Before you depart on a vacation home exchange, by all means tell your neighbors, relatives, and friends about those who will be staying in your home and suggest that they might enjoy meeting them. One German host made a deal with his neighbor: "You may have fruit from our trees and vegetables from our garden if, from time to time, you entertain our guests." (This is known as the VHEFAVAT—Vacation Home Exchange Fruit and Vegetable Arm Twist.)

In all likelihood, soon after you are happily ensconced in your vacation exchange abode and your guests in theirs, you will wonder how they are getting along. Any problems? Is the home information kit clear? If it's a simultaneous exchange, they probably have the same questions. By all means, touch base with them by telephone, fax, or e-mail.

Your guests will appreciate the preparation of your home for their vacation and your introducing them to some of your neighbors. They will be especially appreciative of your taking the time to prepare the all-important home information kit. Extending your hospitality in these special ways will be almost as important to your guests' vacation enjoyment as the key to your front door.

Often, as you may have gathered from some of the anecdotes and recommendations already given, hosts will leave a bottle of wine, a bouquet of flowers, a casserole or breakfast, or some other appropriate gift to welcome exchange partners to their home. A Santa Fe, New Mexico, mother thought the teenagers and their parents who were in her home over Christmas would get a kick out of receiving a Christmas card from the White House. "So, I wrote a letter and filled out a form and, indeed, my exchange family received home-exchange Christmas greetings from the president."

CHAPTER 11

The Key Will Be Under the Flowerpot

"Do you have the key?"

O NE EIGHT-TIME EXCHANGER, AN AUTO SALESMAN in Tacoma, Washington, writes, "I'm not the smartest guy around, but I have learned through bitter experience (twice!) the one most important part of arriving at an exchange home. It was a miserable, rainy night in Birmingham, Alabama, where we'd gone to attend my wife's forty-fifth college reunion; that was the first time. The second time, we had our teenage twin grandchildren along for a couple of exchange weeks in the Algarve region of Portugal. On that unforgettable occasion we spent the first night down the beach from our exchange home in a bed and breakfast! In each of these instances we had a house key screw-up. Tell your readers the most important element in arriving at an exchange home is a very simple one: the house key."

It is a very simple item, but whenever home exchangers get to telling of their experiences, it seems the conversation invariably gets around to someone having had a key disaster of one kind or another.

The lock of an exchanger's second home was changed. For safe-keeping, the key was given to "our neighbor." Which neighbor? The front door key was "the brass one among those on the key ring being mailed you." But there was no brass key on that ring. No problem. "The side door will be unlocked for you." Side door, back door, cellar door, front door—all locked!

Key problems are not necessarily limited to house keys. A medical doctor in Florida writes, "I was asleep in the back of our rented van during the lengthy trip from Madrid to Alacante, Spain. Others in our party of four did the driving and the navigating. We lost at least an hour endeavoring to follow our exchange partner's challenging driving directions.

"Finally—at midnight in the pouring rain—we reached the unmanned security gate of the holiday condo complex where we'd be staying.

"Oh, we had the key to the condo all right but no key to the electronic security gate. We'd no sooner pulled over to the side of the road to assess our dilemma, when along came a garbage truck. With key in hand, the driver opened the swinging security gate. 'No problem,' said my wife, as our van passed through the gate immediately behind the garbage truck. We were so indebted to that driver, we invited him and his helper in for a drink. In faltering English, he said, 'No. We have work.'"

From Chicago, a financial planner writes, "When embarking on an exchange in Paris, we arrived with a house key that didn't work. The substitute apartment superintendent was no help. The correct key was finally found with the help of a Berlitz phrase book through a phone call to family members residing nearby. We finally entered the apartment with the right key—five hours later."

Vacationers from Ohio, on their very first exchange, arrived after dark at their exchange home on Sanibel Island. The house was on a canal in the midst of many shrubs, flowers, vines, and the like, and the key was not where it was supposed to be. "The three of us fumbled, stumbled, and clattered around, trying to figure out a way to get in—all the while trying to avoid walking into the canal in the dark and becoming a midnight snack for an alligator. Finally, we noticed that the transom over one of the doors was open. We boosted our young son up and he

wriggled through—falling with a very loud thud to the floor on the
inside. When he looked up, he saw an older man and woman standing
there in night clothes, staring at him wide-eyed and panic-stricken,
apparently convinced it was their last moment on earth. They were the
previous week's exchangers, who had gotten their departure-date signals crossed. After profuse apologies were exchanged, we withdrew to
the car to search out a motel room. A very inauspicious start to what was

not only a great vacation week but to what has become a fifteen-year-and-counting 'career' of home exchanging!"

A Sarasota, Florida, couple finally arrived in San Francisco at 1 A.M. after a lengthy weather delay and realized the directions to their exchange home were on the table by the front door at their home in Sarasota. "There we were in the middle of the night trying to reconstruct our map from what we recalled of telephone conversations and correspondence. We did remember the street name, and a convenience store clerk in the next town from our destination was able to direct us. We slowly cruised two blocks of the street using the garage door opener at each house; finally, a garage door opened and in we drove. The day before, our hosts had left us freshly brewed coffee and a coffeecake for our brunch-time arrival—good even at 2:30 the following morning!"

"We exchanged for a chalet at a ski resort and were given a map indicating that our destination was the fourth house from the corner," write exchangers from Kaneohe, Hawaii. "When we arrived after what appeared to have been a rather healthy snowstorm, the snow had been plowed into vertical walls at least eight feet high with no way to tell where the first house was, much less the fourth. We finally cut steps into the wall of snow and climbed up, only to find at least waist-deep snow on the other side and the suspected home another two hundred yards away. With sunset upon us, we only had time for one try, but we lucked out. The chalet was absolutely lovely, but the snow was so deep that we couldn't even get to the slopes, much less ski. We decorated the yard with snow angels, got fat on snow cream, and had a perfectly wonderful time."

Keys can be a problem. Somehow, house and car keys are so far down on an exchanger's checklist that the topic is forgotten completely in the excitement of working out vacation plans. It is of critical importance to arrange for the exchange of keys during the latter part of the correspondence, and the best way to exchange keys is to simply mail an extra set (which you have tested and know works) prior to the exchange date. If not handled in this way, then very specific, detailed, written, cast-in-concrete, and confirmed instructions must be given the exchange partner (and the selected key-provider, if any) as to the whereabouts of both house and car keys.

Among the first things some exchangers do is to have at least one duplicate set of keys made, whether they receive them by or pick them up on arrival. This allows both members of a couple to have a set and/or provides a set that can be stashed for emergency use.

Arriving at an exchange home can be quite interesting, even with the right key. "Having been burgled quite recently, our exchangers now had the most heavily secured home you can possibly imagine," writes an elderly English rare-book dealer. "They gave us specific directions for disarming the system and warned us that, within thirty seconds of opening the front door, an alarm would sound if we failed to key in the code on the little console. Since we arrived in total darkness without the foresight to bring a flashlight, we could find neither the light switch nor the alarm keyboard. Sirens shrieked, the dog barked hysterically, and we made the noisiest entrance of all time."

Although most exchangers would never complain about not being met on arrival, the majority would agree that being met is a godsend. If it is not possible to have someone at the airport or station, one British exchanger recommends sending details of alternative ways to reach the destination and, if possible, times of trains, buses, etc., plus the fares. This information might be good to provide anyway, in the event that the best laid plans don't always work.

Being met is nice; being met by your partners is even nicer. Two retirees from Santa Fe were met at the airport by their Toronto partners and given a complete tour of the city and dinner at the country club before the host couple left the next morning. Other travelers tell of being met by partners and taken from the airport to neighborhood welcoming parties thrown in their honor. Still others report that the host's chauffeur picked them up and they had his services available throughout their stay. Yet others describe neighbors who adopted them, introducing them to friends, the neighborhood, stores, etc., in addition to including them in parties, barbecues, and other local events.

Met at the New Orleans airport by their host's son, a couple from Colorado was driven to their exchange home just across the border in Mississippi. "This home was gorgeous—all the luxuries, including an indoor-outdoor pool, and fabulous view of the Gulf of Mexico. We had the use of a Cadillac, and our hosts had provided tickets for one of the Mardi Gras balls, a tuxedo for my husband, and a corsage for me. Wow!"

Helping the meeting process along is the recommendation made by university faculty members in Rincon de la Victoria, Spain. "Exchange partners should share family photographs prior to the exchange date. This accomplishes two things: first, it helps to inspire confidence in these 'strangers' and, second, snapshots can be very helpful to the hosts or anyone else planning to pick up the new arrivals." Snapshots would have been most helpful in the Prague airport for the Clichy, France, couple who waited an hour with the prearranged yellow scarf in place with no one appearing to meet them. Finally, when they were the only passengers left, their host materialized, sheepishly admitting that he had no idea what *l' echarpe jaune* ("yellow scarf") was.

A couple from Brevard, North Carolina, fared a little better—according to them, quite a bit better. Their host picked them up at the train station and took them to "a home that looked only vaguely familiar—quite unlike any pictures we had ever seen. The house was palatial! The scale of the snapshots combined with our partners' modesty had led us to believe their home was as ordinary as our small, two-bedroom summer cottage. On top of that, they'd decided at the last moment to invite another couple to come with them. We offered to back out, but they would have none of it. . . . I suppose, however, that it's just as well we had declined the use of their Rolls Royce; we had left our newly polished pickup for them."

Several people in addition to the Santa Fe couple favor the idea of one couple or the other arriving a day early. Not only do they have a chance to meet and get acquainted in person, but home orientation—at least on one side of the exchange—is easier. Two retired teachers from Stoney Creek, Ontario, write, "On the advice of our very first exchange partners, we avoided passing each other mid-Atlantic, and we continue to make an effort to do that. On that particular one, we spent a few days in London before the exchange began, met our hosts, and got oriented to the house and neighborhood."

"We were with relatives who lived close to our exchangers during the week before the exchange," writes a retired secondary schoolteacher in Kingston, Ontario, "and were able to visit our guests in their home before we moved in. We had several good visits, and I liked getting to know the 'real people' (as opposed to the 'on-paper people') as well as getting used to the layout of their home."

There's another school of thought that would maintain that these kinds of arrangements take all the fun out of getting there. A Baytown, Texas, host tells of his English exchanger driving down the two deep ruts in the middle of nowhere that are the road to his isolated house in the Texas hill country at three o'clock in the morning: "Steep drop-offs on either side and so much worse than your average washboard road that your lights are either pointing straight up or straight down. As he tells it, he got to the house, saw our mud shoes by the front door and began to wonder just what he'd gotten himself into. . . . What kind of people go away and leave their shoes behind? . . . Wonder what else they've left behind. Intrepid Englishman that he was, he unlocked the door and proceeded with his vacation."

An exchange couple from Somerset, England, shared this remarkable story. "In northern Portugal we found ourselves after midnight in a rural village with no hope of locating our exchange cottage. But a fiesta was still going on, and ever the teacher that I am, I thought I would try out my rudimentary Portuguese in hopes of getting some directions. Well, I unintentionally set in motion an elaborate chain response involving half the town! . . . A shopkeeper made a phone call and woke up someone living close to our mystery destination. . . . A truck driver led our car out of town through woods, up a mountainous 'road,' then abruptly abandoned us with a cheerful message. Five minutes later a pretty teenaged girl appeared out of nowhere (full of smiles—even at 2:00 A.M.), got in the car, and guided us to a remote habitation up an impossibly rocky track, helped us negotiate the secrets of the lock, showed us where to switch on the water pump and electricity, and pointed out the bodies of four dead rats in the bedroom. . . . Then, presenting her face to be kissed by each of us, she wished us *'Boa noite!'* and ran off into the darkness, assuring us that her father was waiting for her in his truck close by and that they were looking forward to our visit to their farm that week."

The best story about getting off on the right foot comes from Vero Beach, Florida, from whence a couple once embarked for southwestern France without so much as a single piece of paper confirming their exchange. Their potential hosts had warned them of a mail strike in France. In telephone conversations, it had been agreed that the Florida couple would call on a specific date to arrange to be met the following day. After failing to reach the family by phone, they spent a rather uneasy night in a French hotel, three thousand miles from home, wondering what their next step should be. The following morning the phone call went through; the previous day the phone had been left off the hook.

CHAPTER 12

Successful Living in Someone Else's Home, Part 1

VACATION HOME EXCHANGING IS A LIVING-IN experience—living in someone else's home. Muriel Osher, in Cincinnati, Ohio, shares these thoughts: "How curious it is to live in someone else's home. Someone whom we have never met and perhaps may never meet (although we shall make the attempt). And, of course, it is a strange home in a strange country, filled with family pictures of strange people. But from the first day that the four of us arrived, we seemed to immediately fit into this English exchange home. Without hesitation, we adapted ourselves to the accouterments in the kitchen, bath, and bedrooms, following the detailed written instructions from our host. His generosity was unbounded, inviting us to help ourselves to his bar and larder. On the table in the living room was a large map of the area. Different colored pins designated pubs, walking paths, and points of interest.

"This home was like a metaphor of the people who live in it. It smacked of comfort and easy charm with no attempt at contrived decorating. There was no effort put to blending colors in the upholstery, but aesthetically everything worked very well. The home was a functioning machine filled with clues to the interests of the occupants, that is, books, records, and indoor and outdoor plants. The gardens seemed actually to be a part of this house. Each window offered a visual treat of blooms and green lawns. There was a small greenhouse (used mainly for growing tomatoes and grapes) alongside a kitchen garden where there was a patio with table and chairs.

"Of course, our host's books told the whole story. Most all of them were inscribed inside as 'a gift from Annie,' usually for a birthday with an affectionate note. The library was categorized by subject: history, botany, music, art, old and new novels, etc.—all of which told us of this family's lively and widespread interests.

"There was a large kitchen table. I'm sure it is the gathering place for our host's family just as it was for us.

"I truly felt that harmony and love were so strong in this home that it just spilled over onto us."

The Golden Rule tells us to treat others as we would have them treat us. This abiding truth is also a basic element of the home exchange concept: care for your host's home as you would have him care for your home.

Along with applying your own good judgment to home-related matters that might come up during your vacation stay, probably the best guide to the care of your vacation home will be found in the information about this home prepared for you by your host—the home information kit. In this, you will find everything your host wants you to know about your vacation home, and it is of paramount importance that you carefully read through this material very soon after your arrival. If by chance this is your host's second home, then it may not have been occupied immediately prior to your arrival. Indeed, it may have been vacant for some weeks or months before your arrival, in which case your host's instructions will be basic: opening the storm shutters, turning on the furnace, water heater, and/or air conditioner, and other ways of preparing the home for your use. More than likely, however, this is your host's primary home, and as such it will have been occupied by him immediately prior to your arrival and the more basic aspects of the home's operation will have been taken care of.

First things first, and if your arrival is in the late evening or during the night, the first thing you and those with you will want to do is get some sleep after the long drive, flight, bus or train trip. You will not need the architect's drawing to find the home's bedrooms and bathrooms.

When you are ready to sit up and take notice the next morning—perhaps after enjoying breakfast or some other meal from the kitchen staples your host has left you—you and each member of your vacation group should take an exchanger's tour of the house. Check out all the rooms, noting the drawer, closet, and storage space you are to use. Explore the basement, attic, garage, and other inside facilities. Then take a walk around the property to familiarize yourself with this vacation scene, to get the lay of the land. While you are thus wandering about, no doubt some of the neighbors (your host has told them all about you) will introduce themselves.

An eight-time exchanging telephone engineer in Fort Worth, Texas, suggests that exchangers "bring along the correspondence file for that particular exchange. More often than not, you'll then have at hand good information about your exchange host, his family, his home, his neighbors, and about the area in which your home-away-from-home is situated."

If you are vacationing in an apartment or condominium, during your first day or two by all means introduce yourself to the superintendent and/or staff in the condominium management office. Should you have an emergency of some kind, these people and your neighbors could be of tremendous help.

Generally, home exchange hosts leave their guests ample room for clothes and other personal items, but such is not always the case. One Australian couple faced a space problem on arriving at their exchange home in England. "Our host left us one small closet and two tiny drawers—very inadequate. As we cleared drawers and made closet space for our things, we felt like intruders." Another family arrived at their vacation home only to find every closet and every closet shelf and every drawer in every bedroom filled to overflowing with the host family's clothes and other personal items. This exchange couple and their three teenage sons had brought along golf clubs, tennis racquets, fishing equipment, their personal items, and lots of clothes—a whole carful of stuff with no place to put anything. A little creative rearranging solved that problem.

Creative rearranging was certainly not possible when a six-foot Kansas City exchanger was at his host's home in Ipswich, England. The challenge here was a beam across the center of the living room ceiling with a clearance of only 5' 8". Ten colorful neckties draped over the obstacle didn't quite match the room's decor, but they certainly shouted out a warning.

On some cruise ships and in most hotels (even at New York's palatial Waldorf), there is little space for storage, so travelers spend two weeks stumbling over their empty suitcases. Not so on a home exchange vacation. You simply put these items out of the way in a closet, the mud room, or the basement (but not on the basement floor, as experience proves that two-thirds of the world's basement floors are damp to one degree or another).

Your vacation home may not have all the appliances you have in your own home, and it may have some your home does not have, but in due course you will be using most or all of the appliances in this home. If you have problems with any of these appliances—and you probably will—check out the home information kit or the manufacturers' booklets. More than likely, these instructions will provide you the help you need.

But even with instructions, sometimes things go awry, according to this Corpus Christi, Texas, exchanger. "We told our European guests never to open the windows when the air conditioner's on. Windows the next A.M.: wide open; air conditioner: on. When reminding our guests about this, the wife beamed, 'It's okay. We turned off the air conditioner.' She pointed to the ceiling fan."

Most exchangers prepare most of their meals at home. "But not my wife. On vacation, no slaving in a hot kitchen, no self-catering for her!" writes a seasoned English vacation home exchanger. Early on in your stay, after you have familiarized yourself with the house and its accouterments, you should take stock of the available food staples and get together a shopping list (See? Just like home.). Off you go on your initial vacation food-shopping expedition, perhaps with some where-to-buy-it suggestions from your host or the neighbors. You view the shopping scene, getting some ideas on what shops are available nearby.

You may be using many of the food and household staples left by your exchange host. A fifteen-time home exchanger, a wife, mother, and teacher, in Seattle, Washington, writes: "Our arrangement has always been to keep paper and pencil handy in the kitchen to make note of each item (with brand names) we use, so we can replace those things."

Homemakers—wives and husbands—often become very attached to their own particular kitchen utensils, to the extent that there are just no substitutes for their good old reliable vegetable parer, favorite knives, wine-bottle opener, or some other utensil that has passed the test of use and time. If you are traveling by car, bring these items along with you. Do not forget half-a-dozen boxes and bottles of your favorite spices, scissors, a few plastic travel glasses, and an apron or two. If you go by plane, however, don't pack your scissors or kitchen knives in your carry-on bag. An exchanger from Virginia did this and, after passing through the airport gate metal detector, had an extended conversation with a security officer.

In most cases, making the transition from one's own home furnishings to those in an exchange home is relatively simple, like getting accustomed to the furniture in a hotel or a rented vacation cottage. But as in hotel living, sometimes beds are a challenge. The beds in your host's home may be just right for him and his family, but too hard, too soft, too saggy in the middle for you. Experienced exchangers have learned that nearly all bed problems can be solved by placing a folded blanket or bedspread strategically between the bed's mattress and springs, boxed or otherwise. This procedure did not solve the bed problems some American tourists had at the Ritz in Paris, so they simply flopped the mattresses off the twin beds and slept on the floor. Yes, it

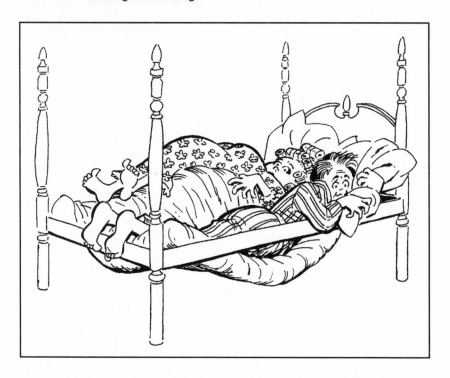

was at the Ritz, and yes, the next morning the chambermaid exclaimed, "*Mon Dieu!*"

Home exchangers from New Jersey had a similar experience while exchanging in Nuremberg, Germany. The bed was marvelous—very comfortable. But it was a mechanically controlled "do-everything" bed. The head could be raised, the foot could be raised, the middle could be raised. A push of the control sent the bed into its act, but it got jammed with the head and foot low and the middle very high. Off went the mattress onto the floor—a good, firm bed in the shadow of the nearby tent-shaped monster. The host later instructed the New Jerseyites on the proper use of that bed's controls.

"My husband's real weird. He has this thing about shirts. Won't wear 'em unless they're 100 percent cotton and he (thank God) irons 'em," writes a Seattle, Washington, retired book publisher's wife. "Our exchange apartment in London's Covent Garden had the iron, but no ironing board. He'd never pay a laundry to do the shirts, so in desperation I said, 'For heaven's sake, go across the street and borrow one from the Senior Care Center. Surely they have an ironing board lying around.' So he did just that, and the lady at the center said, 'Sure, here's a new one; keep it as long as you wish. The cost? Oh, there's no cost, sir.' So, several weeks and many ironed shirts later, my husband made a modest contribution to the center's newly established ironing board fund."

Sometimes other elements of the exchange home—furniture or decorative accessories—take a bit of getting used to. For example, prominently displayed in the living room of a London exchange home was a three-foot-high glass case containing a large stuffed dog. What an interesting way to remember a beloved pet, said the exchange guests from the United States. "No," said the host, "we just have him there to shock people."

While much can be said for taking vacations at times other than the summer months, the survey showed that the majority of home exchangers prefer to take their vacations in July and August. In the Northern Hemisphere, where most vacation home exchanging takes place, these two months are generally the hottest months of the year.

Apparently, there is an unwritten international statute stating that no two air conditioners can be manufactured or operated alike. Yes, all air conditioners (or "air-cons," as a Hong Kong home exchange host calls them) are different. But like traveling salesmen who motel it five nights a week, the experienced home exchanger becomes an expert in operating air-conditioning equipment. A Phoenix, Arizona, exchange host learned his air conditioner was quite okay, as were his instructions for operating it. His German exchange guests just liked it better with no air conditioning and the windows wide opened. Even the 90°–117°F temperatures did not change their minds.

CHAPTER 13

Successful Living in Someone Else's Home, Part 2

YOU ALREADY KNOW THAT YOUR EXCHANGE HOST'S neighbors and other friends can play a very important role in the vacation home exchange picture. Hopefully, your host has left you some information about his nearest neighbors, and this will help you as you meet these new friends. More than likely, you will be hearing the most widely used phrase in the vacation home exchange world, one which here can be attributed to the neighbors: "Be sure to let us know if we can do anything for you folks."

A Baltimore, Maryland, couple writes, "Our home exchange host in Wales arranged a catered party aboard his beautiful fifty-two-foot motor yacht. Among the many other guests, we were introduced to the Marquis of Anglesie. Never heard of him, but we endeavored to demonstrate awe and proper respect."

A Virginia exchange couple writes: "In Scotland, our host's gardener stopped his work to drive us to a bus stop for a day trip to Edinburgh. We worried that perhaps his boss might not appreciate his spending this time with us instead of doing his gardening work. 'No problem,' he said, 'At age eighty-two, I'm my own boss.'"

From Sunset, Maine, another exchange couple wrote: "We contacted two couples with whom we had negotiated but not exchanged in Scotland and in England and met them for dinner. On both occasions we were nervous and wary, but the two evenings were high spots of our trip. The first couple lived in a suburb of Edinburgh. They fed us a great meal, poured endless wine, and educated us in Scottish history. The second couple lived in a stone cottage on the moors in the Yorkshire Dales. He was a rock musician and chatted amiably all evening. She was tall, dressed in black, and had long red hair. She cooked a wonderful meal but barely spoke the whole time we were there. She wrote

131

Harlequin-style romance novels. We have continued a lively correspondence with both of these couples and each has invited us back for a visit."

A Santa Fe, New Mexico, couple who own a retail shop and have exchanged five times—Hawaii (twice), Florida, England, and New Zealand—write: "We met people who had not previously exchanged but who expressed an interest in exchanging with us at some point in the future."

Pride of ownership is a key factor in the good care you take of your own home and possessions. Apply this same practice in your care of your host's home. In cases of rain (or threatening rain), do not leave the windows open—respect the furniture and use of same—do not track mud, sand, or whatever through the house (that doormat is there for reasons other than saying welcome)—keep the appliances clean and in good working order—follow through with the arrangements made for cleaning the home, watering the plants, and caring for the property.

A Vancouver, Canada, business couple arrived at their Minnesota vacation home and found that their host had made ample drawer and closet space available to them. There were clean linens everywhere, and the entire home had been beautifully cleaned. "But there was an antique silver tea set, sterling silver flatware, and lovely crystal everywhere in the dining room. In the living room, there was a huge selection of expensive wines and liquors and a humidor filled with Havana cigars. And the refrigerator? It was fully stocked—enough food to last the two of us for a lifetime. We found some 'regular' china and silverware and endeavored to replace all of the food items we used. We don't drink or smoke. We put all of the valuables out of the way, endeavoring to return each to its proper spot when we departed."

Those who have had more than a few home exchanges know that occasionally (even with careful use) things get broken or otherwise damaged. "We had not been in our exchange partner's apartment for ten minutes when one of our kids opened the fridge door too 'exuberantly' and knocked the ceramic kitchen clock off the wall." So writes a Peruvian exchanger. "My husband was mortified, and we set right out to seek a substitute clock. The only store we found did not have exactly the same clock, but we did get one that I liked and left it on the table."

"When we arrived home following a great three-week exchange in Hawaii, we discovered the young couple in our California home had apparently never encountered a microwave oven. They left a note of apology expressing a desire to replace our once fluted plastic bowl that was now a perfectly flat tray. No problem. We still use it."

A Garden City, New York, exchanger writes: "In the 'never take anything for granted' category, we had exchanged with an English family, and upon our return, a neighbor told us how, after having been in our home for over a week, the English housewife remarked, 'I really can't see how they cook very well—with only a pancake griddle.' The neighbor came over, pulled open the pots and pans drawer of the range, and found the usual collection of pans and skillets. The English woman gasped, 'Oh, dear, I thought that was where one lit the oven, and I never bake.'"

As mentioned previously, most basements are damp. Also, many toilets continue to drip water after their water tanks have refilled. You can save your exchange host a few dollars on the next water bill by removing the top of the toilet tank and adjusting the ball (or float). Bend it (or set it) down slightly; this will prevent the water from continuing to flow over into the overflow pipe. See? Once again, staying in someone else's home is just like living in your own.

This from a special education supervisor in New York City: "Our 'new' friends from Menlo Park, California, were staying at our condo in Vermont. We got a phone call stating that the television set was not working. They could not understand the problem and, therefore, called our television repairman. As it turned out, the television set was not broken; it was just not plugged in. Our exchange partners were embarrassed, but we thought it was quite funny."

A nine-time exchanger in Kaiserlautern, Germany (who has a winter home in Fort Lauderdale, Florida) puts it this way: "Be tolerant of your partner's property. And watch the property of partners like your own and you'll never go wrong. Home exchange vacations, I like it, and I will do it again." If you care for your exchange host's property as if it were your own, usually nothing will go wrong and you will have a memorable vacation home exchange.

It is customary for exchange hosts to pay for their basic monthly telephone service; however, home exchange guests always pay the charges for their toll (long distance) calls and pay for local calls they make if the telephone company serving the area charges for local calls. Many exchangers prefer to charge telephone calls with credit cards. If not, in the United States the various telephone companies provide their customers with monthly statements including date, time, and charges for each long distance call. After the exchange takes place, the U.S.

exchange host simply mails his guest a photocopy of the telephone company's statement covering the exchange time; the guest then reimburses the host. Outside the United States, telephone companies follow different billing procedures, country by country. If your overseas host gets an itemized monthly statement, the procedure suggested above can be followed. If not, the exchange partners must decide in advance how the long distance charges should be handled.

　　With access to a variety of dresser and desk drawers, closets, the basement, the attic, and nooks and crannies throughout the exchange home, exchange guests may be tempted to spread their personal belongings all over the house, never quite sure which item went where. Experienced exchangers keep their clothes and personal items together in rather obvious places. If each person in the exchange group follows this procedure, things are not likely to get lost, and certainly the packing at the end of the exchange is a lot less difficult.

When making up the bed in their bedroom some weeks after their exchange partners had returned to Cornwall, England, Florida exchangers discovered a packet of travelers' checks under the mattress. It was hidden so well the departing guests thought they had lost their travelers' checks and had had them replaced.

This story comes from an eight-time exchanger in Albuquerque, New Mexico. "Several months after one delightful home exchange, I was moving furniture to clean, when I found an unfamiliar lady's undergarment. My husband was in big trouble until I noticed that the garment said 'Made in Canada.' Our most recent home exchange was with a Canadian couple. She was glad to get it back."

In a previous chapter, burglar alarms (or security systems) were mentioned. Like air conditioners, every security system is different. Some are operated by keys. You unlock the front door with the regular key, are greeted by a buzzing sound, then rush inside to the control box and deactivate (or disarm) the system with a special key. Other systems are operated by a push-button code, with the device mounted outside the home near the front door or just inside the front door.

A Toronto, Canada, optometrist writes: "Our host had placed a 'barking dog' alarm in his basement. During our autumn vacation stay, the falling leaves from trees next to the home would regularly set off the alarm."

It is always a challenge to get the system disarmed before the alarm goes off. This piercing sound—both inside and outside the house—is guaranteed to wake not only the dead, but the neighbors and the police. Hopefully, your host will have left you clear instructions on how to operate any security system.

If your host's home has a security system, it is important that you activate it each time you leave the home. An American exchange couple vacationing in Barbados writes: "We were robbed very early on a Christmas morning. We had left everything in the living room of our atrium-style home: presents, purses, and other personal items. Everything was stolen, and all because we hadn't bothered to lock the doors. Our advice to other home exchangers in-residence: When you are asleep (as we were) or away, be sure to lock everything. By so doing, you will be taking an important step toward protecting your things and those of your host as well."

A retired U.S. Air Force officer now living in Germany writes that his exchange home was burglarized during a home exchange vacation. "Fortunately, my insurance covered the things I lost, and my host's insurance covered his losses."

Once in a great while, as part of the exchange arrangements, your exchange home will have other occupants. An American exchanger writes: "We exchanged with a family with two children. These people had just hired an au pair from France who was to remain with us at the home while the host and his family were at our home. As soon as our host left, the au pair took over the house—entertaining her friends and always making herself 'at home' in rooms we were occupying. Once she even decided to 'borrow' some of my clothes. A real horror story."

In contrast, a retired senior naval officer in Sarasota, Florida, writes: "On our exchange in France, a non-English-speaking grandmother came with the house but didn't sleep there. Each day she helped with the cooking, the cleaning, and the laundry. During our stay I decided to take her up for her very first airplane ride. As a former U.S. Navy pilot holding many licenses, I was able to rent a little Cessna. My grandmother passenger-friend was thrilled as I conducted a few acrobatics over our little village. Many of her relatives were out waving white sheets, and after we landed this grandmother got on her bicycle and spent the rest of the day telling everyone she could find all about her *trés belle aérien experience!*"

In addition to swimming, golf, tennis, walking trips, sightseeing, and other vacation activities, home exchangers often arrange to get together with other exchangers. Before leaving home for their vacations, some exchangers check out their vacation home exchange directories, making photocopies of those pages covering exchange listings in or near the vicinity of their vacation homes. During the vacation, these exchangers refer to these copies and contact some of the exchangers listed. It is a good way to meet other exchangers and share exchange stories and a good way to make contact with others who might be interested in exchanging with you. Experienced exchangers never leave home without several fact sheets describing their homes, as well as an assortment of exterior and interior photographs to be shared with potential exchangers they meet along the way.

An exchanger living in Hawaii writes: "After arranging our England exchange, but about three months before going, referring to the home exchange directory, I wrote letters to a dozen interesting-looking people listed in the directory who lived in Cornwall, England, and in Ireland, asking if we could visit with them as we were to be exchanging in their parts of the world—to stay overnight. Their hospitality was overwhelming. These people couldn't do enough for us."

A Seymour, Tennessee, orthodontist writes: "Our exchange partner instructed us to eat from the garden. The garden was beautifully cared for and the fruits and vegetables so abundant that our family couldn't possibly use even a small portion of that which was available. We ended up preserving much of the garden's produce for our very kind exchange partners."

Vacation home exchangers are known to respect the houses in which they live and the communities in which their exchange homes are situated. They are good neighbors. "When in Rome, do as the Romans do" is a key phrase in vacation home exchangese!

As you leave your host's home, it is suggested you leave a note—sort of an overview of your vacation at his home. Mention any problems you had while staying there: broken dishes, malfunctioning appliances, or whatever.

You will want to follow whatever arrangements you made with the host regarding the final departure cleaning and the disposition of house and car keys. At departure time too you should double-check the home (closets, drawers, and every room) to be absolutely certain no personal items have been left behind. Home exchanging is rife with tales of articles exchange guests have left behind—clothes, clocks, money, and a veritable parade of children's books and toys. A Seattle, Washington, exchanger writes, "In a mailed carton of things we inadvertently left behind, our exchange partner of the previous week included a half-eaten box of corn flakes."

CHAPTER 14

A House Full of Geckos

*Born in Alberta, Canadian Sid Lowry to date has enjoyed thirteen
vacation home exchanges—some abroad and in Hawaii,
Tennessee, plus four in Northern California. Until her retirement
from the business world, Sid served as an executive accountant-
bookkeeper.*

*"Mert" Lowry was born in Cardston, Alberta. He was a career
airman in the Royal Canadian Air Force. On retirement from the
service, he became associated with Toyota Motors. His permanent
retirement came in 1984.*

*The Lowrys' present home is near Cowichan Bay on Southern
Vancouver Island. In the 1980s, Mert and Sid traveled extensively
in Europe. Their first home exchange, however, was in 1987—
"three lovely months in a small English village."*

Sid Lowry writes:

When Mert came from the mailbox one cold day in February and
informed me that we might be exchanging homes in Maui,
Hawaii, for a month or so in September, I reluctantly agreed that it might
be a nice vacation spot. Had I even had an inkling that we would have
some strange creatures as roomies, I might not have been so quick to
agree.

Plans were completed, and before we knew it we were in Maui and
getting settled into a very beautiful home. It was two stories of pure
luxury on a terraced half-acre with a kidney-shaped swimming pool,
coconut palms, avocado trees, a banana grove, and papaya trees that
supplied us with heavenly tasting fresh papayas for our daily breakfasts.

The lady of the house had left an information book with all the pertinent dos and don'ts on the home, a sort of an "all you need to know
but had no time to ask" manual. I had perused it on our arrival, but when

I came to the chapters on insects, animals, or any so-called creepy crawlers, I must admit to doing so only in a skimming fashion, thinking that any strange beasties would only be found outdoors.

Our first gecko encounter was a few days after our arrival. We had our breakfasts on the lanai and saw these tiny lizards sometimes scurrying into their tiny hiding spaces. They are no longer than two to three inches and are chameleon-like, so their color blends with the background. When we saw them on the brown siding of the house, they were brown. When we saw them on a leaf, they were green, almost invisible. You would get the feeling that something was peeking at you and were only aware that they were there when they would scurry. And dash they would, moving at great velocity.

While doing laundry one morning, I left the outside door open. I saw my first gecko inside the house. I assumed he entered through the open door, and of course tried to coerce him out again. I soon realized this was an exercise in futility when he crawled into a tiny slot-sized space next to a power outlet. The thought that he might be the permanent resident laundry room denizen never crossed my mind. I always looked for him when I went downstairs. Several days later we were in the family room downstairs, and a gecko appeared on the sliding glass doors. We opened the door and he gladly went into the garden. We presumed this was the same gecko.

I was going to pick up the paper one afternoon. Just as I opened the outside door, I felt something fall on my forearm. Panic stations were activated, and it was all systems GO! when I realized it was a gecko—a real live reptile on my body. The fact that he was only a few inches in size did not matter. As far as I was concerned, he might as well have been a boa or an alligator. My fear was just as intense. I invented the new fast version of the Maui hula, and now that I look back, realize how silly I must've looked. I was jumping, screaming, flailing my arms, and trying to dislodge the tiny critter from my arm. He just would not let go. The more I performed, the tighter he held on. It was as though he was permanently adhered to me with crazy glue and had no intention of leaving. In his own time, he released his death grip on me and went running off into the greenery. I thought I was scared, but just think of how the poor tiny fellow felt. I must've scared him half to death. He was most likely sitting in his favorite spot on the upper doorframe, waiting for some unsuspecting insects to come by for dinner. My opening the door pushed him off and, as luck would have it, onto me.

A few days later, same door, same mission, same command performance. Mert was barbecuing on the lanai and helped remove this one
from my forearm and send him running off. One day in my "zoris," I
was roving about what we called the lower forty, and one of the little
creatures got on top of my bare foot. He fastened to me and would not
let go. After this third episode, I came to the conclusion that since these
little lizards like me so much, perhaps I should become their friend.
They were actually very fascinating to watch, and we did enjoy out-
smarting them (we thought), in that we could actually see them when
they acted as though we did not.

It was time to read up on these tiny tropical soft-skinned lizards, so
I went to the library room downstairs to consult the encyclopedia and
dictionary. They both confirmed most of what I already knew about
geckos from my real-life experiences. Further, I learned that they have
suction pads on the bottom of their feet. One article even mentioned that
some types have nails they can draw out and retract, like cats, although
I did not feel any claws when they clung to me. No wonder they were so
adept at running on the ceilings and walls of the lanai without falling
off. Curious as I was, I was not about to catch one to have a peek at the
tiny gecko soles to see how many suction pads were there, but I knew
that they were very effective.

To this point, we had not seen a gecko on the main floor of the
house, so we did not watch out for them.

I was reading in bed one evening, with only the bedside lamp on.
Mert was still on the lanai. I heard a slight movement beside the dresser,
turned on the overhead lights, and looked behind the dresser mirror. There
was a tiny head peering back at me. I required Mert's assistance in this
great capture, so in he came, armed with a fly swatter. Since all the windows were screened, this posed a dilemma. We did not want to hurt the
little fellow, just get him to the great outdoors. We had to make a gecko
trap. I finally came up with the idea that an empty plastic container and a
piece of cardboard should be effective. The major obstacle to this plan
was how to get the gecko to stay still on a level surface long enough to
cover him with the container. The hunt began—Mert still armed with the
fly swatter, me with the trap. Mert would bang on the mirror, scare the
gecko, and I would run to his new location with my trap in hand. We
soon realized that this gecko was much faster than we were and could get
into tiny crevices that we could not even get near to. We chased this tiny
three-inch lizard all over that bedroom, from one picture to the dresser to
another picture to the window. We were tiring, but not the gecko. Finally,

he stopped on a wall for a moment, and plop, down came the container. Mert gently inserted the thin cardboard between our small buddy and the wall, and he was entrapped. I am sure he was a very happy gecko when we released him into the vines. This performance would have made a prize-winning video for that television series.

We went to bed content in the knowledge that no more unwanted beasts lurked in the tiny recesses of our home. Little did we know.

A few days later, I saw what I thought was a paper clip on the dining room carpet. I bent down and almost had it in hand when the end of the paper clip moved. It was a baby gecko, about an inch long. Again it was time to man the gecko trap and get the baby outdoors. This we accomplished in record time. We put him on a leaf in the vines next to the lanai. He made this his home and settled there, as we saw him on many occasions.

Again we were proud of our capture. That same night we were listening to records and reading in the living room when I heard a slight fluttering noise. I looked up on the wall behind the music system, and there went a gecko scurrying up to the beams above. I calmly said, "There goes one." As Mert looked up nonchalantly, he said, "There goes another." The music must've disturbed them from their favorite resting place. This was getting a bit too close for comfort. Befriending them was one thing, but we did not give them license to move in with us en masse.

This is when I decided that I should fully read the information booklet again, especially the paragraphs on geckos. By now it did not come as any surprise to me to read that since there is no method of total eradication, the residents of Maui have acceded to sharing their homes with the tiny lizards. As they are very shy and completely harmless, there is no reason to fear them, and they do eat insects. At dusk they would appear out of their tiny hiding places and liven up. I watched as several ran across the tops of the huge sliding doors. I raced inside to see them crawling upside down on the inside door frame. They could get in using the sliding doors without even opening them.

With its year-round perfect weather, Hawaii is a great place for a home exchange vacation. When that Hawaii home listing in the exchange directory includes a reference to "lovable small inside-outside pets," potential exchangers will know that's "pets" spelled G-E-C-K-O-S!

With the passing of time, our encounters with geckos were limited to the lanai, where we greeted them each day with, "Good morning, little guys." We even said our good-byes when we left for home . . . and would almost swear they understood us.

CHAPTER 15

Still More People Who Tried It
. . . and Liked It

Prior to his retirement in 1984, Norman Thompson traveled the world as a ship's engineer. Later, he was an equipment supervisor for crews servicing long-distance power lines. Over the years, he had been a Boy Scout leader in addition to serving on the staff of various school swimming clubs. At home, Norman enjoys his workshop and garden.

For thirty years, Dorothy Thompson was a teacher in several Queensland school districts. First she served in a one-teacher "bush" school; later she specialized in the six- and seven-year level—"Where kids discover the excitement of reading," she says. Voluntary tutoring in literacy is one of her retirement interests.

For years the Thompsons' hobby has been travel; among Dorothy's other special interests are collecting Victoriana and theater decor. The Thompsons have two sons, Cameron and Mark. In retirement, they find tropical island life relaxing and travel—vacation home exchanging and otherwise.

Here's the story of a three-month vacation home exchange that started with thirty-one days aboard a Russian passenger liner.

Dorothy Thompson writes:

Norman and I live in tropical northern Australia—Picnic Bay, on Magnetic Island, one of the coral islands of the Great Barrier Reef. Sounds isolated? Well, one certainly might think so, but by fast ferry we are only twenty minutes from the nearest city, Townsville. We island residents thoroughly enjoy a happy blend of peaceful living under the palms and modern conveniences and services.

Much as we love it here, occasionally Norm and I get a wanderlust, and this desire to get away once again was our first step into the world of vacation home exchanging.

Already we had enjoyed wonderful but costly holidays across the Pacific, and for several years we had set our sights on England—and not just for a few weeks. Retired as we are, we would go by ship, spend three months in England, and return to Australia by air. A dream trip it was; however, with costs of hotels or rentals, a good many meals eaten out, and a car for traveling about, being in England between July and October would surely add up to a packet.

The more we planned and figured, the more discouraged we became—realizing that the trip was perhaps a bit more than we could manage—until the former owner of our home "prescribed" home exchange as the solution to our vacation dilemma. The possibility of exchanging homes with someone in England appealed to us immensely, but we were naturally cautious. Strangers living in our home? We floated this idea among various trusted islanders whose English relatives just might possibly be interested. No response, so we decided to take the bull by the horns and list our home in a home exchange directory. We were somewhat concerned that if we were successful in making a contact, would these people properly look after our home, our garden, our swimming pool, and our cat? And what about Norm's beloved Triumph car? I must say that we did take some comfort in the large number of successful vacation home exchanges we'd heard about.

Prior to the distribution of the home exchange directory containing our listing, and quite out of the blue, a friend of ours in Australia received a letter from English relatives—also a retired couple—expressing keen interest in the possibility of exchanging homes with us. Their home was in Bexhill-on-Sea on the south coast of England, not too far from London.

Like us, our newfound English friends had no previous home exchange experience. They and we, however, were quite professional, so to speak, in exchanging letters and information about ourselves, our homes, and the communities in which we lived, with some photographs as well. With each communication back and forth between Australia and England, our mutual friendship, confidence, and trust developed to that point where we said, "Let's do it!"

Finally, there was the matter of cars. Wouldn't it be great if we could also exchange cars? Norm and these folks had a very frank "postal discussion" about car exchange. This was an important aspect of the arrangement for them and for us, so we decided to include our cars as a part of the exchange agreement.

We then threw ourselves into a whirl of preparations as travelers and as vacation home exchange hosts. We installed a garden sprinkling system and checked and double-checked our home, appliances, car, accounts, and insurance policies. And we prepared pages of directions for the use of our home, our car, and our pool (yes, there was also the matter of taking care of our cat), recommendations for shopping and other essentials and services, information about our neighbors, and names of persons to be contacted if anything went wrong. Finally, we arranged with willing friends to add a last-minute sparkle to our home: food in the fridge and fresh flowers for the decor to celebrate the arrival of our exchange partners. Others promised to meet them on their arrival at the Townsville airport. Our near neighbors couldn't wait to greet the people from Bexhill-on-Sea, and island bowlers were enthusiastic about the possibility of two new players. Australian goodwill was overflowing.

In the midst of all these preparations, we received the latest home exchange directory, with our listing included. Immediately thereafter, by letter and by telephone from various parts of England came inquiries from other potential home exchangers—both experienced and first timers, mostly retired—who responded favorably to the possibility of coming to Australia for periods up to three months. From these communications we had our first clue to the reality of home exchanging as a viable and widely accepted approach to vacationing. We were sorry to have to disappoint these people, but, of course, our plans were in place.

Breathlessly, we waved good-byes from the ferry to the well-wishers, and then it was off to Sydney, where our ship was the Russian liner *Belorussiya*. Through the Suez Canal and the Mediterranean, it was a thirty-seven-day voyage to England—a delightful, happy mix of shipboard life and visiting exciting ports of call along the way.

We docked at Southampton under gray skies, too late to catch the through train to Bexhill-on-Sea. Although we were two hours late arriving in Bexhill, like true friends, our English home exchange partners were waiting for us at the station barrier. They recognized us at once, probably because Norm looked so Australian in his broad-brimmed felt hat. After all of our correspondence, what a joy it was to meet these folks in person!

After a lovely picnic-basket lunch on the Downs, our hosts proudly led us up the stairs to Number 16, a delightfully comfortable modern flat, carpeted throughout, with a balcony toward the sea. English flowers bloomed in the landscaped garden. At last, this was Bexhill-on-Sea!

Our English hosts had thoughtfully planned to stay over for two days after our arrival. We were particularly appreciative of their doing this for various reasons. First, we had a chance to get to know the people who were to occupy our home in Australia. Second, our hosts helped to familiarize us with what was to be our home away from home for the next three months. Also, we had hands-on training in the proper use of the flat's appliances (not so different from ours in Australia), met the neighbors who were to become our friends in the weeks ahead, learned about the local services and shopping (including the pick-your-own strawberry farm), and had our first pub lunch at the old smugglers' pub, The Star. In bidding our hosts a fond farewell on their departure from England, we assured them that an equally warm welcome awaited them on their arrival in Australia.

We had heard that in home exchanging the host's neighbors often helped to turn an otherwise enjoyable holiday into an especially memorable one, and this was certainly the case with our neighbors and new friends in Bexhill. We were guided and pampered by our host's stalwart band of past Rotarians and their gracious ladies—coffee mornings, luncheons, and a strawberry tea. They opened their hearts, their homes, and their social diaries to us, and we shall always be grateful for the many courtesies they extended to us.

The English weather? Well, the very months we were there turned out to be England's wettest summer in fifty years (we selected the wrong year, because the next summer was to be England's sunniest). Undeterred by the forecasts of more rain, more clouds, and more wind, Norm and I set out on our wider travels, first to Stourbridge, where hospitable distant relatives proudly showed us the area in which my father and grandparents had lived. Names of places long familiar in family stories came alive for us! Indeed, we climbed through steep banks of wildflowers in the national park to find my father's favorite picnic spot of decades gone by, Kinver Edge. As Dad had told us, from this very spot one had a patchwork view of five different counties. Without delay, I wrote back to tell my dad in Australia of our thrill in experiencing some of these special places of his boyhood. Sadly, my father died unexpectedly just two weeks before we were to return to Australia, so that visit to Stourbridge and Kinver Edge will forever be special to me.

Using our Bexhill home-exchange flat as our base, we also traveled to Wales, Scotland, the Lake District, York, various countries on the Continent, and a week in London. One of the many pluses of vacation home exchanging is that one can pick up and leave for a few days or weeks, always knowing that a comfortable home and friendly neighbors await one's return.

With the passing of time, we became quite adept at managing the flat, shopping, handling the appliances and the car, and just generally living as the English do. There was one minor problem for us: There was no clothes dryer or outside clothesline. However, we did survive those months of folding wet sheets around the hot water system in the cupboard—the "airing closet," they called it—and hanging small items from strings in there. On some occasions, under the cover of darkness, we stealthily hung "drip dries" from a string line in our distant garage and then retrieved them from behind its closed door the next evening. (Drying laundry was never visible at that discreet address.)

While at home in the carpeted Bexhill flat, my handyman husband missed his workshop so much that he found odd jobs to do at our neighbor's bungalow: concreting the garden stairway, cleaning the roof, and in other ways serving as perhaps the original "vacation home exchange handyman."

This exchange story has its share of romance. Back in 1984 our son, Cameron, then an ABC journalist, had brought a lovely lass, Sharen, home to visit us twice. We could see how right they were for each other but later despaired when their ambitions and career involvement seemed to be driving them apart. When Sharen left for an eighteen-month midwifery course in Hastings, England, Cameron went to England to be with her for one joyous week before the course began.

Despite their renewed resolve, their correspondence failed after a year. Cameron was busy at ABC in Darwin, sometimes covering stories in the wilds of the Northern Territory while his spare time was filled with amateur theater and rally cars. In between Sharen's serious study, she had breaks, traveling around Britain and Europe. It seemed to be the end of a wonderful friendship. As soon as I realized that we would be in Bexhill (only five miles from Hastings), my matchmaking mind rang a bell! Unsure of a reply, I wrote from Australia to Sharen to tell her of our proposed visit, so near her hospital. Back came a long, welcoming letter with hopeful references to Cameron. Carefully encouraged, their correspondence resumed during the happy time we spent with Sharen in between studies for her final exams. Her zany humor and extrovert ways were so like Cameron's. After passing her exams, she returned to Australia in October but began to plan further nursing studies in England. While waiting for opportunities, she decided to work at the hospital in Darwin where Cameron was now press secretary to the minister of education. Six weeks later, bursting with happiness, Sharen and Cameron rang to tell us they were engaged. To our delight and theirs, they were married the following April. We know they will live happily ever after.

Never did we dream that three months of our lives could pass so quickly. Yes, October rolled around much sooner than we expected, and it was time for us to bid a sincere fond farewell to our English friends and our lovely flat in Bexhill.

The flight halfway around the world was exciting. It was great to be back in our island home and to find things just as we left them. And it was reassuring too to learn our home exchange partners from England enjoyed their Australian vacation just as much as we enjoyed those months in England. Chalk up one more successful vacation home exchange!

Reflecting over our first vacation home exchange, we have a few suggestions to others contemplating this sort of "live-in" holiday experience:

1. If you plan on listing your home and holiday aspirations in a home exchange directory, do so at least one year before your planned holiday date. We learned that vacation home exchangers often plan many months ahead.

2. Do not be too fixed in your destination plans nor too exact in your holiday dates (if you are retired). Keep your options open for that surprise holiday that might just turn out to be the best you've ever had.

3. Be sure to provide plenty of cupboard, fridge, freezer, and clothing space for your home exchange guests.

4. Make advance arrangements for forwarding or holding personal mail and make advance payments against telephone, council rates, tax, and other regular bills that will come to the house while your home exchange guests are there.

While the holiday home exchange concept is praised worldwide, we are its unofficial ambassadors here on Magnetic Island in Northern Australia!

Residents of South Africa, the Ian Mackay family lives in Randburg, just twenty miles north of Johannesburg. Ian is a property appraiser and lecturer on real estate at the University of South Africa.

Diane Mackay is a primary schoolteacher, currently substitute teaching at various private schools. The two Mackay children are Michael, age twelve, and Kerry-Lynn, age ten.

The Mackays first learned of home exchange holidays in 1989. In the years since, they have exchanged extensively: Hong Kong, British Columbia, Alberta, Ontario, Costa Rica, Scotland, Norway, Sweden, Germany, France, the United States, and Spain.

Ten to fourteen days is the average length of a Mackay exchange. Generally, Ian initiates the correspondence with potential exchangers nine to fifteen months in advance and finalizes the exchange arrangements six to nine months ahead of the actual exchange dates.

> *Ian Mackay writes, "An ample amount of advance planning smooths the way for wrinkle-free home exchanges. Then it's a great joy to experience the coming together of the actual home exchange plans."*

AUTHORS' NOTE: *While away from home enjoying international home exchanges, the fax machine has been the Mackays' number-one method of communication with family members and special friends. The following extracts are selected from some of their more interesting home exchange adventures.*

Faxed from the Greek island of Mykonos:

Mykonos is a rocky, desert island in the Aegean Sea. In the mornings, we take a local bus from the ancient town of Mykonos and then a small *Shirley Valentine* motor launch to the beaches. The color of the sea changes from a light emerald green at the beaches to a pale Mediterranean blue near the rocks to a dark sapphire blue in deeper water. We spend our days suntanning on Paradise Beach and Super Paradise Beach (they truly are) ogling the other nudes, blissfully unaware of what is happening in the outside world. At night we eat souvlakia and Greek salads and drink Greek white wine or Uzo at the many open-air taverns adjoining the narrow, winding passages between freshly whitewashed buildings. Unfortunately, we fly to Rome tomorrow . . .

Faxed from Rome:

Home-exchange traveling with kids (especially young ones) is the only way to go! Generally, they go free on buses and trains and have free access to museums and other sights to be seen. There's oftentimes a 50 percent discount on airline fares. Some restaurants have special rates for children; if not, our kids just share a meal. But, of course, most of our meals we enjoy at our exchange home.

On the metro in Rome, Kerry-Lynn [then five years old], being under three feet tall, was entitled to go free because she could walk under the turnstiles. Michael [then seven years old] ducked under and was caught occasionally. One can pack a hire-car with the whole family. The business-class lounges at the airports have proven to be good classrooms for Michael. We had the immediate past prime minister of Greece come through the lounge in Athens trailed by a gaggle of journalists while Di was trying to teach our son the two-times table.

He is, however, getting good practice in Greece, Italy, and Switzerland converting the local currencies to South African Rand using his two-times table.

Faxed from Burlington, Canada:

We were greeted here with overwhelming hospitality, in absentia, from our hosts who are currently in South Africa. Their fridge was packed with beer, Coke, and wine; further, they typed a comprehensive, indexed visitor's book telling their exchange partners what to do and see, including what to do in the event of having an accident in their Ford Taurus.

The two-bedroom, two-bathroom apartment is absolutely luxurious. It overlooks Lake Ontario (more like a sea than a lake). It has central air conditioning and heating, two televisions, two VCRs, and a CD/stereo. Push button number six on the telephone and the door six floors down unlocks. Access to the underground parking is also by a hand-held remote switch, and entry from the underground parking to the lift area is by push-button code, much to Kerry-Lynn's and Michael's delight. There is an inside gymnasium, Jacuzzi, sauna, suntanning room, tennis court, swimming pool, and outside gas barbecue (which we tried out on our first night!). We were also invited to a friend of our partner's home for a barbecue, where the kids enjoyed three hours of swimming in their large outside pool.

Faxed from Calgary, Alberta:

We always believed that South Africans were the most generous and hospitable hosts in the world until we met Canadians, Swiss, and Germans. Picture yourself arriving at the airport in Calgary during the week of the annual Stampede and being picked up at the airport in a huge Buick driven by a fully dressed-out cowboy who turned out to be our home exchange host. He drives us back to his neat twelve-room suburban home and stays elsewhere for the night. He flew to the East Coast on holiday last night. He may not even come to our condominium in South Africa because of a health problem. [We later learned he was suffering from terminal cancer and died six months later.] On the dining room table are two bowls of fresh cherries, peaches, nectarines, and a range of other fresh fruit. In the sitting room are brochures and maps of Banff, Jasper, Waterton Glacier Park, and Drumheller. On the kitchen table are bus timetables and a fully equipped picnic basket.

There is a bottle of California "champagne" (extra dry) in the fridge alongside two cold, crystal wineglasses. Attached is a welcome card reading, "Here's hoping that you all have a super time." He also left the usual milk, eggs, and breakfast cereal. On the patio are chairs, umbrellas, and a *braai* [barbecue]! In the garden are fresh lettuce, tomatoes, and carrots. Before he left, he introduced us to his neighbor, in case we have any problems. His son will come and mow the lawn during the fortnight. In the driveway is a Chrysler Colt automatic, filled with petrol for our use.

After three months of traveling, Kerry had her first feeling of homesickness yesterday. She sobbed for everyone back home, getting progressively more miserable with each person she remembered. Soon got over it!

Faxed from Brookings, Oregon:

At the end of the Oregon trail, our vacation is certainly turning out to be the holiday of a lifetime. After spending ten nights in a different bed each night, we have finally arrived in Brookings, Oregon, a small town on the Pacific Coast a long way from South Africa. (Yes, you are right, nobody in America has heard of it, either!) We have just been out picking wild blackberries, and Di has baked her first blackberry cobbler, which we used to celebrate Michael's eighth birthday. Michael and Kerry-Lynn and their parents are about as close to heaven as they ever will be! Our home exchange host stayed in our condominium in Cape Town last February. His double-story second residence is on a volcanic cliff overlooking the Pacific Ocean with a magnificent 180-degree panorama of the coastline. Constructed entirely of laminated Douglas fir, with walls of either red cedar or glass from floor to ceiling, it has seventeen beds! The huge twenty-foot-by-forty-three-foot living-dining room directly overlooks a private sandy beach below that is closed off at both ends by high cliffs. The beach house has direct access via a seventy-three-step, redwood staircase to the beach below. Only four other houses here have similar access. Michael, Kerry-Lynn, and Rachel (our host's granddaughter) are building sandcastles below while I type this fax on my laptop. Their shouts of joy and the crashing of waves is all I can hear. We fully realize that we are traveling in an idyllic world that does not exist in real life, only in holiday exchange life!

Our seventy-seven-year-old home exchange host and his companion came to the house to see us settled in. He took us out in his boat into the Pacific Ocean. Unfortunately the fog came in and we had to return to the harbor before we could start fishing. The temperature drops at night, but a log fire in the sitting room allows the kids to toast marshmallows over the glowing logs.

Faxed from Paris:

Paris must be the most beautiful city in the world, and Di's French lessons are proving very useful. She is able to communicate in a basic way, and we have found the Parisians very friendly and helpful. I desperately look at Diane when someone speaks to me in French. Last night we took the kids to McDonald's for supper, dumped them back at the apartment to watch television, and then walked the St. Germaine area on the Left Bank where we enjoyed a lazy supper.

**Faxed from our home exchange converted barn
in rural Montflanquin, southwest France:**

We are staying in a seventeenth-century stone barn! Our home exchange host converted the interior into a delightful double-story cottage with his own hands. We are finding the rural countryside outside this medieval village to be extremely relaxing. We buy our fresh provisions in the open-air market—held every Thursday since 1251. More than seven hundred years later, we sit here enjoying worldwide television coverage piped in from the satellite dish on the roof of the barn!

That little piece of plastic called a MasterCard, which I was issued back home in South Africa, can be used in the ATM in Montflanquin, which spurts out French francs with gusto.

Traveling on the narrow country roads takes some getting used to, though, especially coming from a country where we drive on the left-hand side. The roads are about as wide as our driveway at home, hardly wide enough for two cars to pass simultaneously. A truck bearing down at high speed from the opposite direction really gets the adrenaline pumping!

Faxed from Mijas Costa on the Costa del Sol, Spain:

We returned from a long, hot day touring the Rock of Gibraltar to find that we had no municipal water. Because of gross overdevelopment during the 1980s and 1990s and overcrowding during the peak holiday season, the water reservoirs have run dry, apparently as a result of a burst old and rusty water main—the seventh occasion this season. The locals tell us that last August they were without water for eight days, and we are running out of clean clothes. The temperature is a hot, cloudless 91.4°F during the day and a very warm 80.6°F at night. We are using the swimming pool at the complex to keep clean and flush the toilet with a bucket that we have to carry one hundred yards up a hill. I rushed out to buy bottles of drinking water and paid 1,545 Pts (about $20) for a few liters.

After five days the water came back on again, but we were amazed to see all the garden irrigation sprinklers in town going full bore in a determined effort to ensure that the reservoirs run dry again!

On the other hand, the beaches are quite attractive (especially the topless ones!). You do need to put flip-flops on before venturing into the Mediterranean to get across the first eleven yards of dirty, rocky water's edge before reaching the less murky sandy patches, and you have to be on the lookout for spiky sea urchins.

Looking ahead to the Christmas holidays, we have purchased APEX air tickets on Cathay Pacific to fly to Vancouver, Canada, via Hong Kong and Anchorage and are looking forward to a six-week exchange with a retired couple who will use our condominium in Cape Town over this Christmas period. The price was less than flying via New York or London but, of course, it's much farther. We thought it would be more fun for the kids, as they have not visited Hong Kong before. We will break our journey in both directions with stopovers on the Kowloon Peninsula. Kerry-Lynn is tickled by the prospect of spending the whole night on the plane and arriving in Vancouver on the same day five hours before we leave Hong Kong! She says she will "feel just like Alice in Wonderland."

Reflecting over our home exchange holidays to date, we feel as if each was touched by Alice herself. We believe this will also be true with our exchanges in the years ahead.

After residing in various different parts of England for the past seventeen years, the Douglas family now lives in Northamptonshire, where Philip is local government manager for the county council. His primary responsibility is the organization and supervision of services for the county's elderly, disabled, and mentally ill persons.

With pupils aged sixteen to sixty, Lidia Douglas teaches English at the local College of Education. The Douglases have three daughters and two sons.

Philip and Lidia first learned of home exchanging from a magazine article seven years ago. Every year since then, the entire Douglas family has enjoyed a two- to four-week home exchange, visiting five European countries.

Lidia Douglas writes:

When our children were very young, we always spent our holidays somewhere in Britain, very often at a family seaside home. While we all enjoyed those holidays, we sensed the growing importance of our children's becoming aware of different countries and different cultures and having different life experiences.

But European travel involving hotels and dining out was prohibitively expensive for our growing family. Also, this type of travel raised an endless list of practical, day-to-day family concerns—to say nothing about our cat and the four rabbits!

It was, therefore, fortuitous that I happened to come across a magazine article describing the holiday home exchange concept as well as sharing the experiences of some real, live home exchangers. I thought, holiday home exchanging . . . what a great idea for us!

This article seemed to answer all our problems. We would only need to pay for the journey across the channel and any extra treats. Daily living costs would be the same as at home. The more we thought about it, the more attractive it seemed. We would benefit from a garden, toys (so we wouldn't have to pack many), a retreat (if it rained), proper beds (with sheets provided), hot running water all the time, my own cooking. We could pace ourselves exactly as we wanted. It seemed perfect. There were, however, a few drawbacks. What could we offer in exchange? All the pluses seemed to be on the other side.

We did have one big advantage. We could offer a really comfortable Victorian house with lots of toys and lots of space. Our town, Wellingborough, is convenient for visiting all the well-known sights: Oxford, Stratford, Cambridge, and London. Locally we have all the amenities necessary for families—good shopping, swimming pools, tennis courts, lots of walks, attractive country houses, thatched villages, plus a nearby castle. So we began to feel a little more hopeful.

Our first attempt was quite careful and restrained. We decided to try somewhere nearby and play it by ear a little. Germany was our first choice, as there seemed to be a large number of properties there and I could speak German; so we prepared our campaign. As soon as the directory came out, I marked all the homes with six or more beds (the baby had his own cot) and immediately wrote to the owners by hand, as I thought that would be more personal. I was staggered to see thirty letters go off in the post covering all possible areas and properties. We waited for a response, not expecting much, but in a couple of days we started to get feedback.

A week later, a telephone call from experienced exchangers clinched the matter. They were keen to fix a date and since their English was so good, we were amazed at how easily things were settled. They sent us more detailed information about their house and family and area. Since it was in the Black Forest, an area neither my husband nor I had visited, we were happy to go ahead. The dates fit, the family appeared nice—there was nothing more to hesitate about. In all, we got about eight offers—most from families who had responded to this appeal in our listing. One made a particular impression by the friendly nature of their letter, and we kept in contact, although we have not exchanged with them as yet.

There were obvious apprehensions about the preparations and the journey—and as the time came nearer, whether we were doing the right thing—but, as it turned out, it was a wonderful holiday. The house welcomed us with jam, chocolates, and wine on the table. The neighbors were an aid and support and have remained in touch ever since. In fact, one afternoon while we were out, the pet rabbit escaped, and they spent two hours chasing it round the garden. Our biggest anxieties were (a) whether we would kill the pet bird off and (b) whether the children would break anything. The breakage, when it came, was in the middle of a huge storm, when a picture blew off the wall and the glass broke. We luckily got a replacement quite easily. My most wonderful memories are of the neighbors bringing a present for one of the children's birthdays and then waving us off in traditional style when we left. Our saddest feeling was that we never personally met that exchange family apart from our long telephone calls, but we knew they had enjoyed themselves and were amused to find that the four rabbits we left behind had multiplied to ten by the time our partners left! Their youngest daughter remains a good pen-friend to our oldest one.

After that, we became more adventurous and spent the next summer in Sweden, which was extremely memorable for the journey there through Norway and back through Denmark. The house was the most remarkable one we have ever stayed in—a perfectly idyllic one for a family. It was the family's summer house by a lake, with its own beach, boat, and sauna in the garden. There were bicycles for the bigger children and a little ferry up the road. The whole area was utterly safe for children to play and enjoy themselves. We met that exchange family in England and also when they got back. They were absolutely charming. Our great embarrassment was on the last night when, in our excess of enthusiasm and helpfulness, I tried to wash some sheets for them and inadvertently overloaded the washing machine. Our exchange partner was very calm in response to a frantic 11:00 P.M. phone call and dismissed the problem. He was, in fact, very capable, and we found out that he had fixed *our own* washing machine himself when it backed up!

Other exchanges have seen us in Spain right beside the sea, where the children had all the opportunities they wanted to swim, and three trips to different areas in France, a country we enjoy immensely. Our favorite place there was a second home in a tiny village with a beautiful large garden—and no television! The children were horrified at first. While we were there, my mother-in-law and youngest sister-in-law joined us for ten days. We were immediately befriended by a German neighbor who, after one meeting, gave us her key and asked us to look after her house and dog while she went to visit her daughter. The house was not a problem, but the dog was so enormous and boisterous it became a task of ingenuity to slip out of the garden without his knowing and pinning us to one spot. When his owner returned, she invited my mother-in-law over and overwhelmed her to such a degree with her generosity and nonstop conversation that we had to go to the rescue after two hours in response to pleas for help coming over the road!!

So far we have never had any problems with finding places. This year for the first time we tried a short exchange over Easter with a family in Belgium whom we had contacted a few years ago about a future Easter exchange. Some of the families with whom we haven't yet exchanged still write and keep our address, as we do theirs, so there are always future possibilities. As the children grow older, we look forward to being able to take shorter breaks more frequently and eventually going much farther afield to New Zealand and Australia. Next year the children have all decided on Italy!

My oldest son, Andrew, has said, "What I like about home exchanging is being able to see how other people live. It is quite exciting to explore a new house, sleep in a different bedroom, and play with different toys. It makes a refreshing change."

We feel home exchanging has been a broadening experience for all our children and enabled them to use some of the languages they have been studying at school, as well as learn words and phrases in new languages. We have also been lucky enough to find enormous houses, so other relatives could join us for one or two weeks. Our exchange families have been extremely nice, even though we have not managed to meet all of them, and we have always been greeted by special offerings on the table. We have also found it marvelous to leave our animals to be looked after (we now have extra guinea pigs and goldfish), as well as all my plants and the house itself. We have always found it beautifully cared for and tidy on our return. (One family even bought me a bucket and mop for the kitchen floor!) Home exchanging has enabled us to see how other people live and experience life in a much more realistic way than if we were isolated in a holiday camp or hotel.

On the down side, I spend weeks preparing the house—painting all the shabby patches, cleaning all the cupboards, tidying all the shelves— making sure it's all perfect. I also prepare food so our exchange partners find everything they need in the fridge. There are also copious notes to write giving information and instructions. Another source of anxiety, and sometimes surprise, centers on all the gadgets in the exchange house. Washing machines are always approached very gingerly, as are cookers and boilers. It takes some time to come to grips with all the technicalities and read instructions in foreign languages!

And there are always worries about whether everything is going all right in your own house, yet in all our years we have not been disappointed. We regard it as a matter of trust, and we look after our exchange home exactly as we would look after our own. It's a two-way process, and we have always found that our exchangers have looked after everything in our house very carefully and been very grateful for the use of it. When you spend time in someone else's home, they cease to be strangers, and we feel that we have made friends and grown in understanding. We also feel that our children have been very privileged to have seen so many different countries and experienced so many different life styles. We cannot recommend it highly enough and have been so pleased that some of our friends and family have started exchanging as well—and so far they have felt exactly the same.

The advice I would give anybody starting is to make the first move. As soon as the directory comes out, pick the places that interest you and write immediately with information about your home and family. It's a first feeler, and if there is interest, then repliers will ask for more details. Most of the information you need is in the directory listings. A firm offer is oftentimes made within three or four weeks. Anything coming in after that tends to be from disorganized, last-minute flappers who don't read details properly. Once a firm offer is made, you can relax and do your journey planning at a more leisurely pace. You also know that, if there are any questions, the exchange family is only too happy to supply details. If by any chance nothing turns up in the first directory, we have another two to choose from—and each year there seem to be exciting, new holiday destinations to be explored.

CHAPTER 16

Keeping Yourself Covered— Insurance and Home Exchanging

I N BUSINESS, FAMILY, AND PERSONAL FINANCIAL PLANNING, insurance is a budgeted item of paramount importance. Regardless of where one may live, adequate insurance coverage has become a must. With each passing year, the insurance industry has developed innovative ways in which (1) families and single persons can have more comprehensive insurance coverage and (2) companies can better serve their employees through group insurance plans.

Furthermore, within the framework of acceptable policy premiums, competing insurance companies endeavor to design elements of their policies to better meet the needs of their policyholders. This procedure has a profound effect on all who purchase insurance for protection in countless different situations.

First and perhaps foremost is life insurance. Then follows medical/travel insurance, home insurance, liability insurance, auto insurance, theft insurance, and scores of other types of insurance keyed to benefit people in all circumstances and all age groups. Volumes have been written to help people select the right insurance coverage at the lowest rate.

From the survey, it's crystal clear that vacationing home exchangers are seeking advice and policies in the following rather broad areas:

    medical/travel insurance

    auto insurance

    home insurance

Reviewing many current policies offered in these key insurance categories, it is quite apparent home exchangers and their families may not be adequately covered. The result? Questions aplenty from those in the home exchange community . . .

> What if a member of our family becomes ill, incurring doctor and/or hospital bills?
>
> What if my exchange partner, due to ill health or some other circumstance, must cancel the exchange on short notice? Am I stuck with a long-standing, paid-in-advance plane or rail ticket?
>
> What if we damage our exchange partner's car?
>
> What if we damage something of value in the home of our exchange host?

While those in the insurance world have high praise for the low risk in home exchanging and no one wants to think about confronting serious problems while on vacation, the fact is that accidents happen. Ultimately the bedeviling question arises: Who pays for the costs of medical emergencies, car repairs, and home-related damage?

Home exchangers who have arranged for adequate insurance in advance have a ready answer to that question: My insurance company pays.

Insurance policies differ greatly in the forty or so countries in which home exchangers enjoy their vacations. It would not be possible in this one chapter (or even an entire book dedicated to this subject) to evaluate available insurance coverage designed to meet the needs of home-exchanging travelers. However, we can provide an overview of insurance home exchangers should investigate—useful insurance-related information for the benefit of exchangers residing in the United States and Great Britain. These two countries have been selected for this exercise because (1) they represent the largest number of home exchangers per country and (2) there is as much or more home exchanging activity between these two countries than between any other two countries in the world.

Medical/Travel Insurance

U.S. home exchangers contemplating a single exchange or a series of exchanges outside the United States must bear in mind that neither Medicare nor most group and/or individual insurance policies cover expenses incurred by policyholders while traveling outside of the United States. A long weekend in Canada or Mexico is one thing, but what about a U.S. family (possibly including small children) or an older couple exchanging for a month in Edinburgh, Scotland?

There are a number of extremely reliable U.S. insurance companies offering policies keyed to the medical/travel needs of home exchangers traveling abroad. Among the many benefits of such policies are:

medical expenses, including hospital   personal accident
ambulance service   loss of baggage
personal liability   legal expenses

Designed for short-term travel—up to two months—the rates for these policies come under schedules; that is, a certain per-day rate for one week of travel and possibly a different daily rate for travel over two weeks, a month, and so on. These insurance companies cover their U.S. policyholders during most of their travels, worldwide. For complete information about this type of coverage, exchangers should contact their home exchange clubs, regular insurance brokers or agents, the American Automobile Association (AAA), or travel agents.

As in the United States, various British insurance companies offer policies keyed to the needs of British travelers. Some innovative British insurance companies have included in their policies elements of special interest to home exchangers residing in Great Britain. Under certain circumstances, policyholders can recover the cost of air and rail tickets paid in advance if the host partner is forced to cancel the home exchange arrangement due to an extenuating situation. Neither exchange party desires such a problem, but if such a situation does happen, policyholders with this reimbursement clause in their policies could recover a considerable portion of the money advanced for air or rail tickets.

Whereas most U.S. medical/travel policies offer coverage on a per-day basis, some British insurance companies offer coverage on either a per-day basis or by the year. This alone could be a very real advantage to those British home exchangers making more than one exchange trip during a given year.

Most British medical/travel insurance companies cover policyholders traveling throughout the world. Since the fees for home exchanger travel/medical insurance are based on the number of people traveling and the countries where the exchanges will occur, the cost of covering exchanges in Great Britain would be less than those in the United States.

It is recommended that home exchanging couples (especially those with children) and exchangers traveling alone give earnest consideration to securing medical/travel insurance. This would apply in particular to those traveling to the United States, where medical and hospitalization costs can be considerable. The experience of a home exchanging family residing in South Wales underscores the vital importance of medical/travel insurance being a part and parcel of the home exchange holiday.

"Ours was a two-month series of home exchanges in Florida—one month in Miami Shores and two weeks each at Amelia Island and Sanibel Island.

"While swimming in the Atlantic, Helen (in her mid-thirties) was attacked by a man-of-war, a particularly dangerous type of jellyfish that characteristically emits a poison through its tentacles. Initially, Helen felt relatively little pain. But the next day (a Sunday) she developed a severe rash and an unusual amount of swelling over much of her body, and she was experiencing an almost unbelievable amount of pain.

"She was rushed by ambulance to the emergency room at Miami's North Shore Hospital, where her condition was immediately diagnosed: an allergic reaction to the poison from this jellyfish. Helen was admitted to the hospital, where the immediate danger was the possibility of kidney failure. Happily, her kidneys were okay and the prompt, proper medication and care by the hospital staff stabilized the condition and set the pace for convalescence and a complete recovery.

"After a fortnight, this experience was a decidedly unpleasant memory. Then came the shocker—medical and hospital bills totaling more than $6,000!

"We praised God for Helen's complete recovery. And we praised Him too for the fact that before the trip we'd signed up with Kingfisher Medical/Travel Insurance (through HomeLink—Great Britain, our home exchange club).

"And the bill—the $6,000-plus? It was all paid for by Kingfisher."

In a June 1995 article, the *London Daily Telegraph* recounted several medical/travel horror stories. The following advice was given: "Travel-medical problems can best be solved with some good medical/travel insurance." The writer suggested, "HomeLink—Great Britain has an arrangement with Kingfisher Insurance, one of the few companies offering cancellation coverage for home exchangers with its travel policy."

Automobile Insurance

Of the experienced British and American home exchangers participating in the survey, approximately three-quarters include their automobiles as an important part of their exchange arrangements. While not many home exchangers get bitten by men-of-war, great numbers of drivers—in their own cars and own countries—have an accident or two (usually minor ones) during their driving years. It is imperative that all drivers have proper auto insurance; indeed, in many states and countries this type of insurance coverage is mandated by law.

Thinking about the right-hand-drive/left-hand-drive challenge—plus the U.S. freeways and British roundabouts—it is doubly important for U.S. and British exchangers to be certain that they have auto insurance coverage when they are driving each other's cars.

Are U.S. registered and insured cars covered when driven by exchangers from Great Britain? This question can best be answered by the following clause from the automobile policy of one of the largest U.S. auto insurance companies. After the policyholder, his or her spouse and friends and/or his relatives, an insured person is "any other person while using such a car within the scope of the consent of the insured and his or her spouse." This is simply to say that anyone driving such a car is covered by the car owner's insurance, provided this car is being driven with the permission of the car's owner, the policyholder. A clause similar to this is included in the auto policies of nearly all U.S. auto insurance companies.

Are there any exceptions? Yes.

1. The driver of the car must have in his/her possession a valid auto operator's license issued by the motor vehicle authority in his/her country.

2. The driver of the car must be twenty-five years of age or older.

3. The driver of the car must have in his/her possession a document authorizing use of the car and signed by the car's owner. (See reference section.)

4. The car must be driven under "legal" conditions established by the state in which the car is registered.

While the above provisions apply in nearly all policies written by U.S. automobile insurance companies, before including a car in a home exchange arrangement, the U.S. car owner must confer with the car insurance broker or agent to confirm that the exchange partner is properly covered by the car owner's policy.

Over the years, British automobile insurance companies have differed in their exclusion clauses from companies in the United States and oftentimes differed from each other as well. For example, some insurers in Great Britain will not cover friends of the insured. Others will not cover a driver over a specified age, while still others will not cover drivers who have resided in Great Britain for less than two years—a restriction ruling out all exchangers not living in Great Britain. While company-owned cars cover the driver and his or her family, in many cases this coverage does not include friends, such as home exchangers.

The position many British auto insurers have taken has created a real problem in the exchange arrangements between British and American exchangers. In many cases, exchangers confronting this car insurance dilemma have rented cars. Rental cars solve the car problem in Britain, but the U.S. exchanger then has to add significant amounts to the vacation exchange budget.

A sales executive in Cleveland, Ohio, writes, "At the last minute, we learned that the policy of our near-London exchange host covered only this gentleman and his wife. Then we went on to Wales to find that we were not covered under our host's policy there, either. Having to rent cars during that five-week series of exchanges blew a $1,500 hole in our travel budget."

Recognizing that home exchangers as a group have fewer auto accident claims and observing that the home exchange concept is decidedly on the upswing among British vacationers, some auto insurers in Great Britain have modified their policies to include coverage for U.S. exchange partners. By shopping around the British auto insurance marketplace, some British exchangers have been successful in finding those firms that extend auto insurance coverage to U.S. exchange partners.

Home Insurance

Nearly all U.S. residents have home coverage known as homeowners insurance. These policies offer blanket coverage, including:

accidental damage to buildings and property

personal property

personal liability

damage to property of others

medical payments to others

theft/fire

Most U.S. homeowners' policies offer protection to the homeowner, his or her family, and his or her friends and to anyone who encounters home-related problems necessitating reimbursement by the insurance companies. This includes home exchangers as friends of the insured.

In Britain, homecover insurance policies offer similar coverage and are issued by a number of insurance companies. Some of these British companies include in their coverage specific benefits to home exchangers. Especially recommended to British home exchangers is a Kingfisher homecover policy, one that can also be arranged through HomeLink—Great Britain.

Very much like seeking advice from the directors of a funeral home, one does not like to think about health, auto, or home accidents and the expenses of such accidents while traveling. Nevertheless, if one is confronted with some sort of an accident, it is reassuring to place the problem in the hands of an insurance company.

Home exchangers are rightfully concerned about insurance coverage—medical/travel, automobile, home—so it behooves all home exchange hosts to give careful attention to these insurance matters, thus fully protecting themselves and their home exchange partners.

Those British home exchangers who are members of HomeLink International are fortunate in that HomeLink offers its members—through the Kingfisher Insurance Company—medical/travel and homecover policies keyed to meet the insurance needs of home exchangers residing in Great Britain. Furthermore, HomeLink has researched those British auto insurance companies that provide insurance to car-exchanging home exchangers. For further information, contact:

Heather Anderson, Director
HomeLink International
Linfield House
Gorse Hill Road

Virginia Water
Surrey GU25 4AS
England
phone/fax: 01344 842642

In the United States, the Vacation Exchange Club (affiliated with HomeLink International) provides its members with home exchange–related information. For information, contact:

Karl Costabel, Director
Vacation Exchange Club
P.O. Box 650
Key West, Florida 33041

phone/fax (toll free U.S. only): 1-800-638-3841
phone/fax: 1-305-294-1448

Now, on a somewhat lighter vein—and all seriousness aside—there is this holiday-related story making the rounds in home exchange circles:

On its maiden voyage, the world's newest and largest cruise ship—three thousand passengers and fifteen hundred crew—was approaching the Bermuda Triangle during a full moon on a calm sea. It was midnight, and the Davy Jones Locker Lounge was filled to capacity. All eyes were on the featured performer as Señor Magic went through his mystifying bag of tricks, assisted by his parrot, Survivor. After the magician made a red handkerchief disappear, the parrot asked, "What'd you do with the hankie, Señor M.?" A few seconds later, the handkerchief was found tied to the wrist of the Captain's wife.

Next came a live chicken in the big black hat. One minute it was there, then whoosh it had vanished. The astonished parrot asked, "Señor M., what'd you do with the chicken?" With a flourish, down the aisle came the chief steward pushing a gilded food trolley, displaying a large silver serving tray with the steaming hot, fully cooked chicken.

Then came an explosion. The spotlights went out, the band stopped playing, and the hundred-thousand-ton cruise ship sank, taking with it the full complement of passengers and crew. All were lost, except— floating on a life raft—Señor Magic, his parrot, and a middle-aged couple from Kokomo, Indiana. "Okay, wise guy," the parrot asked, "what'd ya do with the ship?" Señor Magic answered, "I haven't the foggiest notion what happened to the ship!"

Hours later, as the four half-drowned survivors were lifted aboard a rescue vessel, the gentleman from Kokomo was heard to say, "No more cruises for us. Next time, we'll take out a full-coverage travelers' insurance policy . . . and go on a home exchange vacation!"

CHAPTER 17

Stress-Free Holidays with Kids—
Well, Almost

PERHAPS MORE IN THE 1990s EVEN THAN IN THE 1980s—and certainly more than in previous decades—parents are bombarded from all sides with vacation opportunities for their children. Schools, churches, service clubs, Y's, and health clubs offer baseball, soccer, hockey, and other sports camps. There are wilderness camps, music appreciation camps, happy-jolly-fun camps for overweight underachievers, happy-jolly-fun camps for underweight overachievers, church camps, and computer camps. There are dude ranches, national and international student travel groups, short-term overseas and in-country missionary projects, the more ordinary several weeks with relatives or friends, and, yes, even some genuine, old-fashioned camp camps. This comprises a veritable classified section of diverse ways to keep children and young people happy, healthy and occupied during school vacations—especially summer vacations.

Despite all this youth vacation opportunity hype, the truth is that family vacations are still very much the "in" thing to do. It is the prospect of doing things together as a family that is behind these family vacations—looked forward to and enjoyed by both parents and children and other relatives who might go along.

While parents traveling with children represent a less than large part in the total home exchange picture—the majority being older couples—the growth pattern of exchanging families moving through the 1990s is formidable. Why? Certainly a factor here is the continually rising cost of conventional (motel-hotel-restaurant) vacations confronting those parents preferring to vacation with their children. An exchanger in Minneapolis who vacations with his wife and six children writes, "This vacation home exchange idea is g-r-r-r-eat! It sure beats hotels, motels, and buying twenty-four restaurant meals each and every vacation day!"

"Envision for a moment a trip in a minivan from Virginia to Canada with our then six-year-old and two-year-old, my husband, myself, and my younger brother," comments a Virginia consultant. "After a series of nondescript, crowded motel rooms, my unmarried sibling described the trip as 'the vacation from hell.' (Of course he tends to overreact to everything, even such normal occurrences as the two-year-old dumping spaghetti all over himself, his brother, and the restaurant booth immediately after knocking over a full pitcher of milk.)"

"Boring" and "cool" are two of the most frequently spoken words by children and teens, especially young teens. Watching television in a cramped motel room with parents is boring. Waiting to be served meals in real restaurants is boring ("Why can't we have all our meals at McDonald's?"). Long hours spent driving to some Civil War battlefield or remote shot tower ("because you're going to be studying the Civil War next year in school and you need to visit Antietam") is—you guessed it—boring.

While vacation home exchanging does have some negative aspects (kids' clothes get just as dirty as at home and teenage boys still have what appear to be bottomless pits for stomachs), one thing it is not is boring. Watching television and playing Nintendo "just like at home" is cool. Helping dad barbecue ribs for the new friends from next door is cool. (Playing with their kids is cool, too!) It is cool to pack a picnic lunch and take a short drive and a boat trip from "our" house to Fort Sumter. There's a different feel, even for kids, about having a home in which to stay and from which to take off for excursions. It's not the same as staying in an impersonal motel or hotel room.

An Edinburgh, Scotland, mother writes, "Following our first home exchange, our eleven-year-old son won his school's holiday prize for his two-volume account of his experiences in the towns and areas of the country we had visited. He was especially pleased as it was his first holiday abroad and had been eagerly anticipated. He is now studying German and economics in university and teaching in Germany this summer. His brother will be studying French and economics at the same school."

A doctor's wife from El Paso, Texas, shares this story. "While staying at our home, our exchange partner's little girl learned to ride our daughter's two-wheeled bicycle. She did so well that when they returned home to California, she received her first very own bike."

Much has been written in previous chapters about the responsibility exchange partners must have for each other's homes and personal property. When children of any age are a part of the exchange, a special burden of responsibility rests on the shoulders of the respective exchange parents. More often than not, home exchangers with children seem to exchange with partners who also have children; this makes it easier all the way around. Indeed, within the world of vacation home exchanging, a fraternity of home exchangers who vacation with their children has developed. Most in this group are aware that children will be children.

However, all of us have seen—both in public places and in peoples' homes—parents who, for want of a better way of putting it, seem to feel that children will be children and there's not much I can or have to do to control them. They'll grow out of it. The children of these parents are the ones who race back and forth in hotel lobbies, who can't stay in their seats in restaurants, and who finally (after sufficient whining) get a candy bar in the grocery checkout lane. Hopefully, these parents are not vacation home exchangers.

Special precautions should be taken for the protection of the homes and property of both parties to the exchange. These precautions start with the preparation of the home for exchangers with children. Ample drawer and closet space should be provided for the kids' use to store their clothes, toys, games, and other things they may bring with them that are can't-be-without items. Special attention should be given to putting away all treasured family possessions, bric-a-brac, and especially breakables. Your kids may know not to cut the corner from the front hall into the living room—they may have even helped you place that piece of sculpture on the glass shelf—but your guests' children are new to your home. They don't have the same home-care history as your children.

If the child or children involved are infants or toddlers, the host partner should anticipate the needs of these little guests and make an effort to provide for them. A checklist might include:

- ☐ crib
- ☐ playpen
- ☐ highchair or booster seat
- ☐ car seat
- ☐ stroller
- ☐ rubber bed pad (or inexpensive vinyl tablecloth)—even a toilet-trained child tends to forget with the excitement of visiting
- ☐ baby-sitter contacts

"We spent three and a half months on an exchange in New Zealand with our three-month-old son," writes a geophysics engineer in Kernen, Germany. "The reception we got from our exchange host's relatives and friends was magnificent. All the necessities for Jonathan had been made ready. We had the use of a crib (with mosquito netting), a baby's bath-tub, a changing table, and even some clothes. Our host had registered us for the local baby care program (visiting nurse) and many other services. We felt completely at home there."

If the exchange hosts themselves have or have recently had young children, many or most of these child-related items will be readily at hand. If not, perhaps some can be borrowed from family members or friends. As a last resort, any or all can be rented, with arrangements being made during the pre-exchange correspondence and the guest-parents being responsible for all rental fees.

If older children are included, rules should be established in writing regarding the use of the hosts' bikes, skateboards, roller blades, and other sports equipment, including basketballs, soccer balls, fishing tackle, and so on. Rules should also be laid down concerning the use of the VCR and stereo. If the host allows the use of his VCR, then its instructions should be in the home information kit along with the location of his cassette library (if available) and the name and phone number of the nearest video rental store.

Regardless of whether children accompany their parents on a conventional vacation or on a home exchange vacation, experienced dads and moms know that one of the most important elements of a successful vacation with children is keeping them occupied. To this end, host partners can be a real help to their guests by providing them with complete information about the activities for children and young people offered in their communities.

Some host families with memberships in health, country, or racquet clubs arrange for their guests to use their club guest cards, enabling the visitors to enjoy tennis, swimming, golf, exercise programs, spas, and other facilities. Most communities provide a wide variety of recreational opportunities for young children and teens, from baseball and soccer to Red Cross swimming and life-saving lessons. There are the YM/YWCA, the YM/YWHA, local playgrounds, museums, children's summer theater programs, miniature golf, amusement parks, picnic facilities, boat trips (those exchanging in New York City report "the best sightseeing value anywhere" for kids or adults is the Circle Line's trip around Manhattan), and fishing—be it lake, river, or deep sea.

Home exchangers vacationing in condos often enjoy a parade of activity opportunities—tennis, swimming, barbecues, recreation rooms, as well as planned and supervised events geared to children of all ages. "At our Washington, D.C., exchange condo," writes a mom in

Minneapolis, "my sons and I enjoyed playing table tennis on evenings we had no other plans. Sure beats sitting around a boring motel room."

In previous chapters it's been recommended that exchange hosts provide their guests with specific information about the home and its appliances—what to do or not to do—as well as general information about neighbors, neighborhood, shops, sightseeing, and other such facts and/or opinions that will help the guests feel at home in the community in which the home is situated. This should all be available in the home information kit.

In addition, a similar kit should detail for exchange partners with children the type of child-related information set forth in the preceding paragraphs. Included in this kids' information kit should be the names, addresses, and telephone numbers of a dentist, a pediatrician, a family physician, the nearest hospital emergency room, and the closest walk-in clinic that accepts patients without appointments. While some of this may be in the home information kit, it will be easier for an upset parent to find the information here should the need arise. Hopefully, this special information won't be needed, but having it at hand would be a tremendous help, should a medical emergency arise.

This was certainly true in the case of a Hartford, Connecticut, mother who related, "While on a home exchange in Dayton, Ohio, overnight our six-year-old daughter developed an unexplained, unusually high fever. Fortunately, our host had left us a referral to a nearby pediatrician who saw us almost immediately and took care of our child."

Now to the other side of the vacation home exchange coin: guidelines for exchange guests traveling with children. Heeding these should assure the entire family of an enjoyable, memorable, and "cool" vacation. First and foremost, it is doubly important that the arrival of the exchange guests with children be without incident. Nothing is as unnerving as arriving at the exchange home with the wrong door key at night, in the rain, with travel-weary, screaming kids. To avoid this or some similar near disaster, both parties to a home exchange involving children must be especially careful in their arrival arrangements—arrangements that must be clearly understood in advance by both the host and the guest families.

"We arrived at Heathrow Airport on a Saturday morning in August along with several thousand other people," says a mother from Lynbrook, New York. "It took forever to get through customs. The children were getting very tired, we were increasingly edgy, and we wondered if the car service our swap mates had sent would still be waiting for us.

We didn't see anyone holding up a sign with our name, so my husband left me with the luggage and our three little ones while he took off to find the information booth. All at once, a man came up to me and asked, 'Mrs. Johnson—from New York? Going to Bromley?' He took the suitcases and headed off almost before I could answer. I asked how he knew it was I. He looked a little flustered and muttered something about knowing we had three children (right—like we were the only people in Heathrow with three children).

"A week later it clicked. In Trafalgar Square we ran into another American couple like us—white, with adopted Korean children. It dawned on me that I had seen only one other Asian person all week. We're so used to living in New York, where people don't look twice at us, that we forget that in some places, we might be more than a little conspicuous!" Conspicuous isn't so bad, however, when being met by a stranger in Heathrow.

In many respects, preparing for a vacation home exchange with children is quite like preparing for a conventional vacation with children. The amount of luggage space will dictate just how much kid stuff can be taken along—security pillow or blanket, dolls, stuffed animals, games, Mickey Mouse Band-Aids ("Bump-Aids," as one exchanger's four-year-old calls them), and other special things—probably last on the parents' list but sometimes of prime importance to the children.

A child's initial reaction to an exchange home can be somewhat less than positive, thereby putting a damper on the first day or two of a vacation. An attorney and his wife, traveling with their two young children, arrived at their delightful sixteenth-century farmhouse not far from Paris and heard this as the kids got out of the car: "Yuck! This place is disgusting! There's nothing to do here! We don't want to stay here!" Of course, they were crazy about it soon thereafter.

Immediately after arriving at the host's home, guests should look for the home-related, child-related material—the home information kit left by their exchange host. Depending on the ages of the children, house rules should be drawn up and understood by all—what to do, what not to do, where to go, where not to go. "No feet on the furniture"—"No food or drinks in the living room" (the room with the deep pile, off-white carpet)—"Wet towels on hooks, not in a heap on the bathroom" (or bedroom) floor—"Keep the volume on the stereo down"—and so on.

A Seattle couple volunteers, "We always put away any bric-a-brac that our hosts may have missed—bouncing balls seem to come out of the woodwork. Also sometimes we put bath towels or perhaps an extra sheet on light-colored upholstery when we get to our 'new' home as an ounce of prevention. Finally, in assessing the house we look for cracks in windows and any other apparent damage and note it in the home information kit, so we know what we did and did not do while living in this particular house."

Home exchanging with children should definitely be a family affair; everyone has to pitch in so that everyone will enjoy this adventure. Depending on the ages of the children, a job schedule should be drawn up—who does what when—just as it's done at home. Even when there's not a schedule at home, having one on vacation adds to the fun. Mom shouldn't always wind up doing all the chores. New skills may be learned, and best of all, the day's activities can commence earlier if everyone helps. "The youngest children in our ménage learned how to clear the table and wash dishes without leaving a greasy film on them; the next age bracket discovered the secrets of one of the family's favorite (and simple) meals and prepared it; and 'last one up in the morning' had to gather up all the trash and get it ready to take out," writes a doctor's wife in South Carolina.

A professor in Coeur d'Alene, Idaho, recommends contacting the neighbors early on, particularly those with children. "This always makes us feel a little more secure—an extra set of parental eyes, if you will." If the ages are similar, the kids will get to know each other quickly—new friends, new toys. A mother in McLean, Virginia, reinforces this: "While we've been to Europe several times, our best exchange was in Halifax, Nova Scotia. Next door there were kids roughly the same ages as mine, and they were kept busy with their new friends. I had a real vacation! The 'next door mom' has since visited us in McLean."

A salesman in Kentucky with an only child reports taking one of his son's good friends along for company after realizing on their first exchange that the ten-year-old frequently wasn't interested in the "exciting" plans his parents had made for him. Several exchangers tell of taking their regular sitter along. This is particularly helpful with very young children who get worn out long before Mom and Dad do. Most teenage sitters have not traveled all that much and would relish the opportunity to do so in return for playing shepherd or shepherdess.

From a child's point of view, vacation home exchanging—a different vacation home every year—can be a marvelous, memorable, mind-expanding experience. A Danish exchanger says, "Our children learned both to accept people different from us and to use a different language frequently." A London couple adds, "We were out in the country in Normandy, surrounded by fields of corn and a herd of cows. Our five-year-old soon made friends with a neighboring farmer's grandson and played for hours—communicating with gestures, playing games, and repeating the half-dozen words of French he'd been taught in play school. Children simply haven't learned our adult inhibitions yet; they just get on with it."

"Our neighbors in Holland got as big a charge out of our kids running around in their newly acquired *klompen* as the kids did themselves. Apparently, no one in the Netherlands has worn wooden shoes since Hans Brinker!" laughs a Canadian couple.

From a parent's point of view? New Yorkers write, "We love it! We can see the world with our children, and we all enjoy our vacations on different levels. With the children along, we tend to slow down the pace and really absorb our surroundings, sitting more often in town squares and city parks while the children play." Parents from Rutland, Vermont, add, "With the money we save home exchanging, we now take our kids along and spend four weeks on vacation, not just the previous two or three." A couple from Tampa, Florida, says, "With our small children, home exchanging will be the best way for us to vacation for years to come."

We highly recommend *Take Your Kids to Europe* (Mason-Grant Co.), a book devoted entirely to traveling with children. Its chapters contribute greatly to ironing out some of the many wrinkles that can crop up when children are along, either on a home exchange vacation or a more conventional one.

CHAPTER 18

The Animal Kingdom

O N THE SURVEY SOME PARTICIPANTS WROTE THAT their two Persian cats spend holidays at a cat hotel while their "parents" home exchange. If cat hotels (kennels in the United States; catteries in Great Britain) are as expensive, relatively speaking, as people hotels, it is apparent that cats, dogs, and other pets must be a part of many home exchange arrangements.

However thoughtful the Persians' parents might be, moving pets to a kennel or friends or wherever may not be the best solution. A Fort Myers writer, discussing her beloved four-legged family member, said, "I like to think that Annie Laurie is well cared for and has no fleas—that is, we've taken all the appropriate steps. But I would never presume to guarantee that there are no fleas in my house; this is, after all, Florida—she is, after all, a long-haired cat. If I board the cat out, on whom are the fleas that remain in the carpet (be they adult or hatching two weeks after treating the house) going to live? On my guests, of course."

Under no circumstances should pets ever be a surprise to the incoming family. First, based on some previous life experience, they may be terrified of or even have a strong dislike for your animal. Second, it is to your pet's advantage for your guests to know early on about him or her. "We didn't know about our partner's cat until our arrival at his home. We have bad allergies, so the cat spent two chilly weeks at Christmas on the very cold porch while we tried to remove cat hair from every nook and cranny of the house." That was the experience of a television producer in Kaneohe, Hawaii.

What two instructors in Falls Church, Virginia, went through may best illustrate the problems related to pets. "My wife is allergic to cats. We had a great exchange planned and knew the people had cats. The cats had been boarded out, however, well before we arrived, but we soon found that that technique doesn't work. Within two days my wife was

179

having trouble breathing and sneezing almost continuously. Fortunately, the exchange garden had a tiny, brand-new hideaway cottage (and also fortunately it was summer) where, apparently, the cats never went. We moved out there, using only the kitchen, bath, and outdoor patio of the main house. It was delightful—reminded us of the days when we were very young, too poor for hotels, and stayed in a tent or trailer in campgrounds, using their facilities."

If you have pets, you have pets. Moving them out two weeks before guests arrive doesn't create an instant no-pet household. In addition, "We had a dog who refused to eat while at the kennel and a cat who developed the very worst flea problem he ever had while at the best kennel in town," according to a doctor in Greenville, South Carolina.

However, most pet and animal stories are very positive. Baltimore exchangers, for example, "developed a close friendship with our exchange host's dog. It was a sad parting for both dog and us when our vacation ended."

Then there's the story of a Dutch family that had never had a dog. "But one year we exchanged with a family that did. The children loved it; their grandfather wasn't so enthusiastic. He announced that he had no intention of walking or playing with the dog—that if the children wanted to, that was fine, but not him. . . . Who was walking the dog every morning at 6:30 by our last week? It wasn't the kids!"

Pet care on a vacation home exchange is usually not one-sided. Each pet-owning exchanger cares for the pets of the exchange partner. In fact, this is an integral part of many exchanges, and exchange pets are often loved almost to the point of being members, not just of one, but of two or more families.

The care and feeding of the pets would, of course, be among the most important elements of a pet-centered focus of both exchangers' home information kits. Other essential information would include:

> What are the pet's likes and dislikes?
>
> Is this an inside or outside pet?
>
> Where does he/she sleep, eat, exercise?
>
> Where does the pet do his/her business? What are local regulations related to this necessary aspect of pet care?
>
> Does this community have a leash law?
>
> Is there, by chance, a neighbor he or she dislikes?
>
> Who and where is the veterinarian familiar with the pet?

If the home exchange guest is to be away for a few days, who is to take care of the pet?

What about fleas?

A Boise, Idaho, exchanger shares his foolproof test for the presence of fleas: "Wearing white athletic socks only, take a walk around the house—basement, kitchen, porch, all the rooms. Then check your socks. If they're covered with little black specks, you've got flea problems." You must deal with the problem before the other exchangers move in—including a new flea collar for the dog or cat, a supply of whatever kind of flea killer you prefer used for followup, and the name and number of your pest-control company as a last resort.

These suggestions from fellow home exchangers are in no way intended to disparage pets. However, pet owners should be aware that Murphy's Law may apply to pets as well as humans. "In France we were asked to give the cat a birth control pill every day in her food," reports a couple in Wales. "Initially, the pills could not be found, which led to a most amusing conversation with signs, drawings, and body language between our neighbor (who knew no English) and us (who knew no French). Eventually, we found the pills but then could not get the cat to eat. For three or four days she consumed neither food nor pills. Kittens? We never heard."

A family from Scotland looked after their exchangers' chickens and rabbits in Germany. Unfortunately, one of the rabbits chewed a hole in the screen fence and was caught and eaten by a fox. That was bad enough, "but you should have heard us—with no facility in German at all—trying to explain to the neighbors (much less our hosts) the fate of the escapee."

Normally, pets are lots of fun and can provide both love and laughs, even if—or more exactly when—they do the weird things they are wont to do. A couple exchanging in Maine tells the story of returning home one evening and finding Nellie the cat sitting straight upright next to the garage door, "just like one of those ceramic fireplace cats. Even when we tooted the horn, she didn't budge, but when we opened the garage door with the remote control, out popped Nellie. Her long tail had been caught under the door as we closed it when we left. . . . She'd been stuck there all evening."

A veteran traveler in Saint Croix, Virgin Islands, with sixteen exchanges behind her, tells of dearly loving her Dutch exchange cat. Apparently, the feeling was mutual "because one evening Pushkin

followed us to a local outdoor concert, sat with us and listened for two hours, then followed us back home."

Not everyone has cats. Some people have a cat and a something else. "On our last exchange in London, in addition to the expected family cat, we also found a rather motley old goldfish in a tank in the bathroom. Being old, the fish spent many hours nearly catatonic, appearing dead. My wife feared the worst: we'd be accused of not looking after their beloved pets. Despite my protestations that most fish die of overfeeding, she fed it daily, just to see it move. She worried incessantly about the heat in the bathroom: the prospect of cold baths loomed! Eventually, after consulting with everyone in the area on the subject of old fish, she called our exchangers on the pretense of talking about the cat and incidentally about the fish's health history. 'Phoof!' said the other wife, 'It's old, it will die. They all do, you know.'"

Other people are owned by dogs, not cats. "Our friends in Albuquerque had a German shepherd puppy," writes a couple in Lower Saxony, Germany. "'Twasn't very bright: it liked to swim but couldn't get out of the pool. One morning at about five o'clock we heard a huge splash! "The dog's fallen in the pool! The dog's drowning!" Out of bed we leapt and ran to rescue the dog. After we pulled it out, it raced around us a few times, then shot straight for our bedroom and up on the bed— water everywhere: all over the bed, all over the walls, all over me, all over my wife, all over the floor. . . . So much for waiting 'til daylight to get a bath."

People in Murrells Inlet, South Carolina, had to learn to reprimand a terrier in French—"an absolute riot," they say.

A Santa Barbara couple are experts at quick thinking in the face of possible disaster. "Our exchangers had a beautiful standard-size female poodle—show-dog quality, I would guess. It took a couple of days for us to realize why some really ugly dog was scaling the fence to come play with our foster poodle. When we did, we moved very quickly and got the dog to the vet for a morning-after shot that fortunately worked."

A family in Bologna, Italy, had arranged to care for their host's large, black, and seemingly ill-tempered wolfhound. After a day or so of creeping on eggshells around the dog, they discovered that, apparently, the owners had left only a large bag of dog biscuits in the way of food. "So we cooked up some of the recipes we used to feed our dog when we had one—homemade Italian dog food. The bad temper went away, and we became great friends. Perhaps he likes home exchanging now, too!"

Both cats and small dogs use pet flaps to gain access to their homes. So do neighbors' cats and dogs, according to some reports, as well as baby raccoons, as a couple in Oakbrook, Illinois, found out. Fortunately, not all the neighborhood animals wander in and out at will. From Calgary, Alberta, comes this story: "Our La Jolla exchange partners asked us to feed their outside cats each night. No problem. They had a couple of inside-outside cats, too. Every night around midnight we watched and admired the beautiful black-and-white cats from the patio door . . . until we realized that we were also feeding a family of skunks!"

But pet exchange is a relative term. Pets are definitely not just dogs, cats, and goldfish. "Our Australian exchange," reports a Steamboat Springs, Colorado, family, "included the care and nurture of six goats, six sheep, one donkey, four pigeons, nine chickens, one duck that thought it was a chicken, two ducks, and two cats." At one home exchange in Oahu, there were 201 plants to care for. A lot of exchangers apparently have chickens. "Great feeding them and eating the fresh eggs, but rounding them up when they're AWOL down the main road is a different story."

Then there's the management consultant and his wife in Warwickshire, England. "First night: 'We'd better get the hens in the coop: foxes, you know.' The next hour was spent chasing chickens—whooping, waving blankets, and exhibiting assorted other mad behavior. Second night, while discussing methods of improving our technique: Hens troop military fashion, under the watchful eye of the rooster, into the coop. Last one in undoubtedly shut the door."

A shopkeeper in Devon, England, a city of some size, once swapped with a family that had sheep ("most days it was twenty-five"), riding horses, laying hens "that produced wonderfully for us and had to be locked up at night, and two geese. The female was on the nest, incubating her eggs, and they both became violent if anyone came too close—not a problem until they ran out of water. My valiant husband, the solicitor, in two long-sleeved shirts and an extra pair of pants to protect his arms and legs, managed to avoid their huge wingspans and snapping beaks as he maneuvered a big dishpan (it left the house, at least, full of water) into their enclosure."

From San Francisco comes the story of Mother Nature at work in an English exchange home. "One night we heard a great commotion in the sitting room and crept out to investigate. A very large winged creature was fluttering around what we had thought was a terrarium. We called our host's local relative who informed us that this was a very rare and beautiful Brazilian death's-head moth whose emergence the little boy of the house had eagerly awaited for weeks before his departure. The creature was supposed to live for three days, mate, and die. It performed two of the above three functions quite well."

A couple in Washington, D.C., reports that a potential exchanger in Venezuela assured them that a neighbor would come in daily to feed mice to the pet boa constrictor held hostage in the basement. A Canadian couple made the acquaintance of a corn snake that had adopted the Florida family they exchanged with about a week before the exchange. "'Fang' dropped in on us the first time from the ledge over the front door, making like Medusa on my husband's head." Alligators are very visible in Florida also—occasionally showing up crossing streets, in pool enclosures, and frequently seen basking on lake, river, or canal banks. It is against the law to feed or harass them: if one is harassing you, call the police. Most law enforcement officers in the state are trained to deal with them. Remember, big and lumbering as an alligator may appear, it can outrun a grown man and regards a curious unleashed pet or wandering inquisitive child as merely a tasty tidbit.

Sometimes pets aren't part of the exchange but are an extra bonus of the trip. A large pot-bellied Vietnamese pig that was curled up under the carpet in a Santa Fe art gallery amazed a couple from Kent, England, who were told that was the way Piggy kept warm when it was chilly outside.

In scanning the vacation home directories, smokers don't consider those with a no-smoking rule, parents pass over no-children-please listings, and those home exchangers who prefer not to avoid pet care clearly note that in their listings. But, as has been mentioned, most pet-sitting home exchangers are also pet owners and pet lovers, so they are generally familiar with what may be expected. Moreover, they are accustomed to having pets of one kind or another around the house. Just as they appreciate the companionship of their own pets, so they will enjoy living with those of their exchangers. They may even introduce them to Italian food . . . or perhaps even rename them briefly. A Canadian couple, for example, renamed their German feline adoptee "Der Schnitzenpusser."

CHAPTER 19

Coping with Culture Shock, Part 1

I
N THE PRECEDING CHAPTERS MUCH HAS BEEN WRITTEN
about the global nature of home exchanging—that by adopting the
home exchange concept, vacationers from everywhere can go anywhere. According to the survey, they do just that, vacationing in
hundreds of cities and towns in more than fifty countries.

Prior to and in the years immediately following World War II, most
international vacationers stayed in hotels in either major or tourist-
oriented cities or in resort areas that featured beaches or sports-related
activities. This type of vacation was and is expensive, especially for
families traveling with children. Cruises? Only the idle rich could afford
cruising the seven seas.

The vacation world was ripe and ready for package tours, with a
fixed fee covering travel, hotels, and, in many cases, meals. Initially
these tours were also relatively expensive. With the advent of the jumbo
jet, carrying three hundred or more passengers, and forty-five-passenger,
living-room-comfort motor coaches—combined with the tremendous
growth in international recreational facilities and keen competition
among tour operators—vacationers everywhere benefited. In the past
ten years or so, large cruise ships carrying a thousand or more passengers lowered the cost of cruises. Today, travelers from all over the world
are able to enjoy longer and better-value vacations. For a wide variety of
good reasons detailed in these chapters, international vacation home (or
even motor home) exchanging is a viable alternative to hotel and resort
stays, cruises, and even package tours.

Home exchangers walk one step at a time in the footsteps of other
cultures, and to one degree or another culture shock is inherent in all
international travel, particularly vacation home exchanging. "In Holland
our home was one of those tall, narrow, picture-postcard houses, and the
stairs leading to the upper floors were very steep and very narrow—a lot
steeper than we were used to," writes an Ontario exchanger. "Within an

hour of our arrival, each member of the family had managed to tumble down the stairs at least once."

Ours is a world of differences: from living in accommodations quite different from one's own and trying to cook on a "foreign" stove to starting an English car (some have manual chokes) or using a clothes dryer in Sweden. There is a veritable parade of other differences—currency, dress, customs, landscape, shopping, church life, languages, telephones, emergency services, and even the temperaments of pets.

These and a hundred other aspects of international exchanging are the underlying causes of what some refer to as culture shock. It is how one handles these differences that makes or breaks the home exchange vacation in a foreign country. "Sometimes my wife and I are sure we will lose our minds when we're exchanging outside Belgium," writes a florist from Brussels. "In Canada, the States, or even nearby Holland, everyone appears to dance to a different tune—one we just can't seem to catch on to at first. But early on we get used to it, and once back home, can't wait for the next year's exchange directories (we list in three) to arrive."

An experienced exchanger in Northampton, England, says, "What impresses the English (or Welsh in my case) about the United States is the scale of everything—houses, residential developments, roads, and cars big enough to carry three British families. The service and the politeness (albeit a bit plastic) beats ours hands down. Combine these with good old American know-how (the 'Nobody does it better, folks!' attitude) and the sun—always the sun!—and one has an irresistible holiday exchange experience. Our American friends, on the other hand, tell us that the flowers, the lack of stress, the flowers, the greenery, the flowers (!), and the sheer storybook feel of England all combine to make them want to settle here. 'Maybe we should just swap homes permanently,' they say."

"One of our exchanges was in the Alps with a steep mountain trail complete with a wooden bridge and a waterfall," writes a vacationing judge's clerk. "We travel with our two teenagers plus two little ones who were thrilled with the surroundings—'just like Heidi,' they proclaimed, and our neighbors had a baby deer that they all loved. We expect to keep on home exchanging in the future and have given some thought to the possibility of 'child exchanging'—our teenagers for theirs, giving both sets of kids the experience of living in other countries and learning other languages. These aspects of home exchanging are very important for young people around the world."

An author-artist in New York City chimes in, "Our first exchange in 1973 was in a fifteenth-century Irish castle. In the years since, we have had seventeen other exchanges in England, France, Portugal, Spain, Mexico, Canada, and seven U.S. states. Wonderful life experiences for us and our two (now grown) children."

From Sparta, New Jersey, comes this comment: "While we were in Australia, our hosts took us to their second home, 185 miles west of Sydney, to the bush in Mudgee. At this house, named Land's End, there was no electricity, no telephone, and no plumbing—but a river in which to bathe and swim, gold miners' falling-down shacks, kangaroos bounding around, and a real sense of being in the Australia of a century ago. This was, as you might suspect, the highlight of our trip and something we would never have experienced as conventional vacationers."

A book publisher in Mahwah, New Jersey, writes, "While home exchanging recently in Sellebakk, Norway, we happened to meet the pastor of a local church. He invited us to attend his service the following Sunday evening. As we score a zero in Norwegian, he arranged for a church member–translator, who was kind enough to translate the entire service for us—sitting as she did in a chair between my wife and me. It was a memorable spiritual experience—highlighted by a full band and a singing group of four young people. By coincidence, this church happened to be the one of which our exchange host and his family are members. The following day we were invited to attend a football game, in which our neighbor's son played ('we' lost). While exchanging in foreign lands it's always fun to become a part of the local scene, local community activities."

It's quite evident most international vacation home exchangers view their experiences less as culture shock and more as challenge and adventure, an exercise in international living and learning.

"During the past ten years we have exchanged in England a number of times," contributes a Saint Louis, Missouri, salesman's wife. "Not only have our hosts' friends and neighbors been gracious and helpful, but we've made friends also through regular church attendance on these trips. In Cornwall several years ago, for example, for three weeks in a row we were two of a twelve-member church congregation. This year in Suffolk, we were part of a family-centered service during which the pastor asked my husband to share a bit about church-family life in the States. We find ourselves warmly welcomed and very 'comfortable' in these church-related situations."

Home exchangers who travel abroad report that consummating the arrangements calls for more homework on their parts as well as on that of their exchange partners. A year is not too soon, they say, to begin setting international exchange plans into motion.

In chapter 7, reference is made to the different schools of thought regarding use of the telephone in making home exchange arrangements. All, however, concur in that the telephone can play an especially important role in international arrangements—this because of the excessive amount of time it takes for international mail to go back and forth. Writes a retired government personnel officer, a thirteen-time exchanger now living in Carmel, California, "I would recommend the importance of using the international telephone system to call good prospects as soon as the new directories come out. Better to nail down a good prospect immediately than wait the time needed for correspondence to flow back and forth. Of course, you follow up with letters, photographs of the home, etc., but 'strike while the iron is hot,' we say. The cost of the call is minimal compared to the ultimate saving and fun involved in getting exactly what you're looking for. Don't worry that you will have difficulty with the language. Most European exchangers have someone in the house who can speak a little English. Perhaps you know someone who speaks the language needed or, at worst, you can use your broken French, Italian, or German to at least make the initial contact."

Many Americans traveling to Europe arrange for a chain of exchanges. "After all, once you decide to go that far," comments a Riverdale, New York, accountant, "you might just as well line up several exchanges. Last year we had two weeks each in London, Geneva, the south of France, Javea in Spain, and the Algarve region of Portugal. Sure, this takes a lot more advance planning and arranging, but we figure, 'Hey, why not?' Yesterday they said, 'Join the navy and see the world'; today we say, 'Grab a home exchange directory and see the world.' We are long since retired and not going to live forever! Culture shock? No problem."

From Fayetteville, Arkansas: "We've taken various holiday tours in the past. No more. We are now confirmed vacation home exchangers and have no desire to vacation any other way. Last summer we took our daughter and three grandchildren to Germany and had a wonderful time. The children played soccer and computer games to their hearts' content with the neighbors' children, and even though neither side could speak the other's language, they managed to understand each other very well. With luck, back we all go to Germany next year."

From West Wales, United Kingdom, come these comments: "Our first home exchange in 1988 was a great success. A retired couple from Florida spent a month in our house in Cornwall, and later in the year we stayed in their lovely holiday apartment on Sanibel Island, Florida. The contrast with a conventional holiday was enormous. Our hosts, who lived nearby, introduced us to their friends, took us fishing, sailing, to a concert, and generally made certain we had a marvelous time. Apart from having to abandon the apartment due to a threatened hurricane (it petered out later to become nothing more than a tropical storm), there were no problems. The possibility of the odd alligator crossing the road at night just meant it was advisable to drive to our local restaurant rather than walk. Now our friends from Florida are staying with us again. This time they are in our new home in Wales, whilst we live in a self-contained annex. In October we shall be off to Sanibel once more. We are completely sold on home exchanging, and next year will have three couples from the United States, each spending four weeks at our home. This will enable us to spend February-March and October-November in different areas in Florida. We are already planning for the following year and hope, at that time, to do a 'round-the-world home exchange trip. The world of international home exchanging has been a most exciting discovery for us and has made a great change to our way of life."

CHAPTER 20

Coping with Culture Shock, Part 2

THOSE HOPING TO ARRANGE HOME EXCHANGES abroad face an added communications challenge over and above making their arrangements clear. They must spell out precisely, in typed or hand-printed form, step-by-step instructions for the use of all appliances in their homes: stoves, microwaves, clothes washers and dryers, dishwashers, disposals, televisions, VCRs, or whatever they have. The survey revealed that whenever home exchangers get outside their own environment, they almost inevitably have appliance problems of one kind or another.

An American in Spain "nearly blew up the house trying to ignite the stove's pilot light," and an English family in the United States "almost filled the kitchen with bubbles the first time we used the dishwasher."

The microwave's control panel completely mystified a first-time French exchanger ("The directions in English only made it worse"), and an American in Guadeloupe found the French instruction manuals for her appliances equally mystifying.

"My wife singed her hair attempting to light a water heater in a German bathroom—walked around wafting that burnt-hair smell all through the house for several hours."

Americans in Holland "couldn't figure out why the washing machine left the clothes soaking wet until we discovered the spin dryer was a separate appliance."

A couple from Paris visiting England were "perplexed by the dishwasher's strange behavior. We put the dishes in after dinner, pushed the buttons and turned the knobs just as the instructions said, but nothing happened. We tried again—nothing. We gave up, went to bed and found the dishes washed and dried when we got up in the morning. Seems the machine was on a timer to operate during the night when the utility rates were lower."

At least one brand of English clothes washer has its own water heater: if the incoming water is not hot enough, it waits until it is—quietly soaking the clothes (and baffling the house guests)—then proceeds to agitate and go through its cycles. Most Americans are familiar with this feature in a dishwasher but would not necessarily think of it in a clothes washer.

Another complication an exchanging couple ran into in Scotland was the separate circuit that served the water heater, which "until we discovered the breaker in the off position, provided us with several days of sixty-five-degree showers."

"In France we were told that, instead of a dryer, there was a 'drying closet,'" says a Riverside, Connecticut, couple. "A correct description, but what we weren't told was that clothing emerges from it so stiff it can stand on its own. And in Germany the 'trocken' got so hot it scorched a sock almost to the point of flames and reduced one of my husband's T-shirts to a size two."

But a Texas airline pilot's story is hard to beat: "We were in a flat in a Stockholm apartment house that had a communal laundry with all the latest equipment. To use the dryer, you fed in the garments one at a time. They traveled on a heated drum, and after one revolution of the drum, the dried clothes spilled out. I had fed in all my underwear piece by piece, and the first pair of dry shorts was about to emerge when the dryer grunted and stopped. I could grasp the emerging end of the shorts but could not move the drum. Our host had left us English instructions on 'How to Dry,' which I had with me, but nothing on 'How to Repair Dryer.' Our designated helper (named in our home information kit) was away for the weekend. Back to the apartment I went with no underwear. 'Where are your clothes?' my wife asked, reasonably enough. 'The machine ate them,' I replied. The next morning I went back to the laundry prepared to do battle again and found all my underwear dried, neatly folded, and stacked next to the dryer. Somewhere in the building was a very nice Swedish person whom I never found, but to whom I am indeed grateful. The dryer never grunted again."

There are yet-to-be solved mysteries of some popular U.S. appliances: the combination convection-microwave oven—the wonders of the fancy coffeemaker that may or may not have the morning coffee ready at the time for which it was set—or the absolutely baffling instructions for the highly touted self-cleaning feature of a stove's oven.

"When we exchanged for a thoroughly modernized thatched cottage in Cheshire, England, I had to learn to cook on a fascinating device called an 'Aga,'" says a woman in Pickering, Ontario. "An Aga is a two-burner (one very hot, one simmer) and two-oven (one hot, one warming) stove. As you can guess, I burned quite a few meals before devising an appropriate cooking technique. The thermostat was an almost invisible gauge on the front with a scratch in the middle denoting the correct temperature, regardless of what one was cooking. It did boil the kettle quickly yielding a good hot cup of tea and, once I got it right, turned out some great meals. Since you never turn it completely off, it keeps the kitchen area comfortable all the time, even on chilly English days." An exchanger in Montreal West, Quebec, perhaps says it best. "Homemaking in another person's home is a variety of challenges. . . . What is simple and second nature at home becomes a grand adventure while on exchange."

For example, from a Sausalito, California, couple comes the story of a charming little English cottage that had a heating system that stored heat at night when the rates were lower and dispensed it during the day. "When we decided to ferry to France for a few days, we turned off all the radiators so as not to waste electricity. On our return the house was absolutely icy, so we turned everything back on, expecting warmth by morning. Wrong. We apparently had blown a fuse by turning everything on at once, and the house remained freezing all day and until the next morning. The system must have kicked in during the second night because the next day there was most welcome warmth."

A Brownsville, Texas, couple tells the tale of a "stone cottage perched on a mountain above Lake Maggiore, in Switzerland, only three kilometers from Italy. The appliances in that house were the ultimate in miniaturization. The refrigerator was under the counter with a freezer that would maybe hold one quart of ice cream or two ice trays. The bathroom (roughly 5'x5') had a curtained shower, toilet, sink, and combination washer-dryer all crammed into it. I've never seen a washer-dryer like this one: one sheet almost overstuffed it. The most fun was the lack of closets; a small wardrobe stood in one corner—too narrow in which to hang our hangers. We had clothes draped everywhere—over chairs, doors, doorknobs, stair rails, etc. (Being typical American tourists we, of course, had taken too many clothes in too much luggage.) Getting dressed each morning was an adventure, kind of like a scavenger hunt."

A London family that sallied forth to Norway relates their experience in a large and lovely environmentally "green" home that had all the usual conveniences—plus chemical toilets in both bathrooms. "We had been told about them before we went, but we didn't quite appreciate what was being described—perfectly normal-looking toilets until you lifted the lid and discovered a yawning hole. The written instructions declared that, under no circumstances, were the lids to be left up. Of course, our four young children didn't always remember, and the entire house soon reeked with a ghastly odor. We were also told that if two flies went in, a week later a million would come back out. Naturally, with the children's lapses, this made us even more anxious. So we changed our game plan: first thing in the morning, we were up, out, and in the car headed for the closest public toilet—which, being in Norway, was always immaculate. Then back to the house for breakfast, baths, and the day's planning session. A little strange, perhaps, but it worked for us."

As stated elsewhere, most exchangers look at glitches as challenges, not difficulties, and figure "they go with the territory." They really don't have to: mechanical problems can almost always be stopped before they start, provided the host leaves detailed operating instructions. In addition, the host should not fail to leave names and telephone numbers of electricians, plumbers, and others who do various home repairs. After all, it is the host who benefits from having his home and possessions properly cared for.

When the host has not left proper instructions, neighbors can be a real help—especially in foreign countries where the language barrier comes into play. Until the world has one language, English will have to do, at least for most Americans. Exchangers can nearly always find someone who speaks English. Apropos is the story told by a Spanish family exchanging in Holland: "Something went very wrong with our plumbing, and although our host had left us the telephone number of his plumber, we wondered how we would explain the problem to the man. Much to our amazement, the plumber spoke better English than we do."

Of course, speaking English does not solve every problem in every quarter. A Peasenhall, England, retired naval officer writes, "The children were amazed by the apparent strange diet found in Germany. 'Spaghetti' turned out to be multicolored ice cream put through a ricer and yielding a spaghetti-like mix topped with strawberry sauce, and 'diesel' was the local name for a mix of Coke and lemonade." To say nothing of the fun a Bartlesville, Oklahoma, couple faced in Lingerich and Markdorf, Germany, when they needed to buy a valve handle *(ventil griff)*, fine sandpaper *(fein sandpapier)*, and a vacuum bottle filler *(thermos)* by means of a German-English phrase book plus sign language.

Generally speaking, Europeans, Far Easterners, and families elsewhere in the world seem to employ domestic help—maids, cooks, gardeners—to a much greater extent than is true in the United States. In

England, some of these domestic servants are called "dailies" and work by the day or half-day cleaning houses and sometimes doing washing and ironing as well. "Our London host had a maid who came in once a week," writes a New York City account executive. "A delightful Italian, she did a great job but was terrified of the vacuum cleaner. We helped with the vacuuming, which Britains call 'hoovering.'"

Six-time exchangers from Florida added, "Some of our exchangers had cleaning services—daily in Portugal and twice-weekly in Spain and

England. This was a nice luxury feature, and it was considerate of our hosts to continue the service while we were there."

In the Far East, many homes have live-in domestics. In Hong Kong, for instance, these live-ins are frequently from the Philippines, working under two-year contracts. "Our host said the live-in maid would do the food buying, cooking, cleaning, and washing," writes a Nuremberg exchanger, "and, if you left your underwear lying around, not to be surprised if it's washed and ironed within the hour."

When domestic help is part of the home exchange arrangement, it is important that the host makes it clear to his exchange guests just what the maid's responsibilities are—what she does, what she doesn't do, and/or what you can ask her to do. Also, is the host or the guest responsible for paying the domestic's wages?

Some European parents (and increasingly American parents) with small children engage the services of au pairs, usually young women between the ages of eighteen and twenty-four. Generally, the au pair's responsibility is to take care of the children and occasionally do light housework and/or fix an occasional meal. She gets her room and board, usually a small stipend, and lives as part of the family. If she is from another country, she learns the language and the customs of the country in which she is working and may even take a course or two in the local college if scheduling can be worked out. Obviously, traveling with her employers is an added bonus to her, as well as to her charges' parents.

The European employment of domestics and/or au pairs is but one in an endless list of customs one finds when traveling the world. "Last time we were on Sanibel Island, Florida, we went to a fancy cheeseburger place our friends had recommended," relates a Bruges, Belgium, couple. "We each ordered their pounder with all the trimmings and a pitcher of beer. The waitress said they didn't have pitchers; they had buckets. So we ordered a bucket. Imagine our surprise when she brought to the table a real bucket, filled with ice and six bottles of beer. The bottle opener was attached to the bucket handle with a string."

A Carrollton, Texas, foursome laughs as they tell of their first trip to Manchester, England. "The American addiction to iced drinks seems to be incomprehensible to the English mind. We arrived at our exchange home about 4 P.M., and the two husbands took off after groceries for dinner and ice for drinks, while Barb and I stayed behind to settle in. After three hours we were getting more than a little concerned about our husbands' whereabouts and their safety. Sometime later, they staggered in . . . they'd spent thirty minutes food shopping and the rest of the time trying to find ice. They had finally found a pub that gave them a couple of sandwich bags full of ice. The next night we all walked over to the same pub for dinner and asked again to buy ice. This time one of the waiters had a better picture of what we needed (he thought) and brought out a large green trash bag with about forty pounds of ice that had to be carted home before it melted. We finally found out about those plastic 'baggie' disposable ice makers with small cube-shaped compartments into which you drip water, then seal and freeze. It takes approximately one hour each night to remove the cubes made last night and prepare tomorrow night's batch. We each, on more than one occasion, gave some serious thought to dropping the cocktail hour entirely."

Americans exchanging overseas should probably take along a few plastic ice trays—either standard size, with earrings or other small things stashed in the cubicles, or the smaller minicube variety. You can always leave them as a house gift if you don't have space to bring them back.

A retired accountant in British Columbia also laughs as he recalls his family's first experience with meals in Germany. "Our exchange host met us at the airport. His maid had dinner prepared when we got to his home—white German sausage. Never having had it before, we weren't aware we weren't supposed to eat the casing. I really didn't like them at all and wound up shoving them around on my plate while discussing the exchange with our host, but my better half soldiered through, ate casing and all and never touched another bite of sausage the whole time we were in Germany."

"In the Netherlands the kids were riding bikes the way they do in our neighborhood at home—all over the road, up on the sidewalks, down the curbs, figure eights, etc.," adds a Kimberley, Ontario, mom. "It seems that the rule in Holland is to ride on the right side of the road only, obeying all traffic signals. Needless to say, our kids were stopped by the police who eventually gave up on their lecture when they realized not a word was being understood by our non-Dutch-speaking children."

In Ireland, Americans ran into what can best be described as a combined language-and-custom puzzle. Two local lads came to the door one day and asked, "Any turf today?" "What's turf?" "It's what you burn in the fireplace." But the American couldn't quite make out the sense of what the boy was saying and consequently responded, "No, thanks." He did, however, clearly understand one boy say to the other as they walked away, "Stupid foreigners—these are just as dumb as the ones who were here last year!" (Turf is a type of peat burned in fireplaces—a very common practice in Ireland.)

From western Canada, a home exchanger writes, "In Germany, some of the women were dismayed at our 'scandalous' clothes (shorts, T-shirts, and so on); at the same time, they were unfailingly helpful when it came to directions, shopping advice, etc."

A multitime exchanger in Texas shares these thoughts about exchanging in another country, "The first thing we do after reaching a foreign destination is ask our neighbors if there are areas of town to avoid. Sometimes both male and female exchangers who come here do thoughtless things like going out in skimpy athletic clothing or wandering off alone at night—occasionally to areas we'd never visit—and we feel like shaking them when we hear them telling about their adventures. One may be able to do things like that in a remote, peaceful beach community or a tiny Italian mountain village, but not in a U.S. city.

"We had to tell three exchangers who arrived before we left that men here do not go out to dinner wearing shirts unbuttoned all the way down. As I said, it may be different in some areas, but here we dress for the occasion rather than the weather. There's nothing wrong with this attire, if they want to soak up more sun, but dressing differently from everyone else marks one as a tourist and, under certain circumstances, as one courting unpleasant consequences.

"Here are a few other things we tell our exchangers from abroad:

1. American bars are not the same as English pubs; sometimes 'informality' would be a masterpiece of understatement! Do your drinking in hotel or restaurant bars or lounges.

2. Underscoring the above, take steps not to call attention to yourself. Observe what others are wearing and then dress accordingly.

3. Don't flash money.

4. Don't park in the dark. Either use a well-lighted, established parking lot or select a parking spot under a streetlight.

5. If you use public transportation in the evening, be sure you know the time of the last run.

6. (Perhaps the best rule of all): Don't ever be embarrassed to ask questions!"

"Hey, their money is different from our money! How do we handle that?" Any discussion about "swapping" cultures must include some reference to money.

Some exchangers recommend that travelers use credit cards, travelers' checks, or bank ATMs. Some say foreign currency should be acquired from the international sections of travelers' banks. All recommend that one travel with limited amounts of cash. This latter is true, very true. Those traveling abroad with cash run the risk of losing it in any of a number of ways.

To be well advised as to the best current procedure in this matter of money and traveling, home exchangers and others traveling abroad are urged to consult with their banks, with their travel agents, with tourist information centers, and/or with their accountants.

Meet Ambassador and Mrs. Belden Bell

Since they have traveled extensively, Belden and Rae Bell are unconcerned about culture shock. The Bells have exchange homes in a Washington, D.C., suburb and on the West Indies island of Saint Kitts. Bell was a one-time Republican congressional candidate from the state of Indiana and served in a number of Capitol Hill executive agency posts, including that of deputy assistant secretary of state. Later he was named ambassador to the Federation of Saint Kitts and Nevis. In 1985, Bell opened the first Organization of American States Embassy in Saint Kitts.

Because it preserves the architectural integrity of Saint Kitts, "Lavington," the island home of Belden and Rae Bell, was pictured on a Saint Kitts postage stamp. Without a doubt, a vacation home exchange first can be chalked up to the Bells: the first home exchangers to use a postage stamp showcasing their own home on envelopes carrying their home exchange correspondence.

When they reached the point of semiretirement, the Bells were very active in the life of their island nation. Their Saint Kitts home often hosted memorable events of diplomatic and charitable importance.

With fewer government responsibilities these days, the Bells report: "Offering our homes in Virginia and on the island of Saint Kitts, we are now looking forward to and are excited about becoming serious national and international vacation home exchangers."

Culture shock? Reviewing this chapter and chapter 19, one must conclude that international vacation home exchangers seem to cope very nicely with culture shock and go on to enjoy the positive aspects of vacationing in foreign lands.

CHAPTER 21

The Kitchen—Toasty Warm in August?

"The Kitchen—Toasty Warm in August?" was created by writer Marillyn Wild of Corpus Christi, Texas. Marillyn and her husband, Fred, had their first home exchange experience in 1984. Since then, they have enjoyed twenty-four exchanges in the United States, England, the Netherlands, Germany, the Caribbean, and elsewhere. Generally, the Wilds exchange for up to four months per year—one month in each exchange home along the way.

Fred received an engineering degree from Washington University, served with the U.S. Air Force in England, and then held a civil service position for some years.

Marillyn served in the WAVEs in World War II, was a teacher for some thirty years, and now has a busy career as a writer for a variety of magazines and newspapers. For ten years she has taught classes in reminiscence writing at a community college in Corpus Christi and to various Elderhostel groups.

Marillyn's writing skills and her years of home exchange correspondence uniquely qualify her to present this overview— from one side of a home exchange correspondence that might have been.

"Perhaps we are not typical exchangers," Marillyn writes, "but our idea of a perfect afternoon is sitting in a churchyard of the charming English town of Saffron Walden and listening to the organist practicing—thus condensing all we know and love of England into one experience."

Dear Mr. and Mrs. Huntington-Green,

We noticed by your listing in this year's home exchange directory that you want a seaside location. We may have just what you're looking for—miles of beach and relatively few people. Although we don't actually live at the water's edge, our comfortable three-bedroom home is within sight and walking distance of Corpus Christi Bay.

Our listing in the directory gives information about our house and area. If, after reading it, you are interested in further discussion of an exchange, we will be delighted to hear from you.

Dear Bernard and Margaret,

What a thrill it was to receive a telephone call from England last Sunday night!—followed so promptly by your letter agreeing to an exchange for the month of August. I hope we made ourselves clear about the temperatures in Texas in August. We realize you were, as you said, "looking out the window at a bleak gray landscape" but you may feel quite differently when you step off the plane into a blast of 98° heat. However, you said you'd love it so we'll take you at your word.

To answer your question, Margaret, "modern kitchen" means a stove, refrigerator, dishwasher, and garbage disposal. We have all of these plus a microwave oven and a food processor. The refrigerator has a separate freezer section and there's another freezer in the garage. The kitchen has many convenient features—a slide-out pantry, lazy susans in both upper and lower corner cabinets, and a built-in breadbox. What is your kitchen like? About the same, I suppose, since your listing says "modern kitchen," too.

Would you mind looking after our three adorable pets? Dagwood is our little terrier and the cats are Mimi and Musetta. They're absolutely no trouble at all.

No, dear, our house is nowhere near a forest. That's just the way they name streets here. I'll bet your house isn't covered with roses either, is it? They'll do anything to sell a house these days, won't they?

P.S. Next time, dear, would you mind calling a little later in the day? It was 3 A.M. here.

Dear Bernard and Peggy,

Okay, Peggy it is, and you must call us Bunny and Skeeter. You don't mean it! Your house is really two hundred years old! There's nothing in this town over a hundred years old. Hurricanes, you know. Do you realize your house was built in the same year we got our independence? Oops! No offense. That was a long time ago, wasn't it?

And your house is covered with roses! Well, that shows how little I know about England. I always thought it was ivy that climbed around on houses over there.

I enjoyed the description of your kitchen, Peggy. I'm glad to hear you also have a dishwasher. Who wants to waste their vacation washing dishes? What exactly is an Aga cooker? Is it gas or electric? Also what did you mean by "an ingenious means of drying your clothes right in the kitchen." Is that where you keep your clothes dryer? Mine's in the utility room.

In answer to your question, a lazy susan is a sort of turntable that lets you get at things in a corner cabinet that you used to have to hunt for on your knees with a flashlight. It would take too long to describe it but you'll love it.

Is there a supermarket near your home? I'll want to stock up on groceries when we arrive so I won't have to waste time marketing for weeks. No, we don't prefer frozen food. Why would you think that?

Listen, guys, forget *Dallas*. Texas is not like that television show. We don't even know any millionaires. You may see boots and big hats, but believe me that doesn't mean you're looking at cowboys. As for Indians, the only one I know is running a Honda dealership in Oklahoma.

I hate to discourage you but some of your plans are simply not going to work out. You really can't "run down to Big Bend National Park" or "pop over to New Orleans" some afternoon. Grand Canyon is a bit out of one day's driving range from here, and Washington, D.C., is out of the question. You'll have to see your cousin some other time, I'm afraid.

Things are getting quite pretty here. The wildflowers are in bloom—also our peach trees. I hope your weather improves soon. Enclosed are some photos of our house and a map of the United States. Please note the scale.

Dear Bernard and Peggy,

It was great to talk to you again yesterday morning. I hope we set your minds at ease about hurricanes. There's not a thing to worry about as long as you stay in the house away from bits of roofs blowing around and live electric wires. Besides, they are infrequent, like the shark attack at Padre Island last week.

I'm glad you enjoyed the photos of our house. Yes, those really are banana trees with real bananas hanging on them. What you call the garden is what we call the yard. You needn't worry, Bernard, about how large it is to keep mowed. We've hired a neighbor boy to do that.

I'm sorry to be so stupid, Peggy, but I still don't quite understand about the Aga cooker. You say it keeps the kitchen toasty warm. How can it do that unless I keep it turned on all the time and why would I want the kitchen toasty warm in August?

Of course, we will feed your cat, Hildegard, and give her lots of "cuddles." She sounds like a dear and she'll help us not miss our pets so much. One thing I forgot to tell you about Dagwood. If you scold him or try to make him get down from your lap, he rolls over on his back and urinates. You will watch out for that, dear, won't you?

It's awfully nice of you to offer to leave breakfast things in the fridge for us. What do you mean by "what kind of bacon?" Thick or thin-sliced?

Spring is really here now. We went for our first swim of the season yesterday. The tomato plants are waist-high, and the peaches are beginning to turn pink. Sorry about the blizzard and the burst water pipes. Will the repairs take long?

P.S. Yes, your call did wake us up, but don't give it a thought. We'd only been asleep about an hour. Please send photos of your house, especially the kitchen.

Dear Peggy,

No, that wasn't a "Texas tall tale" about the shark attack, but you really needn't get upset. This was the first one in eighty-five years, after all.

That many kinds of bacon! I don't know what "streaky" is but it's a good description of the kind we like so that would be fine. And smoked, please. I've never heard of unsmoked bacon.

Thank you for the packet of photos. Now I understand about it not mattering if there was a supermarket nearby. We had a fridge just like that in our RV. I'll market every day as you do.

I still don't understand about the Aga cooker—the picture seems to be blurred—but I do recognize the dryer hanging above it. My grandmother had one like it back on the farm. She dried her dishtowels on it and I loved the way they smelled of bacon.

Isn't that funny? I thought you meant an automatic dishwasher. I have one of those little sprayers, too, but a dishwasher here is a machine. Yes, I'll bet Bernard does get a lot of laughs with his joke about not needing a dishwasher because he married one.

The bedrooms are adorable—all that lovely Laura Ashley fabric. Isn't it funny what film does to colors? The kitchen looks purple and the living room walls look brown.

One thing, dear, and I'm not intending to be critical but where were the lamps? We only see one tiny one, like a night light, on the bedside table and none at all in the living room. Excuse me, the lounge. Skeeter and I are great readers, so good reading lamps are important to us. No doubt they were in other parts of the rooms that didn't appear in the photographs.

You're sure we won't notice your lack of air conditioning? In August? Well, you would know best, of course, but we couldn't sleep a wink here without it.

I'm having so much fun getting my wardrobe together for the trip. I found the smartest yellow sunback dress and sandals to match. All I need now is a couple more pairs of shorts. Most men here wear guayabera shirts everywhere in summer so Bernard won't need to bring jackets and ties.

Well, I must close. We have so many peaches this year that I can't give them away. I'm going to put some in the freezer. We should have tomatoes in a couple of weeks. Still bleak there?

Dear Peggy,

Isn't it exciting? Only three more months!

About the Aga cooker? What do you mean "solid fuel"? The only solid fuels I can think of are wood and coal, and of course no one under eighty would know how to cook with one of those anymore. So what solid fuels are you talking about?

We had a picnic on Padre Island yesterday. It was Mother's Day so there were hundreds of families enjoying the water. We had a good time but everyone got sunburned.

I'm so disappointed about the yellow sundress. Are you sure it won't get any warmer than that? A guayabera shirt has lots of tucks and embroidery and is worn outside the trousers. Bernard can get some here; he'll love them.

Dear Peggy,

I really don't think you need to be so huffy. I certainly didn't mean to "lord it over you" about our weather and my kitchen. I can't help it because it's warmer here. Why do you think we want to come to England? I suppose you'll get mad again if I say I hate hot weather but actually I do.

The photos did make the kitchen look purple. How was I to know it was "grape"? And now that I look closer I can see the lights in the living room—in those little sconces on the wall.

I apologize for sounding "bossy." If Bernard likes to wear jackets and ties in hot, steamy weather, who am I to tell him to wear a comfortable cool guayabera shirt? You told me not to wear a yellow sundress.

You weren't very straightforward about the Aga cooker either. I don't care what you say. I'm sure I'll never learn to use a coal stove, and Skeeter hates cold cereal and peanut butter sandwiches.

I started my suntan today.

Hi, Peggy,

I'm so glad Bernard and Skeeter took over the correspondence and worked out all those tiresome details, aren't you? The only thing is— I've missed your letters.

I'm getting so excited about seeing England at last. I can hardly believe that in less than three weeks I'll be having one of those heavenly cream teas you described at the Victoria Tea Shop in Hampton-on-Dean and sleeping under a two-hundred-year-old roof.

It is really hot here now. Bring plenty of suntan lotion. The bananas are getting ripe now. I hope I have prepared everything to make you comfortable. I've left you plenty of storage space for your clothes and a small stock of foods to carry you through until you get to the supermarket. There's a chicken casserole in the freezer with directions for heating taped to the lid. Have a wonderful time in Texas.

P.S. Musetta has been bringing in lots of lizards lately and one of them ran down into a burner pan this morning. It's down in the stove somewhere so watch out for that, dear, won't you? It might jump out at you some day while you're cooking.

From England

Dear Peggy,

We love it! Rose Cottage will be such a happy memory for us. It's toasty warm in the kitchen and there's a lovely pork pie heating in the Aga for our supper. Cynthia and Jeremy have been seeing to it that we see everything!

We enjoyed seeing the photo of you two having dinner with Pat and Doug at Snoopy's Fishhouse. Bernard looks great in his guayabera shirt. Sorry about Musetta bringing in the baby possum.

CHAPTER 22

And Still More People Who Tried It . . . and Liked It

Home exchangers since 1988, the Roland Poelvoorde family live in Belgium in the West Flanders seaside town of Knokken-Heist. Roland received his master's degree in chemical studies from the University of Leuven in Belgium. He is now general manager of the New Holland Company, manufacturers of agricultural machinery.

For the past twenty-two years, Katharina has been a teacher. Geography and biology are her subjects today. Her students are in their midteens. A difficult age group? "Not at all," she says, "in my relationship with my students I have a 'listening ear' . . . and consider them all to be in the wonderful age of enthusiasm for life!"

The Poelvoordes have two sons. Lieven (sixteen years old) excels in math and science, loves sports, and plays the violin. Fourteen-year-old Wauter's best grades are in math and economics; he plays the side flute and enjoys working in the garden, reading, and playing squash.

Katharina Poelvoorde-DeSment writes:

When we heard about home exchanging, our first thoughts were that this would be an interesting holiday idea for us for many reasons. We would make new friends—our exchange partners and their neighbors. In hotels, where you're just a number, I always feel very lonely. Yes, an exchange is much better than a hotel. In an exchange home, you don't have to worry about the children keeping quiet, and you have space in which to enjoy your holiday weeks. Children have more fun in a home than in a hotel, and if you are an international exchanger, you actually live in a different culture that is an exciting, informative, learning experience for all members of the family, regardless of age.

We learned of the home exchange concept at the very time we were building a new home, and money was tight. Our holiday choices were no holiday or home exchanging, so we chose the latter.

To date, our exchanges have included an enormous home in a Marin County town, near San Francisco. We called that the "five-ketchup-bottle" house, because our exchange partners left five opened ketchup bottles in the fridge. One of our California neighbors stayed with us later during their visit to Belgium. We had another wonderful exchange holiday in Norway. While there, the sons of our neighbor took our boys hiking up to a big hill to watch the sunset. We learned how to pick eatable berries, saw many colorful flowers growing in the wild, and saw our first reindeer in the woods. Because it's so far north, it gets very cold in Norway. What was the highlight of our visit to Denver, Colorado? Of course it was a driving tour of the awe-inspiring Rocky Mountains.

We like to exchange in different countries and always had a burning desire to visit Russia, but there was no Russian listing in the home exchange directory. I said to Roland, "Why isn't this possible, now that they have *perestroika* and *glasnost?* They have a great culture, and we cannot share this because of some foolish ideology." So that night I sat down and wrote a letter to Mr. Gorbachev at the Kremlin in Moscow, inquiring about the possibility of our contacting a Russian who might be interested in exchanging homes with us in Belgium. That was in February 1988; the answer came the following May. The authorities accepted our suggestion and said they would recommend a family to exchange with us, the man, an engineer, and the wife, a teacher, just like us. It was the first time that a whole Russian family could do this. In the past, one family member always had to stay in Russia. Because in Russia the home exchange arrangement is too difficult, generally Russians select hospitality exchanges. When we were there, we were interviewed on Moscow radio, and our Russian exchange family was interviewed on Belgian television. It was a great adventure for all of us.

Our Russian exchange partners spoke a bit of English, and we spoke some Russian. Our stay was a great success as far as our two families were concerned. You know, the Russian people have a great heart, once they have accepted you. The home of our partner was a three-room situation. It was too little but very neat and clean. We only had two kinds of meals during our fourteen days in Russia, but our partners showed us as much as they could of their country. We even went to Leningrad on a very beautiful night train. In Leningrad there was a student, Olga, who helped us, and one evening she went to the circus with the boys. She studied Dutch, so she spent the whole evening with her dictionary and our boys, and it was an enjoyable evening for all.

Several years later we went back to this home in Russia for a hospitality exchange week. While Moscow had improved in many ways since our first visit to Russia, living was still difficult. For example, there was no electricity or clean water beyond the Moscow city limits. On this trip we did notice more food in the shops, lots of fruit—only one has to pay a lot of money for everything.

In our home exchange experiences through the years, we've found the neighbors of our exchange partners to be friendly and helpful to us in many ways. This was also particularly true in the "new" Russia.

We always tell people to take young children with them while exchanging because when they get older they may prefer to take school trips or do things with their friends. When our boys are at the university stage and I am not teaching anymore, probably just Roland and I will do the traveling. Then we can be much more flexible in making our home exchange plans.

In our communications before the actual exchanges, we always explain that we will be very careful with the private property in the homes—the furniture, the glassware, and other fragile things. And we expect our exchange partners to also take good care of our things. This is an important part of every exchange, and we have never been disappointed.

Then there is the matter of smoking. Our son Lieven is very allergic, so we do not permit smoking in our house. (This is a good idea, too, because of fire!)

Our friends and neighbors here in Belgium often ask about the condition in which our exchange partners leave our home. We tell them that in five years of exchanging, not only have our exchange friends taken good care of our home, but they have also left it clean and neat for our return. And we have always done the same thing with their homes.

This book suggests people should leave a small amount of food to "greet" their exchange partners. We always do this. Also, we have in our country more than three hundred kinds of beer (including sixty in our own region), so we always leave our incoming exchange friends some beer and cheese. They always appreciate this.

Planning ahead, we hope to have future exchanges in France and Italy. Doing this, we will have the advantages of living in two cultures quite new to us.

I now want to say we feel the most important part of home exchanging is the matter of trust. Remember, you are giving your partners the use of your home, just as they are giving you the use of theirs. In the beginning, you must trust each other to be honest about your homes— what it contains, what it offers. Then while in each other's homes, you need to take care of the home just as if it were your own.

As Roland and I always say, "The very best holidays are a product of the worldwide holiday home exchanging experience."

For thirty-three years, Neal Schattauer was with AT&T—initially in Des Moines, Iowa, and then in Orlando, Florida. In 1988, he launched Neal's Wood Technics—home repairs and carpentry— and later Schattauer Enterprises—consumer goods distribution. Although retired, this is one very busy man.

As a registered nurse, Eunice spent fifteen years on the staff of Iowa Lutheran Hospital in Des Moines. Later, in Orlando, she was school nurse, worked in a nursing home, and served as R.N. coordinator in the office of a healthcare provider. Their home is in Englewood, Florida. These folks have three sons, a daughter, and four grandchildren.

Among Neal's hobbies are woodworking and barbershop singing, Eunice is an active church worker, and both (when there's time) enjoy boating and fishing.

Neal and Eunice Schattauer write:

We first learned of vacation home exchanging in 1986 while participating in a barbershop singing convention. Several years later, one of our friends (who also did some home exchanging) shared the benefits of home exchanging with us and urged us to look into this vacation concept through the vacation exchange club that had helped them "enjoy vacationing more than ever before!" Look into it we did.

In 1989 we arranged for our home to be listed in an exchange directory, and it has been listed every year since. Up to the present date we've had twenty exchanges, some hospitality and some regular. In fact, as I write this, we have an English couple with nine-year-old twin boys in our house as hospitality guests for two and a half weeks.

In brief, here is an overview of our home exchanges to date:

July 1990. Brisbane, California. Our very first home exchange—fourteen days with an exchange car. While we were at their home, our exchange partners were on a camping trip. We selected this area in California because we wanted to attend a nearby barbershop convention. This exchange home was lovely—its five levels were on the side of a mountain overlooking Brisbane Bay, and the home was only a ten-minute drive from the Cow Palace, site of the convention.

July 1990. Makaha, Hawaii. Fourteen days in a small, very comfortable condominium overlooking the ocean. While we did not meet these exchange partners because they were traveling elsewhere, their daughter and her family spent ten days at our home in 1992.

October and November 1990. During these months we were in Australia and New Zealand. A couple from western Canada was to have occupied our home for three weeks. During this time, they wrote that they'd like to extend their stay to a month; later to two months. Our home was well attended while we were traveling "down under."

June 1991. We spent fifteen days at the second home of exchangers—one built out over the water near Pine Island, in Matlacha, Florida. Great for relaxation and fishing!

July 1991. Two Fort Myers couples made use of our home while we were away. Then three years later, we stayed at their lovely golf condo. One of these couples had us over for dinner and let us dock our boat in their slip and familiarized us with most of the local waterways. This was over and above conventional home exchange hospitality.

July 1991. For a barbershop convention in Louisville, Kentucky, we stayed at our exchange partners' second home.

August 1991. We hosted exchangers from Rustenburg, South Africa, for a week. They were on a tour of parts of the United States, and Walt Disney World (only a few miles from our Orlando home) was high on their must-see list. We look forward with great anticipation to visiting South Africa at some time within the foreseeable future.

March 1993. This was a weeklong simultaneous exchange. Our exchange partners' main home is in Evansville, Indiana, but we occupied their second home in the Florida Keys.

June 1993. We hospitality-hosted a couple from England and their parents from Ireland—just five days.

August 1993. Another hospitality exchange—this time a family of five from Holland.

September 1993. While we were away, an Arizona family of four occupied our home and car for six days. With a near perfect record of finding the house in excellent condition following exchangers' departures, this was the single instance in which we found both home and car dirty and untidy. It took us a full day to get things back to normal. We didn't appreciate this, but we know—from our experiences and those of others—this type of occurrence is very, very rare in the home exchange experience.

October 1993. An English couple was with us for a short time.

February 1994. Hosted a couple from Vestal, New York, traveling with a gentleman friend.

May 1994. Two couples from Denmark were with us for a short time.

August 1994. Barcelona, Spain, was the home city of a single gentleman who stayed with us for a week while he thoroughly enjoyed Walt Disney World.

October 1994. A family of four enjoyed a two-week stay here in Orlando.

Looking back over our home exchanging experiences, we are reminded that we rarely have had simultaneous exchanges. Generally, our exchange partners are at our home first. Later, at some mutually convenient time, we stay at their homes.

Our eight-week October-November trip to Australia and New Zealand was truly a mountaintop experience in exchanging. First, we traveled in Australia for some weeks as part of an international barbershop singing tour. Then we home exchanged our way through New Zealand—Christchurch, Greymouth, Picton, Wellington, Levin, Rotorua, Ngongotsha, Auckland, the "Bay of Islands," and Kaitaia. That was quite a trip!

Rather than risking getting stranded along the way in Australia or New Zealand, we made all our singing tour and home exchange arrangements before our departure from Orlando. Someone once said the success of any home exchange trip has a direct relationship to the amount of time the exchange partners put into advance planning. Believing this, we endeavor to allow a full twelve months for the exchange planning stages. In fact, we are now beginning to set up plans for exchanges next year and the year after—England, Holland, Denmark, and France. We have friends on Florida's Gulf Coast who spent nearly four years arranging for a seven-week home exchange in Hong Kong.

Hermann and Gudrun Lippold both work in the ZDF Television Centre in Mainz, Germany. ZDF is the public broadcasting system of Germany, producing both television programming and Deutsche Welle, a worldwide radio service. Gudrun is an assistant editor for television movies, and Hermann is the head of video maintenance for regional studios, studios in foreign countries, and the remote broadcasting vans. He is also the German representative to the European Broadcast Union and chairs an international EBU Commission for the standardization of measurements on serial digital television. (EBU is a broadcast standardization body that also serves as an exchange point for news programs around the world.)

The Lippolds' hobbies include reading and classical music, both recorded and in concert. They like raising summer flowers from English seeds, travel, and the worldwide correspondence that home exchanging entails. Gudrun even keeps in contact with some near exchangers—people they have tried several times to exchange with but whose schedules have never quite meshed with theirs.

When they first started exchanging, they traveled with their teenagers. Their daughter Antje, now twenty-seven, has a master's degree in economics and is studying art in Barcelona, and their twenty-nine-year-old son lives in Bamberg, Bavaria. Ralf finished his master's in early 1995.

Hermann Lippold writes:

We first learned about home exchanging from a radio program, but I was leery of the idea, although Gudrun really liked it. After two years, she finally pushed me forward, and we put an ad in one of the home exchange directories. We took no action and had no immediate response, so we booked a holiday in Spain. Just before leaving we received a call from an English engineer working in Frankfurt who wanted to have his family come over for a visit. I told him we'd already made arrangements for our holiday but, really pushing myself now, I told him he could stay in our house while we were gone.

The following Sunday I went to the station to pick him up. I immediately sized him up to be the person we were looking for and walked up to him, saying, "Good morning, Mr. Bennett." It soon became apparent that there was some confusion: we'd spoken in German on the phone and "June" and "July" got mixed up, and we were only to be away for twelve days of their planned visit. Gudrun found the solution: a neighbor working in the United States for IBM was home with his family on holiday but would soon return to the States. They were familiar with the home exchange concept and said our guests could stay in their house when we came back from Spain. Our exchangers thus became our next-door neighbors for another six weeks. At the end of the summer, I counted the empty wine bottles in the basement . . . we had spent many a long, warm summer evening together and since then have become close friends.

We have made six exchanges in England and six in the United States, in addition to one in Canberra, Australia, one in Vancouver, British Columbia, and two here in Germany.

We like to make lots of contacts during our exchanges and sometimes become very close to the friends and neighbors of our hosts. When we vacation, we always visit friends in the area. One year we stayed in Oregon and visited several friends in Vancouver. One friend there gave a party for everyone we knew in town. On the way back to Oregon, we stopped to see someone in Seattle who had written us, and we arranged an exchange for the next summer.

When going to England, we always drive our car and ride the ferry. Immediately on arriving in the country, one comes face-to-face with a customs officer. We had always been lucky, and they'd just waved us through. Therefore, one time we took thirty-six bottles of Rhine wine with us for our friends in wine boxes in the trunk.

"Would you please open your trunk?" the officer asked.

As I was very slowly opening the trunk, the two brand-new bikes on top of the car caught his eye, and he wanted to know about them. I told him that there would be two bikes at our exchange home and we needed these two for the other members of the family.

"Home exchange? What's that?" he wanted to know.

I explained and then casually closed the trunk. My family welcomed me back into the car like a returning war hero as the officer waved us through, and we all had a good laugh about this newfound benefit of home exchanging.

Our very first exchange was in England, in Wellwyn Garden City. We were all excited and pleased with both the house and the area. The first morning I got up very early to check on the newspaper and milk deliveries. The top of the front door was glass, and as I reached to open it, a strange man appeared in the opening. I was startled, but I pulled myself together and in my very limited English told him that we didn't need to buy anything, that we were only guests in the house.

"No, no," he said. "I'm Derek, your next-door neighbor, and I'm just checking to make sure everything is okay and there's nothing you need."

We had been chatting awhile when a woman came through the bushes and said, "You sound so nice and friendly. I guess I should come over and meet you, too." She was his wife.

Our host had put up a notice in the library that we wanted to meet English families. Albert was the first to call. He said he wanted to paint his kitchen the next day, and he was sure the children would want to help. With my limited English I couldn't talk him out of the idea, and the next morning we received Albert with mixed feelings (since, indeed, the children had no such sentiments). But he had forgotten all about the kitchen and instead suggested a guided tour to the homes of all his relatives in the area. What an interesting day that was!

On another trip to England we really liked our next-door neighbors and invited them over to "our" house. We soon realized that they had never been in the house and that, in fact, our hosts would not speak to them. It turned out that the reason lay in the distant past: the day our hosts moved in, the neighbor's dogs had stolen all the sausages (meant for the moving staff) from the kitchen counter. We all laughed, and Gudrun suggested that they try for a new start by preparing a sausage dinner for the four of them. We hope they did.

As is so often the case, we had quite a bit of correspondence with our first American home exchange partners. By the time the exchange date was a week away, we felt as though these people were longtime friends.

We arranged, as always, for the home exchangers to arrive two days before our departure. We picked them up at the airport and went with them to the baggage claim area. As soon as we neared the area, one of the large boxes began moving and jumping. It was their very large dog wearing a long red scarf. They said that they lived in the mountains and the scarf gave the dog some protection against the crazy hunters. The fact was, the dog didn't want to be without it. Needless to say, when we returned we heard numerous stories from the neighbors.

Our guest was very interested in finding information about his ancestors who came from our area. As a Chicago newspaper writer, he knew how to do research and took this opportunity to check all the old newspapers for articles about his relatives. He was quite successful because his ancestors were notorious—well-known criminals who were hanged, shot, etc. At first, he was upset, but then he thought, "Why not be proud of them?" He made posters out of the newspaper broadsides and hung them on the walls of his home.

Their house was on a mountain and very remote: the closest neighbor was a mile away. They warned us not to set off the burglar alarm system, as it was supposed to be the loudest system in the United States. Once, at 4:23 A.M., the pre-alarm went off, and I jumped out of bed and switched the system off. With the flashlight, I checked the windows and doors, but everything seemed to be okay. As we were trying to get back to sleep after this exciting tour of the house, the alarm came on again. Same procedure, but again everything seemed to be okay. I decided that 4:45 A.M. was much too late for a burglar, switched the alarm system completely off, and went back to bed. The next day Harry from the security company found traces of a lightning strike on the circuit board. Only then did I recall our exchanger mentioning a severe thunderstorm that had taken out three of their six televisions and three of the six phones.

One evening there was obviously a storm approaching. As we heard the wind and rain getting closer, I went upstairs to close the casement windows. To my surprise, one of the windows was completely gone—three levels down! I went tearing out, flashlight in hand, and found it (not even cracked) on top of the bushes under the window. The next day, I put it back together. Some time later our host told us he had never even opened that particular window.

Besides the very real benefits of lower costs and having a home to stay in on vacation, we find that we really enjoy perusing our hosts' books, listening to their CDs, reading their magazines, even trying out their hobbies. Exchanging opens a window on the world that is inaccessible on almost any other kind of vacation.

See Hermann Lippold's "General Information for Home Exchange Partners," in the reference section.

CHAPTER 23

Putting Exchange Wheels Under Your Vacation

THROUGHOUT A LIFETIME OF SPENDING, A PERSON'S single largest investment is his home. One's second greatest outlay of money is probably on automobiles. Obviously, the experts generating these statistics have never sent several children to college, married off a daughter, or had to purchase seemingly endless pairs of Reeboks.

Most chapters of this book deal with exchanging that largest investment—the home. This chapter, however, is focused on exchanging automobiles. Although less of an investment is involved, many people are more protective of their cars than they are of their homes. Yet the survey revealed that three out of four home exchanges worldwide include cars.

"We thought long and hard about including our car in our home exchange," writes a shop owner in Norwich, England. "Strangely enough, we were more worried about someone driving our car than about them taking care of our home and two cats. But we were going to Germany for a month, and the cost of a rental car would have put us in the poorhouse. So, exchange cars we did, and it all worked out wonderfully well. Oh, we had some right-side-driving traffic problems, but our German exchangers had to face the hazards of entering clockwise-traffic roundabouts while driving on the unfamiliar (to them) right-hand side of the car." Apparently, both cars (and exchangers) survived.

In Manhattan, in downtown Boston, in London's West End, or just about anywhere in Paris or Hong Kong, a car is an unnecessary burden. However, the bulk of vacation home exchanging is done not in heavily trafficked cities with no visible parking, but elsewhere, where a car is nearly always an absolute necessity. Renting a car (except offseason in some places) can be frightfully expensive. Whether you are talking about a week, a month, two months (or even longer), car rental involves significant costs. While there are many reasons for vacation home exchanging, there is only one reason for exchanging cars—to save money.

One element in car exchanging that needs to be clarified and agreed upon in advance is where and how far the car is to be driven. A Vero Beach teacher and his wife "put ten thousand miles on our English host's VW camper in England, Scotland, Wales, and the Continent—a seven-week exchange. The English couple enjoyed Florida so much they came back to our home the next year while we vacationed elsewhere in the States. We figured we owed them an additional exchange after putting all that mileage on their camper." Ten thousand miles in seven weeks would seem to be an inordinate number of miles to put on an exchange vehicle, but apparently this was done with the approval of the camper's owner.

On his first home-and-car exchange, a Fullerton, California, retired geologist added seven hundred miles on his Dutch host's car. He returned home to find his partner had put three thousand miles on his car. "Next time," he says, "I will negotiate a set mileage—say, one thousand free miles, then a per-mile charge for any excess by either party." With a difference of twenty-three hundred miles driven between these two exchange cars during a three-to-four-week period, one can well understand why the exchanger at the short end of the deal would want to build safeguards into his future car exchange arrangements.

However, more common is this report from Kattskill Bay, New York: "Our three-week exchange partner in Cubbington, England, made his small car available to us while he drove our larger station wagon. He toured the New York/Long Island area and drove to Washington, D.C., while we went to Stratford, Bath, Wales, and various points in between. All in all, 'twas fair and square."

A rental agent and retired teacher had no complaints about the mileage their guests drove, but they found to their consternation that apparently the exchangers had never checked the oil in the car. It was down to one quart when they returned. What especially perturbed them was that, if the engine had burned up, their car insurance would not have covered it. Homeowner's insurance covers the negligence of a guest, but car insurance definitely does not.

The types of cars and their condition provoked numerous comments from survey respondents. Anecdotes ranged from the sublime to the ridiculous. "Our Spanish exchange partner didn't want to leave us a problem with his seven-year-old car, so he traded it in three weeks before we arrived. Unfortunately, he didn't have the new one long enough to work out all its bugs. We drove it for two weeks and had repair bills of more than three hundred dollars for overheated brakes, seized ignition switch, and sluggish acceleration. So, we called him and asked if he wanted us to continue spending his money on repairs. Within twenty-four hours he had wired us twenty thousand dollars in Spanish pesetas and sent us out to buy a brand-new car, complete with all available options." That tale is from a Victoria, British Columbia, couple.

On the other hand, a San Rafael, California, family found that the only way they could get their English exchange car into reverse was to position four of them around the car, lift it up, and turn it around. "Thank goodness for those small English cars!" A German couple reports that twenty years ago, during their first exchange, they spent hours trying to start their car, only to discover that the seat belts had to be fastened first. Then there was the English headmaster who had been left a whole ring of keys, none of which seemed to work in the car. A helpful neighbor got in and started the car right up. Again the Englishman tried—no luck. "It seems one has to depress the clutch on some American cars before they will start." An exchanger in Perth, Scotland, tells of attempting to start the car left for them (they thought) which, on closer inspection, had no engine. This one had been left in the driveway for the boys to play in. The "real" one was in the garage.

A Massachusetts lawyer offers, not one, but two cautionary tales on the care and nurture of exchange cars in foreign countries. "I pulled up to the pumps at a filling station in Italy and jumped out with a fifty thousand lira note—about forty-six American dollars. Many of the petrol stations there have automatic machines that you put your money in, push a button, and get gas for that amount. It's really a great convenience except that these machines are very finicky: You have to feed them new, smooth money with no wrinkles—the correct denomination, face up, turned a certain way—or your payment will be rejected, and you'll have to start again. In point of fact, you might well be out there five or ten minutes trying to feed your money in, pulling out different bills from your wallet, carefully "ironing" each one on the side of the pump, running back to the car to see if anyone in the car has a newer bill—even asking passersby if they have anything better.

"Not this time! This machine took my wrinkled, dirty fifty thousand lira note on the very first try—threw me off completely. I was so rattled I pushed the button for diesel fuel instead of gas and, of course, there's no cancel button. Fifty dollars wasted. It was Sunday, of course,

and a national holiday to boot. We phoned the number in the station window, only to learn the owner was at the shore for the weekend.

"So we waited . . . and waited . . . and waited . . . for someone to pass by who just might need fifty dollars' worth of diesel. No such luck. Eventually, the caretaker of the farm at which we were staying happened by, saw us, and stopped. I explained to him with sign language, gestures, and so on what the problem was. He went back to the farm, returning with two big, brand new polypropylene containers into which he pumped the diesel to use in the farm vehicles. I then filled up the car, and we were finally on our way; he paid me back the next day."

This New England attorney-exchanger's second story is closely related. On another exchange (two couples, two cars this time), his friend signaled and pulled off for gas, with the attorney and his wife following but staying in the car. "About five minutes down the road, billows of black smoke started pouring out of his exhaust. We could see him slowing down, obviously losing power. We didn't know what was happening, but we definitely knew something had happened to our exchanger's second car. As my friend was barely able to coast off the road and into the next filling station, we realized that he'd put diesel into a nondiesel car. Fortunately, he hadn't driven far enough to do any permanent damage, but it took more than four hours to get the car back on the road again."

He adds, "You really have to be alert as to what kind of fuel you're buying and putting in your vehicle. In other countries, many pump nozzles appear to be all the same size, easily fitting any type of car—unlike those in the United States."

Numerous exchangers pointed out that not only do make, model, year, etc. (as well as any idiosyncrasies) of a car need to be communicated, but size needs to be made clear. "In Italy, our family of four got the smallest car we had ever seen. It looked like a little red bathtub on wheels—an absolutely tiny Renault." This from a couple of New Yorkers. Extrasmall cars must be the norm in some (most?) parts of Europe, because a Repentigny, Quebec, family reports arriving in Germany and finding a "mini for the six of us." On the other hand, a retired schoolteacher by herself in England drove "a huge, beautiful Daimler. I almost never drove it for fear something would happen to it." A Frenchman had three Cadillacs and two boats to choose from in California, and a Hong Kong exchanger still laughs about his early attempts in California to drive "what seemed to be an aircraft carrier with marshmallow wheels—actually 'only' a Pontiac."

When Americans and Canadians exchange cars with each other, they are switching familiar cars and find themselves governed by similar rules of the road. Also, most cars in the United States and Canada have automatic transmissions and air conditioning. In Europe, however, many, if not most, cars have manual transmissions (stick shifts), and few are air conditioned. Most Europeans do not feel the need for automatic transmissions, and their short summers make air conditioning an unnecessary expense. Also, many English cars—even late-model ones—do not have automatic chokes, so one must become accustomed to a manual choke during the first few miles of driving until the engine warms up. It's the answer to the question, Why doesn't this car's engine start?

British exchangers driving in the United States or Canada do not seem to have the problems with cars that North Americans in England report because British vacationers often take their own cars to nearby France and elsewhere on the European continent. There, although their driver's seat is on the right-hand side of the car, they at least become familiar with driving on the right side of the road. Americans and Canadians, on the other hand, are frequently terrorized by their very first driving experience in England—that trip home from the airport.

"Heading to Leomington Spa, about two hours out of London, we arrived at Heathrow in the evening, took forever recovering our luggage, then discovered that car keys and directions were not at the airline desk as arranged," reports an urban planner in Pelham, New York. "We wound up pushing luggage carts all over the airport, finally finding our envelope at Lost Luggage (appropriate), seemingly miles from where we had started. The envelope contained the key, directions, and a map.

An experienced international driver, I was still woefully unprepared for a new and different car, right-side steering, driving on the wrong side of the road, hopelessly confusing directions, grumpy wife, two demanding, know-it-all children (ages ten and thirteen), and a stick shift. The 'journey from hell' was a gear-grinding nightmare. Dad's descent from his normally restrained, confident, exalted position as Head of the Household to the ranks of sweating, clench-jawed mere mortals (who knew a lot of words the kids had never before heard) was, no doubt, appreciated by my three passengers, terrified though they were. But we survived. I got them safely to Leomington Spa, we enjoyed the English bitters and dinner left for us by our hosts, and we had a glorious two-and-a-half-week vacation."

A pointer from a Michigan car exchanger: "We had a terrible time managing those circles (so-called roundabouts) during our Oxford, England, exchange. Finally, I got the hang of it: first, you need to determine before you confront the rotary which road you are taking out of it. Slow down as you approach the roundabout and turn left as you enter it. Important! The cars in the circle—coming from the right—have the right of way, and the drivers assume you know this. They will keep coming. Then, once you're in the roundabout, immediately signal for a left turn again and make your left turn when you reach the predetermined road out of the roundabout."

Quite a few people who cross the Atlantic from west to east for exchanges have taken an additional measure: a large sign in the window notifying other drivers to "Be careful—Confused American/Canadian driver!" One gentleman from Stoney Creek, Ontario, found an even more creative solution. "Especially as I grow older, I find driving in other countries (especially England and Australia) very nerve-wracking. I overcame this problem the last time by taking myself to the government employment center and offering thirty pounds per day for a driver, on a day-to-day basis—five or six days at the most. Within an hour an unemployed aeronautical engineer (husband of the woman I talked to in the office) called—fifty-six years old and an excellent driver. The big plus was that he was a most knowledgeable guide with a good sense of humor who totally charmed my wife and the two ladies visiting her."

But driving woes are not entirely the province of Americans and Canadians abroad. A couple in Chesham in Buckinghamshire, England, writes, "We can look back and laugh, but at the time we didn't think this was very funny. We had gone on a driving tour from Vancouver to the Okanagen Lake district in British Columbia. I had done all the driving on the way there, and my wife wanted to drive back. On the map the highway looked like a major road, but come to find out, it was mainly hairpin turns and tunnels with no passing lanes. She was really doing quite well, a little slow but steady (she had limited experience on an automatic), until a timber lorry came up behind her—right on her heels, in fact—and started blasting his horn. Finally, after about ten miles, she was able to pull over and let the hundred or so cars following her get by. She never got behind the wheel again in Canada."

Regardless of whether exchange cars are old or new models or in what country they are licensed, car exchangers must be sure their cars are mechanically sound, have been recently lubricated and tuned up, and are clean. Eccentricities of the particular car must be relayed to the incoming driver, and the operator's handbook should be placed in the car's glove compartment. Of course, sometimes even the manual doesn't help. "A retired engineer never could comprehend the importance of glow-plugs to the starting procedure in my Mercedes 240D." Then there was the trunk of a late-model Audi that opened easily enough at the market to stow a week's worth of groceries but stubbornly refused to open when it came time to unload them. Not to mention the fancy automatic-everything four-door Jaguar with a rear-door window that could not be raised.

An exchanger in Honolulu tells of "the case of the balky motor home." "After lengthy drives, this vehicle simply would not start. It was a Japanese model with German license plates in a part of France where no one spoke English. We finally discovered that if I got out and pushed it just a little, it would start up again. And it would start every time if I just got out and gave it a bit of a shove. I'm a woman and weigh in at 140 pounds soaking wet, but I am determined!"

All car owners have these kinds of problems, not just exchangers. After all, cars are like people—they're simply not quite perfect. The owner's manual can often be a godsend, but when all else fails, the guest should be able to turn to the home information kit for the name of a local mechanic.

For over-the-road problems there are the American and Canadian Automobile Associations, Allstate, Signature, and several other emergency-service companies on this continent and/or their equivalent outside the United States. AAA and CAA cover towing or emergency repairs for the individual member, not just for a car owned by the member. Individual members may call for help with any car they happen to be driving, be it personal, rental, or exchanged. But AAA and CAA do not serve their members outside the United States or Canada (except reciprocally), and comparable foreign services have different regulations. It is important for all potential car exchangers to inquire about what emergency services may be available to them.

Once in a while, car exchangers have accidents with their partners' cars. "In Dublin, I backed my host's Mercedes into their palm tree. I honestly think they were more worried about the tree." "A deer jumped out in front of the car in California's redwood forest. Sadly, the deer was killed and the front end of the car was badly damaged, but we and his insurance company had it made like new again." Then there was the experienced exchanger from Washington state who tells the story of driving his exchange partner's car through the back of the garage. "He was a very kind and understanding proper Englishman. He was also in the construction business and had no concerns about the damage I had done to his garage. The altercation between his car and his garage didn't interfere with our relationship, I'm glad to say. We still communicate and see each other whenever we are in England or he is in the States."

Provision must also be made for the parking of exchange cars. Normally, garage space is available (that is, if not filled with table saws, lawn mowers, wheelbarrows, and half-empty paint cans) or driveway space. But if no such accommodations exist, the exchange partners must make adequate arrangements for the parking of their respective cars. In Boston, for example, on-street parking is apparently by special dispensation only and ticketing is quick and expensive.

When driving in the United States, drivers must carry their driver's license, the registration certificate covering the car in use, and a current insurance identification card. Usually the latter two documents are kept in an envelope in the car's glove compartment, and the operator's license is kept in the driver's wallet.

An additional document—a "To Whom It May Concern" letter authorizing the exchange partner to drive the car (see reference section)—would have ameliorated the predicament of an Arizona couple. "We were in Portugal. Our host had neglected to tell us about the burglar alarm in his car. We managed to set it off in a busy downtown district—immediately surrounded by police, no papers other than those identifying our host as owner, and no clue to the Portuguese language. Fortunately, someone in the surrounding crowd spoke enough English to forestall our arrest."

Last but not least—more like first—car exchanging partners need to have their respective cars in good condition. Assuming this is so, and assuming each car is driven less than three thousand miles, the partners need only purchase gas and have the oil, water, and tires checked periodically. If the car is to be driven more than three thousand miles (time for an oil change), the exchange partners must agree on what preventive maintenance should be done, where it should be done, and who should pay for this work.

Although there are occasional complaints about second-home exchanging with no car available, three out of four vacation home exchangers include cars in their exchanges. It must work. But responsible exchangers endeavor to make this element of exchanging work even better by carefully checking into the matter of car insurance (see chapter 16), providing information about AAA or its equivalent, agreeing on who is to drive the car and where, having the proper documents accessible to the exchanger, listing what mechanic to use should that be necessary, making specific pickup and delivery arrangements for the cars and the keys, and offering clean, reliable cars in good condition. If these elements are discussed, agreed upon, and provided by car-exchanging partners, and if both parties to the exchange are reasonable and fair, the result is almost certain to be a successful car exchange.

Responsible car-exchanging partners should not only skip that last one for the road, they should not drink at all when driving.

One last thing: exchangers should be sure to leave their partners' car washed and with a full tank of gas.

CHAPTER 24

The Vacation Home Exchangers?
They Went That-a-Way

AND THAT-A-WAY SEEMS TO BE A VERY WIDE-ranging everywhere. As a group, vacation home exchangers tend to have very few limits in their choices of vacation destinations. Much like conventional vacationers, however, home exchangers seem to gravitate toward particular areas for their vacation experiences.

The survey shows, for instance, that over the years 40 percent of home-exchanging Americans who chose to vacation in the United States exchange in the western states—in particular, California and Hawaii. Twenty-eight percent have exchanged in New York, Massachusetts, Washington, D.C., Pennsylvania, and other parts of the Northeast. And 24 percent have vacationed in the Southeast, notably Florida.

As regards future vacation destinations—U.S. regions Americans aspire to visit in the United States during the years just ahead—47 percent hope to exchange in the West, 25 percent in the Northeast, 15 percent in the Southeast, and, interestingly, 11 percent in the Southwest, especially Arizona. With its year-round dry and temperate weather, Arizona has a strong appeal for middle-aged to older home exchangers.

Large numbers of Americans have chosen to vacation outside the United States. Of these, 75 percent have exchanged in Great Britain and Continental Europe, 12 percent have been to Canada and Mexico, and 5 percent have had exchange destinations in Australia and New Zealand. The remaining small percentage have been to countries as widespread as Tahiti, Israel, Colombia, Yugoslavia, and Iceland.

Looking ahead to future vacation home exchanges outside the United States, once again about 75 percent of the Americans surveyed have their sights set on Europe, mostly England and France.

What of those home exchangers who reside outside the United States? The survey shows that, of those who have exchanged in the United States, 39 percent have done so in the western states—California and Hawaii, 28 percent have exchanged in the northeastern states, and 24 percent in the Southeast, in particular, Florida.

The survey also shows that future U.S. exchange travel plans of those residing outside the United States to be quite consistent with those in the previous paragraph, that is, about 40 percent to the West, 25 percent to the Northeast, and 25 percent to the Southeast.

Of those non-U.S. exchangers who have vacationed outside the United States, 77 percent have been to Western Europe, mostly England, Germany, and France. Their hopes for future vacation exchange destinations? Again, three-quarters would choose Western Europe, while the rest are thinking about Australia, New Zealand, Canada, Mexico, and elsewhere.

Like most vacationers, home exchangers generally have a good idea of their vacation destinations; they know where they would like to go. Even so, a surprising number of exchangers—mostly those who are retired and/or have both the time and the airfare—play what is known as Vacation Home Exchange Roulette. These exchangers (experienced, for the most part) have absolutely no preconceptions as to their vacation destinations. In their exchange directory listings, they state they would like to go "anywhere, anytime."

When the directories are issued from December through March, these adventurous types generally receive scores of inquiries from potential exchange partners. They pore over the listings, noting interesting opportunities. This game has only two rules: first, select interesting possibilities, and, second, be sure the listings cover people who have an interest in an area in which the game player has an exchangeable home.

One such exchanger writes: "We never know where we are going to vacation until the directories come, and we get out a bunch of home exchange letters. Each year another vacation 'surprise.'"

A seven-time vacation home exchanger in Boca Raton, Florida, and his wife are also sold on the roulette concept. They list their three-bedroom, two-bath home with swimming pool and spa in the two largest exchange directories and are inundated with inquiries. A typical year's responses: twenty-one from France, eighteen from Great Britain, seven from Germany, four from the United States, two from Holland, two from Canada, two from Spain, one from Austria, one from Brazil, one from Ireland, one from Sweden, and even one from Zimbabwe.

Where in a given country or region do home exchangers prefer to vacation? Nearly one-third of American exchangers seem to prefer places with historical significance, 23 percent head for the seashore, 15 percent go to lakes and/or the mountains, 4 percent aim for ski resorts, and 26 percent are in the roulette category.

Of those who reside outside the United States: 33 percent prefer the seashore, 25 percent go to places with historical significance, 22 percent visit lakes and/or the mountains, 1 percent trek to ski resorts, and 19 percent are in the anywhere column. These numbers do not include the exchange couple traveling from Bangladesh to Florida's Gulf Coast for a two-week holiday.

In summary, vacation home exchangers travel the world—limited only by time and expense. In the vast majority of cases, through their own research and flexibility in scheduling, home exchangers are able to fulfill their vacation destination desires through arrangements with other equally enthusiastic home exchangers.

CHAPTER 25

Red Carpet Guests

ONE OF THE GREAT ADVANTAGES OF VACATION HOME exchanging is its flexibility and adaptability to individual needs and desires. Perhaps the easiest way to home exchange is to arrange a hospitality exchange. A vacation such as this requires as much research as any other type of exchange but the end result is no different from having friends or family as houseguests for anywhere from a weekend to a couple of weeks. Most people already know the basic elements of entertaining as well as being entertained in another's home.

If you are an older couple, siblings, a single person, or simply unsure about home exchanging, a hospitality exchange may be the answer for you. Hospitality exchangers stay as guests in their hosts' homes while the hosts are there, then serve as hosts in their own homes at another time.

There are also special-needs exchanges, in addition to those undertaken solely for rest and relaxation. For example, a retired French physician and his wife are hoping to exchange with an American couple—perhaps a month in France and a month in the United States—so the two couples can learn each other's languages. A couple in Pembroke, Maine, retired to a small farm after years of round-the-world exchanging and is looking forward to trying a farm exchange. Each couple would learn something about farming in another area or country in addition to having a country-fresh vacation. Another couple recommends the Bounding Main exchange: offering the hospitality of their yacht in Chesapeake Bay in exchange for being guests on another vessel someplace else. Because of the complexities of yachting, particularly in unfamiliar waters, it is mandatory that the boat owner host the exchange.

Finally, the terms of some lease arrangements prohibit subletting or exchanging rented apartments or homes. No problem. Assuming one has sufficient room, a hospitality exchange could certainly be the answer.

Bob and Anne Rapley, now living in Paphos, Cyprus, after serving in several capacities in numerous countries, have hospitality exchanged and guested for years. Their recommendations, in addition to the pointers found throughout this book, should assist readers in learning the ropes of this type of home exchange.

A hospitality exchange has much in common with a regular exchange in that one makes connections through the directories, corresponds, exchanges photos and videos, and works to find a mutually acceptable date for the visit. Most hospitality exchanges are for shorter periods than home exchanges (a week or even a long weekend), although one woman from South Africa mentioned that "occasionally people stay a bit too long."

The Rapleys point out that there is no need to arrange car insurance coverage for your guests, clean out the master bedroom closet and dressers, or put away the vintage wines. Your guests stay in your guest room, join you in whatever meals you may agree on, and take part in your family life to the extent that seems appropriate. As a host, you will have more mouths to feed at dinner and some entertaining and sightseeing to arrange, but no more than would be expected when relatives or special friends come to visit. It's a thrill being a tour guide in your hometown. Think of the fun this Isle of Sylt (a resort on the North Sea, off the coast of Germany) host must have had with his Salisbury, North Carolina, guests. His guests reported, "My wife and I were walking on the beach with our host one day during our visit. We were unaware that nudists used this section of beach until one suddenly appeared—a male out for a walk on this cold spring day. We passed each other with eyes straight ahead, but I couldn't help but notice the twinkle in our host's eye, and I've often wondered if this particular 'tour' wasn't planned just to see our reaction."

A hotelier and a teacher from Natal, South Africa, writes, "We live in a small town with not much for visitors to do after the first few days, so when we get exchange requests we respond offering hospitality. We enjoy showing our guests around and advising them on where to go and what to see. As a consequence, we were able to afford a four-month holiday a few years ago in Britain, Europe, Canada, and the United States, plus a fantastic three weeks in Zimbabwe. Our hosts there—formerly total strangers, now good friends—made all the arrangements for visits to Victoria Falls, Kariba, Hwange Game Reserve, and the beautiful Eastern Highlands. They were kindness itself during the days in-between."

Of course, you do not have to spend every minute with your guests. Most guests will enjoy exploring the area on their own with a little guidance from you, then return for dinner and a quiet evening. You may want to go out to dinner to a favorite place or two during their stay or escort them to one or two places of interest you enjoy, but leave them time to be on their own, too. Usually admission prices and meals out should be considered Dutch treat, but this will depend on the circumstances.

Hospitality-exchange experts Bob and Ann Rapley make a point of the fact that there is certainly no need for you to suddenly become a gourmet cook. Regional and national specialties—food not normally available in your guests' countries or hometowns—will always be appreciated. While still in the correspondence stage, do find out if there are any foods your guests either particularly enjoy or cannot eat. Other than that, there is no need to get carried away with feeding them. If you have any doubts, take them grocery shopping. Not only will you glean the information you need, but your guests will discover that (1) it's fun shopping in a different part of the world and (2) one learns a lot about an area simply by checking out the food stores.

In return for your hospitality, you will enjoy your vacation as a guest in their home with no worries about getting lost or suddenly needing to find a doctor, no fears of blowing up the water heater or being surrounded by police in response to a mismanaged security system, and no concerns about buying foods you've never heard of, much less tried to pronounce. You will enjoy home-cooking instead of expensive and frequently dull hotel food, have a comfortable bed every night, and enjoy the company of people who will treat you as friends as they introduce you to their hometowns, neighbors, and friends. You enjoy all of this, of course, at a much lower cost than that of a package tour or the same length of time in a hotel or resort.

Exchanges of hospitality do involve a little more work before a final agreement is reached, since you obviously want to visit people with whom you will feel comfortable. Making a hospitality exchange arrangement will involve more correspondence than a regular exchange for both partners to learn about each other. You will, after all, be living with these people in their home, as will they with you. By the time the visit is consummated, each couple should feel confident that they will not develop any sudden distaste for or antipathy to the other's company.

You'll need to find out all you can about the other's habits, idiosyncrasies, likes, dislikes, children, and pets. In return, be honest about your own home and family. Obviously, you should be a little diplomatic, but some people swear by a checklist (similar to what new patients fill out these days in a doctor's office) as the best way to give and get information about other people. The point is that no one wants to travel hundreds or thousands of miles and be unpleasantly surprised, especially when a minimal amount of tension goes hand-in-hand with being a host or a guest.

Occasionally, one runs into an unpremeditated hospitality exchange. A businessman in Apopka, Florida, returned home from his out-of-state exchange to find "my exchange partner's wife in a local hospital. We had the husband as our worried but delightful guest for an additional two weeks." An English couple received a phone call while still in their partner's home in Florence, Italy, asking, "'Since you have such a large house, would there be a problem if my friend, who does not want to leave yet, stayed on?' Caught like that, what can one say? When we got back, after my furies had abated, I had the gentleman up to supper and have actually gained a close and respected friend."

One also has to watch out for misunderstandings that may arise from language or cultural differences. It is hard to be a good judge of people who are writing to you in their second or third language. A brilliant college professor can sound pretty childish and illiterate in a language he only studied for two years some thirty years ago. Try finding someone fluent in the appropriate language to transcribe your correspondence, translate the potential partner's correspondence, or both. To avoid unintended social blunders, read anything and everything you can get your hands on about the area you are going to visit—culture, traditions, etiquette—(libraries, AAA guidebooks, and tourist bureaus have a lot of this information) or talk to a friend who has traveled or lived in the area you will be visiting.

People who are willing to exchange hospitality with strangers are usually open, friendly, relaxed people, or they would not be involved in this sort of exchange in the first place. Determine the area's customs (hats in church, no shorts on the street, for example) and don't forget your mom's last words before you left the house: Remember your manners. House rules about smoking, drinks (or no drinks) before dinner, and preferred bedtimes should be well understood and adhered to.

A family from Green Lake, Wisconsin, hosted an English couple "who indulged in 'tea breaks' about five times a day. After the first day, with every cup in the house dirty, my wife assigned them each a cup and asked them to use and rinse their own cups rather than getting a newly washed one each time." In other words, it's basically a matter of being as considerate of one's hosts as one would expect them to be in return.

It may take a special kind of person (or personality) to enjoy the unique ambience of hospitality exchanging, and many people will continue to prefer the more conventional exchange of homes. But the benefits of living with another family can be well worth the extra effort involved. If you love to entertain and meet people from other parts of your country or from other cultures, think about hospitality exchanging.

A Chicago Spanish teacher writes about the Australian couple she helped to stay with friends of hers in Chicago. "This pair traveled for one whole year all over the United States with hospitality exchanges only. They own a bed and breakfast in Perth, and I envision that they will be receiving Americans well into the next century to reciprocate for the more than one hundred hospitality exchanges they enjoyed during their tour."

The last word from the Rapleys is, "The biggest kick of all are the lifelong friendships that can develop from even the briefest of hospitality exchanges."

CHAPTER 26

The Upside

PERHAPS THE ONE UNIVERSAL, MOST FREQUENTLY cited advantage to vacation home exchanging is the savings that accrue from not having to pay for accommodations—be it for a couple or for a family of six. Add to that a car exchange (as opposed to rental) and the use of a fully equipped kitchen (instead of three meals a day in restaurants), and the money saved mounts up into as much as many thousands of dollars over a two- or three-week period. In fact, an Arlington, Virginia, couple who took their granddaughter with them on an exchange to Southern California calculated that their two-week vacation (which included a car exchange) had cost them two thousand dollars less than the same trip would on a nonexchange basis. Obviously, an overseas exchange would save even more.

Running a close second to economy is the comfort of a home over the sterility of a hotel room. A Concord, New Hampshire, teacher elaborates. "I love the space, the laundry and cooking facilities, and the feeling of just being settled." Having the ability to relax, sleep late, or even sit and read and not feel compelled to play tourist every minute just to justify the cost of a hotel room are refinements of the economy issue underscored in one way or another by many respondents to the survey.

Two Los Angeles County employees noted: "On European trips, we especially like the fact that we can recover from jet lag—even be sick, if necessary—in a place of our own with kitchen, bath, and the space to get away from each other while feeling absolutely blah! The thought of several days' recovery in a cramped hotel room evokes not only visions of cabin fever, but also of even worse headaches caused by the continuous clanging of the hotel cash register as our vacation money pours into it."

"I have a digestive problem," continues the Concord, New Hampshire, teacher, "that not only makes constantly eating out difficult at best, but also occasionally gets me up in the middle of the night. To wake up at 2:30 A.M. and be able to make a tummy-settling cup of tea is pure heaven." So is having breakfast in one's PJs (or even in bed). So is not feeling guilty about staying put when the weather is bad.

A businessman and his wife in Hingham, Massachusetts, add, "You get much better accommodations for free. Plus, you get a better feel for the area and its culture and have more of a chance to immerse yourself in it, to soak it up." "And," a teacher in Great Britain points out, "it's not only economically good; it's also ecologically sound—much less waste living in a home as opposed to a hotel."

From Australia to Zimbabwe, Key West to Juneau, Cape Town to Vancouver, New Zealand to Norway, and from Middle Europe to Middle America, the positive aspects of exchanging far outweigh the negative. You know you have a place to stay at the end of the day. You can swim in a pool or shoot some pool. You can watch the video you made yesterday or the one you rented just for tonight. You can play the piano, do some sketching, attend a class. You can water the garden or wash the car. You can play golf, tennis, handball, go biking or camping or both. In short, just about anything you can do at home you can do—perhaps even better and with a touch of adventure thrown in, too—while on a home exchange vacation.

A couple in Portsmouth, Rhode Island, is learning foreign languages. They have French down pat and are now working on German. In addition, in England and Northern Ireland they took time to do some genealogical research, found cousins in Ireland they never knew existed, and returned to visit them a year later. "New experiences, new places keep the mind and body in good shape," according to a professor and school librarian in Tucson, Arizona.

People with children—youngsters or teenagers—speak as one with the home-exchanging accountant and his wife in Hertfordshire, England, who flatly state, "Home exchanging is the only way to travel with children." While the expense of housing and feeding a couple of kids and their parents in public accommodations versus at home is certainly nothing to sneeze at, the additional benefits of taking children along almost outweigh the economic factors. "What better education in terms of understanding other cultures as well as the history of the world?" ask two professionals in New York City.

Think about two adults and two kids in a motel room—or even a hotel suite, for that matter. "There's nothing to do here." "The television programs here stink." "You won't let us play in the parking lot." "I'm bored." Poquoson, Virginia, parents say, "Give us a quiet, safe neighborhood with

local children to play with, a house with another kid's toys (always a winner), and a base to return to each night—an arrangement that allows a vacation to unfold and everyone to alternate activity and recovery days."
"Our kids have their own rooms away from ours. They've had games, toys, bikes, and even mopeds—free of charge," volunteers a school principal in Kimberley, Ontario. "In Holland they even had a swing in the attic they could use. In addition, frequently an exchange includes camping equipment, which lends an additional dimension to the holiday."

"Even the smallest town has lots of things of interest to all ages that the average tourist never finds. We do—because we live there," offers a couple in Sequim, Washington. "Our kids (now twenty-seven and thirty years old), whom we dragged along as youngsters, love to travel and both have lived abroad a number of times. Although the younger one is presently here in the States, the older one—in Tanzania with the Peace Corps—just climbed Kilamanjaro and journeyed to India and Bali over Christmas. Home exchanging nurtures the travel bug!"

A town planner and teacher in Edinburgh add, "The money saved—plus having a home base—make many additional new experiences accessible to a family. Teenagers' interest in the world around them—other countries, other peoples, other languages—is greatly stimulated by this kind of at-home, away-from-home exposure."

Another benefit of home exchanging—particularly with teenagers—is the youth exchange, mentioned by several parents as a logical followup to their vacation exchange experience. The home, neighborhood, and prospective "parents" are all known quantities, unlike the arrangements when a youth exchange agency simply assigns a student to an anonymous family. "Some of our best experiences have been not with exchanging homes, but exchanging children. Using the home exchange directory as a resource—utilizing procedures similar to those followed in researching a vacation exchange—works very well," attests a husband-wife exchange team in Carbondale, Illinois.

A different kind of comment on traveling with the kids comes from a Belgian engineer and teacher who have participated in several hospitality exchanges. "Once, we hosted a girl from a youth-exchange organization—a lovely girl, a drama major, but she was always rehearsing. She had to work so hard she couldn't take time to even talk with us. It was good for our children to see that. It was also good for them to witness firsthand how hard living can be in other parts of the world. In Moscow, we and our host family had only two alternating menus for the entire fourteen days. When they came to Belgium every day was a fairy tale."

Last but not least in the advantages-of-traveling-with-children category, there's the German teacher and her physician husband who probably wish their kids would stay seven, eight, and nine years old forever. "On a hospitality exchange near Boston, our hosts bought enough lobster to feed themselves and the five of us. However, the three children were so tired after a long day of sightseeing that they fell asleep without dinner. What a feast we had!"

There is a whole list of things that are available as givens in home exchanges that one doesn't usually find on hotel-based vacations. "Meeting new cats," for example, or "having to really clean my house at least once a year" or "cooking in a real kitchen" or even "doing laundry." Neighbors as a rule are wonderfully warm and helpful with appliances, cars, light switches, and fuse boxes, for example, and especially the how-to's of sightseeing. Neighbors invite exchangers to backyard barbecues, to Easter sunrise services, to play golf or tennis, to pool parties.

"Neighbors get you inside places such as out-of-the-way pubs and local hangouts. We saw museums known only to locals. We got in on bargains such as the Dutch Museum Card, which admits one into every museum and park in Holland. And we were told of the county bus in England that runs to Stratford-on-Avon for a fraction of what the tourist coaches cost. In most cases, we have been adopted by friends and relatives and have even been able to revisit some of them." Such is the warm affection expressed by a couple of teachers in Berkeley, California, toward their exchange neighbors and friends.

A retired teacher from Brigantine, New Jersey, speaks lovingly of the friends and relatives of her exchange hosts in Southampton, England. "They discovered that my favorite author was Jane Austen and made all the arrangements for me to see the different places in which she had lived, visited, and written about. One dear man even gave me a very old leather-bound edition of Austen's *Emma*." Others speak of exchanging greeting cards, ongoing correspondence, and visits from, not only their exchange partners, but also neighbors, relatives, and friends met during their visits.

A couple in Montclair, Virginia, writes, "Our very first exchange house, to our complete surprise, was a true southern mansion—not unlike Tara in appearance—in a small, very southern city. It seems the owners practically owned the town, and the townspeople reasoned that we were close friends and should, therefore, be entertained. Entertained we were—two solid, wonderful weeks of it. Before we left we threw a party for more than one hundred guests—all of whom had been part of our two-week vacation home exchange experience."

An Orlando couple tells of their trip to New Zealand. "Our exchangers had arranged numerous trips and overnights for us with relatives and friends—to a sheep farm, to the coast, to other areas of interest that no tour would have included. They even arranged a day on a dairy farm with their friend who was New Zealand's Farmer of the Year in 1987."

"If you're living in and thus part of a neighborhood," remarks a Tucson couple, "you can find out truly unique things to do by checking out the posters and placards in shop windows and then asking questions. One time we attended 'La Nuit des Caves,' a Beaujolais wine festival celebrated by villagers throughout that part of France and, on another exchange, a Swiss jazz concert, complete with a food festival on the grounds of a medieval chateau."

There are other, more personal moments of elation, too. A Central Florida exchanger was sitting in the driveway of an exchange home in Sedona, Arizona, sketching, when a roadrunner darted across the expansive front porch just beside her. Although a Cambridge, England, woman was not particularly happy about it (somewhat scared, in fact), she nonetheless had the once-in-a-lifetime opportunity to watch numerous kangaroos cavorting around her house in Australia. A homemaker in Hampstead, England, a hundred miles inside the Arctic Circle in northern Norway, was breathless at the sight of reindeer roaming the hills behind her house. A family from Venice, Italy, found it fascinating to watch several young grizzly bears playing in their Montana garden as they and their children enjoyed their breakfast safely inside the house. And what visitor to the J. N. "Ding" Darling Wildlife Refuge on Sanibel Island, Florida, will ever forget his or her first sight of an alligator just lying there, sunning himself? Or the first glimpse of a large flock of roseate spoonbills coming in to roost just before sundown on a March afternoon?

A home exchange vacation does not have a tour leader's nagging whistles, "Time to load up the bus, please," waiting for a lost member of the group, being seated elbow-to-elbow at a U-shaped restaurant table while many complain about the poor service of the harried waitress, avoiding the man who bores everyone with endless tales of his travels and his "remarkable" grandchildren. "Hey, it's a lot different on a home exchange vacation, when one has lots of time to do one's own thing and to stop and smell the roses," says an executive secretary in Birmingham, Alabama.

Beside the new, different, and often delightful surprises—beside the sought-after perks (golf, tennis, beach, etc.)—there are often other amenities in the home exchange experience: a couple of meals ready to heat-and-eat in the refrigerator, garden fresh flowers in one or more rooms, a greeting from the hosts, being met at a strange airport and delivered to the new home. These are but a few of the home exchange benefits.

"On our return home from a super vacation," writes a woman in Arroyo Grande, California, "we found that our exchange partner had been a regular Mr. Fix-It, doing all those little jobs my husband had been putting off, month after month." Of course, there is this potential horror story from an English couple exchanging in Florida: "Frequent late-afternoon showers are a part of life during Florida summers. One such turned into a major thunderstorm, complete with cars pulling off the road, streetlights out, etc. When we finally found our way back to our exchange home and went inside, we discovered water pouring into the house under the patio door. We managed to keep it at bay with every mop and towel we could find, but think of the awful mess our returning exchange hosts would have found had we not been there."

Then there's the gentlemen in Lake Placid, New York, who writes, "The teenage son of my exchangers, apparently somewhat bored with his parents' planned activities, not only tuned up both of our cars and had them running better than they had since they were new, but also repaired my boat that had been sitting in the back yard for four years without being used. Seems he wanted to go water-skiing."

"While we were living it up in Florida," writes yet another exchange couple, "our exchange partners had a dreadful time of it in our home. Our water tank burst, and they found themselves spending most of their vacation supervising plumbers, drying out all our bed linens and towels and, I'm afraid, generally having a miserable time. But, thank God, someone was there—on the spot to deal with what might otherwise have been a total disaster."

In addition to providing the opportunity for later advantageous youth exchanges, home exchanges can bear fruit in other ways. "We remained in regular contact with our London exchangers, and three years later became associated in business together." So reports a computer marketing executive in Dallas, Texas.

"Most of our exchanges were done from our home in Scottsdale, Arizona," adds another couple. "Eight months ago we moved to Tucson, and we credit our home exchange experience for the ease we have had settling in to our new home."

"One of the big hurricanes a few years ago brought us and our Eleuthra exchange partners together again," writes a teacher in Golden, Colorado. "The Eleuthra homeowner is a builder, and coincidentally my husband owns a building supply company. Although the networks did not pay too much attention to Eleuthra following the hurricane, the builder called us to report that much of the island had been wiped out and his home severely damaged. He asked if my husband could donate any materials or equipment to help rebuild the island. Of course he did, and our partner also gave his time, expertise, and hard work to help the islanders."

The expansion of self, the widening of personal horizons, art galleries, spectacular gardens, antique shops, historical museums, architecture, sunny places during rainy winters, the ocean for inlanders, the mountains for beach people, the mainland for islanders, the city for country folk, the country for urbanites—all appear in the survey under the category Best-liked Features of the Home Exchange Concept. "We learn something new with each exchange," states a banker-teacher couple. "Cultures may be different, as are customs and languages, but our basic humanity links us together globally. We all smile, cry, respond to kindness—and a million other commonalities that make us human. Home exchanging makes the world a smaller, more familiar place."

CHAPTER 27

The Downside

SURELY, WONDER THOSE WHO ARE A BIT SKEPTICAL about vacation home exchanging, this home-swapping cannot be all sunshine and roses. There must be a fly in the ointment somewhere.

From Longwood, Florida, comes this experience: "What do we like least about home exchanging? That we can't exchange with everyone from whom we get offers." Or "having to go home" from a California couple. Or "life is too short for us to make all the exchanges and go all the places we want to go." A lot of people respond to the survey's query with a big question mark; that is, they see no downside. Some flatly state, "There aren't six things we like least." Some write "none" across the six spaces provided, and some simply leave the lines blank. "I see virtually no downsides," writes a Washington home exchanger, "Of course, one needs to make certain assumptions—the home will be relatively clean, the car will hold up, and the appliances will work properly."

No vacation experience can be 100 percent perfect, but what the survey's responses reveal is that home exchanging—the idea, the range of possibilities, the benefits—approaches perfection. When the occasional flaw does occur, it is usually related to the mechanics of the arrangement, its logistics and implementation, or a lack of understanding on the parts of the exchange partners.

There is the teacher in Saint Croix, Virgin Islands, for example, who asks, "Why do exchangers always want to come here from January to March? Who wants to go north then?" Another teacher in West Flanders, Belgium, volunteers, "Exchanges between Belgium and the south of Europe are difficult. We have a lot of culture here, but not such a great climate." Included in the survey results were other comments about weather directed mainly toward those exchange partners who did not divulge enough local information for the exchanger to be prepared or who leave neither proper weather gear nor proper instructions for weather exigencies.

The cleaning of both homes was mentioned by a number of exchangers. Although some welcome the annual opportunity to clean and toss, others look on it as onerous and would be more than willing to pay a maid service on both ends of the exchange. "But how do we find a dependable cleaner in our exchange town?" asks an Orlando couple. "No one needs or wants a maid every day but on departure day, while trying to put more stuff than you brought into the original number of suitcases."

Some exchangers have their homes professionally cleaned before the exchange and tell their partners that they are on vacation and are not expected to be maids, "nor will we be theirs. Once over lightly is all we expect on returning home."

Another housekeeping comment in the survey concerned linens— specifically, not enough. It would be a big plus to many people if the beds could be made with an extra set of clean sheets on the last day without having to strip, launder, and remake the beds with the same sheets.

Unrelated to last-day blues, but certainly the ultimate in not enough linens, an exchanger from Scottsdale, Arizona, reported that to enjoy their French exchanger's four homes, they had to take their one set of sheets from one house to the next.

This same woman spoke to another issue. "Cleanliness is a variable. Some homes have been less than clean upon arrival—at least, by our standards. I always wonder if the inhabitants of these homes realize how unattractive they appear and that, while I'm in their homes, how concerned I am about the condition of mine when I return. My home has, in fact, always been in the 'pristine' condition in which I left it, but on one exchange here in the States, I had to call in a cleaning service before I was comfortable in the house."

With the exception of less-than-adequate house cleaning by some hosts, the absence of sufficient storage space for incoming guests and— what could be a biggie—an exchange car that won't run, difficulties are generally referred to as disadvantages, and even these are viewed as challenges, not disasters, in most cases.

"Yes, exchanging is a fair amount of work to arrange," says the Concord, New Hampshire, teacher quoted in the previous chapter. The correspondence can be "tedious and time-consuming," say others; "arranging and deciding on a commitment can be stressful," added someone else. Getting absolutely no response at all to inquiries is justifiably labeled rude by many, and Americans seemed to be the most

frequent offenders. Some survey recipients suggested that, at the least, a postcard should be sent to acknowledge receipt of a letter.

A professional couple in Upper Marlboro, Maryland, with twenty-five exchanges under their belt, pretty well summarized the short list of what might be called global difficulties—one or more of which appeared on many surveys: "bad exchange car, bad or difficult plumbing and/or appliances, unfriendly or too-friendly neighbors, exchangers who don't pay their telephone bills, and exchangers who leave homes uncleaned." To that short list, a retired couple from Bartlesville, Oklahoma, adds, "the logistics involved in the physical swapping of cars (for example, which airport parking lot), timing of arrival and departure, insurance in foreign countries, language uncertainties, and currency exchange rates."

Some correspondents elaborated. "Strange plumbing arrangements—the patience and concentration required to accomplish a simple morning shower, for example" (from scientists in New Brunswick, Canada). "First finding in the parking lot, then driving an English car from Heathrow Airport to the exchange home on the (gulp!) wrong side of the road." Other obstacle courses reported by global exchangers: different washing machines, dishwashers, driers, telephone systems, and Aga stoves (see chapter 21).

Although most exchangers agree with the New York City professionals who like the privacy of a home—"no noisy hotel maids, and you experience the area—not just the hotel," a semiretired Colorado couple expresses concern about "the quality of home, beds, linens, etc. With a hotel you know what to expect and can complain or move." They ask, "Three weeks on a soft mattress really hurt our backs, but what could we do?" This same couple also mentions "a prolonged sort of jet lag and culture shock that makes it hard to get active because one feels overwhelmed by learning new systems for even the simplest tasks—like making coffee. We could not just call room service but had to figure out how to cook, run the appliances, etc." For most exchangers, however, these little discoveries seem adventurous, even a fun part of the exchange experience.

One interesting observation and several permutations of it appeared throughout the survey: "Difficulty finding houses in the open countryside" (San Fulgencio, Spain) and "the occasional isolation in a country home—lovely, but far removed from neighbors, stores, etc." (Garden City, New York). On the other hand, a Boulder, Colorado, couple notes, "In a large city, sometimes your home is far removed from theaters, restaurants, etc. It is frequently time-consuming, frustrating, and a real hassle trying to work things out. Spontaneous trips usually don't happen." Related to both is the comment from a retired Kingston, Ontario, teacher: "Exploring may be difficult when one is new to the area and has no way of connecting with someone who may be able to show one around or relay necessary directions." These comments would appear to have to do with the preparation of neighbors, friends, and relatives done by the host prior to the exchange, but one exchanger wrote that they arrived at their house in Montana and found themselves thirty-five miles from anyone and everywhere. Surely, this extenuating circumstance should have shown up in the prearrangement communications.

Another concern that surfaced in the survey was what might be generically labeled "Surprises." There are, of course, pleasant ones:

"Got to Austria and found we had a maid and cook six days a week . . . expected a small car and found a Mercedes 450 . . . and in Hong Kong we had both a chauffeur and an amah who cooked, cleaned, and even ironed our underwear." The ultimate unpleasant surprise is, needless to say, a last-minute cancellation (see chapter 31). In the case of simultaneous exchanges, many people feel strongly that it should be up to the exchangers who cancel to help make other arrangements for their incoming guests. Not only may these guests hold nonrefundable airline tickets, but they may have no other viable contacts in the chosen community, having corresponded exclusively with this one exchanger.

A Florida couple suggests that international exchangers should post the phone number of someone who speaks the partner's language. Another found the absence of an elevator to her upper-story flat quite disconcerting when toting suitcases, groceries, and the like. "Public transportation information needs to be quite detailed if no car is available," points out another exchanger.

"Moving around furniture, kitchen-cupboard items, and clothing in closets and dresser drawers is our only gripe," write a Sussex, England, multitime exchanger. "On some occasions, we've returned—not to a messy home, thank goodness—but to one totally rearranged by our partners." Now, if the exchange home has no wastebaskets in one bedroom and two in another, dining-room chairs everywhere except in the dining room, and no available drawer space, then, of course, some items must be moved around a bit. However, on departure everything should be returned to its proper place.

Bringing in extra people without prior agreement is a no-no. However, some exchangers plan on it anyway. A couple writes from Devon, England, "On our very first exchange our partners arrived the day before we left and, at some point during the day, received a phone call. I overheard them making all the arrangements for meeting some additional people who were to stay with them. This plan had never been mentioned, and we found out later that several groups of people had been there in addition to our partners. The point is, we probably would have agreed had we been asked, but this 'undercover' operation really left a bad taste in our mouths."

"It is better to manage your partners' expectations carefully and not oversell what you have to offer. For example, living in central London in a townhouse can be a great holiday if you want the convenience of living in one of Europe's capital cities . . . and not a beachfront resort," is the advice from a London exchange couple.

A Boston homemaker's only complaint was that "We ate out seldom, and it was too much cooking and housework and not enough vacation for me," while others mentioned the difficulties they had had with shopping: store hours different from those at home combined with a language deficiency led to some long, difficult trips to the grocery store. A Dallas, Texas, exchange couple wrote, "We found the frustration of language ineptitude more critical when home exchanging than when staying in a hotel."

A university professor in Colorado agrees that his "inadequate knowledge of French and German" is a drawback. But even when people speak the same language, confusion sometimes reigns. "In a conversation about where things were in the English home we were to stay in, we discovered that 'jumpers' weren't used to help start a car; they were sweaters," according to a Virgin Islands couple. "When we told them that the jumpers were in the trunk of the car, they appeared amazed. I guess so. In tropical Saint Croix, one does hardly ever need a jumper-sweater. And certainly not stored in the trunk of the car!"

Those who don't think positively about exchanging homes can always turn up a wrinkle here and there. Like life, liberty, and the pursuit of happiness, there are problems—some sizable, some small—that confront vacation home exchangers. While admitting that exchangers do occasionally have to roll with the punches, a Springfield, Massachusetts, multitime exchanger says, "My wife and I have learned to deal with the few negative aspects of exchanging by focusing on the positive aspects—too many to list here—and, by so doing, we look forward to enjoying home exchanging till death do us part."

CHAPTER 28

Light Up Your Life!

I N THEIR DESIRE TO MAKE NEW FRIENDS, SEVERAL YEARS ago two Detroit couples, each in their sixties, placed an ad in one of the Detroit afternoon newspapers:

> LONESOME? Meet other seniors at the new Friendship Club on Saturday, 8:30 P.M. Cost: $5.00 per person; no reservations necessary.

They closed with the address of the local American Legion Hall. Having absolutely no idea whatsoever how many persons, if any, would respond, the couples arranged for refreshments for as many as two hundred guests. As it turned out, the hall had a mob on its hands when more than one thousand presumably lonesome people turned up.

Most of these people were over fifty years of age. Their children had grown up and moved away. Their grandchildren sometimes thanked them for Christmas presents but were always very busy—camp, school, college, friends. Their latter years—supposedly joy-filled, according to those uplifting books for seniors—were coming into view as their last years.

Happily, adults of all ages have a world of opportunities that tend to lead them away from loneliness and into fellowship and friendship with their fellow men. Among these opportunities are community service organizations, church organizations, high school and college reunions, the American Legion and Disabled American Veterans, golf, tennis, racquetball, boating and fishing clubs, senior citizens' clubs, vacation home exchange clubs, volunteer service, and a parade of other activities, groups, and organizations—even cigar-smoking clubs for men and women.

Opportunities abound for all seniors. Fight the tendency to become a television-addicted couch potato. Get up and get involved in an interesting activity—possibly national or international home exchanging.

Most assuredly not in that line forming to the right at that Legion Hall in Detroit was this seventy-five-year-old bookseller, specializing in rare and second-hand books in Devon, England.

"My first exchange was in 1981, and I've had sixteen exchange vacations since then—all over the States and as far distant as Sydney, Australia.

"I love Christmas because of the cards and letters I get from exchangers everywhere. They are such lovely, friendly people—my exchange partners and their family members, neighbors, and friends.

"Making contacts is always easy, as I have an eighteenth-century home in the country and am open to any offer at any time. I have had as many as fifty invitations in a year's time. Usually I'm joined by one of my friends, but sometimes I travel alone, and in those instances, the whole neighborhood seems to rally around—taking care of me and organizing my side trips. I've had a house on San Francisco Bay, on the waterside on the Keys, a flat overlooking the Opera House and Sydney Harbour Bridge; I've snorkeled in Queensland, and I swam daily with the manatees in Florida. Each of my four grandchildren has joined me on exchanges in California—four excursions to Disneyland.

"Of course, the travel part is fun . . . but the people one meets while at each exchange home are the best part of exchanging. My family generally remain in England while I'm away. Their lives have been enriched by getting to know various of my exchange partners—those who stay at my home when I'm away. My plan is to continue home exchanging forever."

Home exchangers learn early on that exchange hosts' neighbors and friends do indeed play an important role in the exchange experience. "Be sure to let us know if we can do anything for you folks," is perhaps the most often used phrase in the home exchange living situation—second only to Where's the house key? and Does their dog bite? But more often, offers to help come from exchange hosts' neighbors, relatives, and friends.

What's so great about home exchanging? "Lasting friendships," answers a recently widowed, retired schoolteacher from Rhode Island. "Home exchanging has completely changed my life—lifted me from addiction to daytime television to a 'new world' of travel, responsibilities, and lasting friendships."

Floridians, on returning from a three-week exchange in Winchester, England, said: "A highlight in this most recent exchange of ours was the opportunity we had to fellowship with our host's neighbors. Some of these people are retired while others, younger than we, make the daily commute to London. One of these couples invited us to a dinner party at their large and lovely home just down the street—a party to which they invited other neighbors. People two houses away had us in for cocktails, and a third couple took us on a day-long automobile trip to see something of the sights in and around Winchester. We had only known Winchester Cathedral as a song, but after having been guided through this cathedral on no fewer than three different occasions, we found this lovely, historic cathedral to be much, much more than just a song. Not only did these new friends show us the town, so to speak, but they became true friends who added much to our vacation experience."

Exchangers in Concord, New Hampshire, write, "One day while exchanging in France, I spent several hours with our exchange host's neighbor—talking about fishing in New Zealand (my homeland). We didn't speak the same language, but with many hand signals (especially useful when telling fish stories) we managed to impress each other mightily with our rod-in-hand successes. The wine flowed . . . and the fish got bigger and bigger!"

"The hospitality of our host's neighbors and friends has been remarkable," says a London school headmaster exchanger, "particularly those in the United States and in South Africa. We have made some dear friends over the years through exchanging." Lake Havasu City, Arizona, exchangers write, "Our Hannover, Germany, exchange friends liked our home so much they purchased the lot next to ours. Upon retirement, they will move to the United States and build a home on this property. In the meantime, they come to visit their empty lot annually, staying with us for a week or two. We have become fast friends."

From Monkton, Maryland, exchangers—a teacher and an industrial hygienist—write: "During an 'overlay' at our home here, we threw a party for our German exchangers—figuring it would be helpful for them to meet our neighbors up-front in their visit. In Germany at our exchange home, the four adults in our group felt it would be better for us not to be a burden on the neighbors. But it was difficult not to accept an invitation to spend a Saturday in Bremen. So we went ahead and proceeded to have one of the most memorable experiences of the whole trip. Even with the language barrier, we learned so much about how the people live, what they enjoy, and who they are that visits like this are one of the things we now enjoy most about exchanging."

During his first year of full retirement, a British airline pilot at last was able to fulfill his career-long dream—not to travel and to spend the better part of each day in his garden. His wife, on the other hand, had spent untold hours in the garden while he was away, and she wanted to travel, so she engineered two home exchanges—one to the United States, the other to Australia. With some degree of hesitation, he too undertook the trip. This once-again-traveling pilot said, "I'll have to admit this home exchanging experience introduced me to a totally new dimension in world travel."

Several exchangers have something to say about that "new dimension" in world travel. "On a New Year's Day," writes an exchanger in Seattle, Washington, "our two-time exchangers in Belluno, Italy, telephoned just to see how we and our kids were doing . . . and to wish us a Happy New Year."

"When we started exchanging eight years ago, it was our thought not to have repeat exchanges; rather to go to different exchange locations each year. Well, we became such good friends with one of our exchange families—adult and kids alike—we've exchanged with them annually for the past four years."

"We've developed a wonderful friendship with exchangers in Glasgow, Scotland; in fact, we've also exchanged our kids with these folks during the past two Easter school vacations."

"We loved our exchange home near Boston . . . but our exchange host's several neighbors made last year's one of the very best vacations we have ever had. These folks showed us all of the sights in and around Boston, entertained us for meals and at cocktail parties attended by other neighbors, and even helped us deal with a dishwasher problem."

After exchanging in Switzerland, a Florida physician and his wife wrote, "We won't forget those neighbors; from them, we had a daily offering of fresh raspberries."

"Our vacation home exchange was a trip to England with our two college-age young people. We made the exchange to save money," writes a Tampa, Florida, couple. "However, other pluses far outweighed the original reason. For example, our exchange family's next-door neighbors invited us over for cocktails. As it turned out, they had young people our children's ages, and these kids had a grand time together. These same neighbors very kindly allowed us to use their membership at the local yachting club for dinners out where, incidentally, we met other delightful people who invited us to their church worship service and also to their five hundred-year-old home."

A systems programmer and his training-coordinator wife in San Juan Capistrano wrote, "In Basel, Switzerland, the housekeeper came in to clean one day, and I offered her coffee and cookies. She spoke no

English and we no French, so she placed a phone call then called me to the phone. Her daughter on the other end spoke English and invited us to her mother's home in a small village for Sunday dinner. We went, met the whole family, and spent the entire afternoon and evening with them. Since then several of them have visited us in the States."

Berkeley, California, exchangers write, "At first, we regarded exchanging as a cheap way to see new places. Indeed, it is that, but our several exchanges have led to real friendships and repeat visits."

In a most peculiar way, the home exchange relationship seems to sweep away the age barriers of exchange partners. Of their Brussels exchange partners, home exchangers in the Washington, D.C., area write: "We are now in our early seventies while our Belgian exchange friends are in their midforties. Our families have had three exchanges, with them living with nearby relatives while we occupied their home. So, we got together with these folks every few days—family parties, sightseeing trips, and just developing a lasting friendship. Honestly, we see these folks as contemporaries, even though we often remind ourselves that they are the same ages as our son and his wife."

In previous chapters it has been pointed out that U.S. home exchangers—and those from abroad, as well—favor certain U.S. states for their vacation enjoyment—California, Hawaii, Florida, and Washington, D.C. Within these larger parameters, those who enjoy the fellowship, the companionship of other home exchangers seem to gravitate to particular U.S. cities and towns. Santa Fe, New Mexico, for example; Palm Springs, California; Sanibel Island, Florida; Silver Springs, Maryland; and, because of the large numbers of home exchangers in this Florida city, Pensacola is known in the home exchange community as the "no-rent" district.

A Tennessee exchanger writes, "We first exchanged in London just eleven years ago. Although we've only exchanged with these partners two or three times, while exchanging elsewhere in London (which we do nearly every September), we arrange a dinner get-together with these friends. We've seen their two girls grow up and, indeed, recently attended the elder girl's wedding."

Folks from Virginia write, "Our exchange partners in Paris last year were sharing with us the tragic story of their fourteen-year-old son's drug addiction. While we found ourselves to be short on advice, we certainly were long on comforting them and committing their family problem to prayer. They phoned several months later with the joyous news that their son had had a complete turnaround in his lifestyle—that he was back at home and doing well in school. Tears aplenty during that phone conversation!"

The travel brochures extol the benefits of each destination visited—"Four wonderful destinations in an adventure-packed week!" In vacation home exchanging, the talk is not of destinations but, rather, of lived-in, loving homes. Putting this in different terms, two teachers from Germany said, "Vacation home exchanging is meeting a neighborhood, not just a tour director."

Seventy-five percent of those in the home exchange universe are over fifty years of age. Many have retired, sold their homes, moved away from loved ones and friends, or have otherwise been uprooted from the lives to which they have been accustomed for so long—in many cases, for decades. The vacation home exchange concept provides, in a significant way, a means of filling some of these large gaps in the lives of these seniors . . . and younger people as well.

CHAPTER 29

The Inevitable Question

A S ONE CAN SURMISE FROM THE CHAPTERS OF THIS book, to suggest that home exchangers are enthusiastic about the vacation home exchange concept would be a masterpiece of understatement. The vast majority of home exchangers are ecstatic about this way of vacationing—to the extent that they rarely miss an opportunity to talk about it and try to convert family members, friends, and anyone else they meet into believers in this kind of travel experience.

Sooner or later, as they go about their soft- and sometimes even hard-sell efforts, they run into the question, "But how can you possibly let strangers stay in your house when you aren't there? Doesn't that make you very nervous?"

Logical question, agreed—motivated by the fear that strangers might mistreat one's home—red wine on white carpet, broken crystal, cigarette holes in the bedding—or steal things. For those who have not caught the home exchange bug, for the uninitiated, these questions are totally understandable.

So far as out-and-out stealing is concerned, the survey—primary resource for these chapters—failed to turn up even one case of theft. Remember, the survey covered approximately four thousand different home exchanges around the world. Furniture rearranging? Yes. Less-than-great housekeeping? Yes. Occasional breakage? Yes. Theft? No. "People interested in exchanging homes are not 'criminal types,'" says an Ithaca, New York, computer analyst. "Better to have strangers emptying my dishwasher than burglars emptying the safe in my unoccupied house!" is the succinct comment of a Gwent, Wales, exchanger. "Besides," writes a Swedish exchanger, "I don't think an exchanger would rob me. Even thieves take holidays from stealing, don't they?"

The only "stealing" mentioned by any respondents (and usually described in an amused way) were the two or three times when an exchange host's wine or liquor cabinet was raided—a problem that could have been averted had the hosts simply not left their prize vintages readily available. Along with grandma's antique vase, these hard-to-replace items should always be put away.

"'Home exchanging? Sleeping in someone else's bed, my head on their pillow! Not for me!' My husband," reports an advertising copywriter, "had a ready answer (one that should have earned him the home exchanger's Medal of Honor), 'Listen, Jack, you travel a lot. What's the difference between your head sinking into a Holiday Inn pillow—one used by perhaps twenty different men and women in the preceding four weeks—and an exchange home's pillow used by one or two people during the past year?'"

Regarding the care and nurture of the hosts' homes and personal property: of the more than one thousand survey participants—all experienced exchangers—nine out of ten reported that their exchange partners had taken excellent care of their homes and belongings; most of the rest reported very good care. Only a handful rated their guests' care of their homes as less than good. As one might expect, on the other side of the coin respondents claim that, when they are guests, they take excellent care of their hosts' homes and property. That claim may well be true—numerous people state that they return to homes that are in "pristine condition" or "cleaner than we left it."

Nervous about strangers living in your home? "I do think the first time you hand over your house keys to a complete stranger, it can be just a bit unsettling. Our first exchange," writes a retired airline engineer from San Francisco, a veteran exchanger, "was in Hawaii. We had arranged to meet our partners at a hotel, exchange keys and maps, drive them to the airport, then go to their home. My stomach was in absolute knots. I thought, 'What are we doing?!' But when our hosts arrived, they were just like us, and by the time we had driven them to the airport, we were like old friends."

A Winchester, England, exchanger adds, "I'm far more nervous that my home won't live up to my guests' expectations or that my cat will prove a nuisance than I am about actually having them live there." From Indian Wells, California, "In thirty-one years of home exchanging (scores of exchanges everywhere), we've never had anything damaged or missing."

An Israeli couple have not yet come to full agreement on this issue: "I am only a little apprehensive, but my wife is still quite nervous about

it, so we prefer to exchange our second home in Ein-Hod, an artists' colony overlooking the Mediterranean near Haifa."

"How about strangers using the items in our home?" asks an exchanger in Belgium. "For the short time we're here on earth, we consider ourselves only as users of these things. So, why shouldn't others be allowed to use them?"

In other words, responses to the inevitable question cover the gamut from a point-blank and without-comment "No! Not in my house!" and "Listen, no one's stranger or more destructive than our kids!" to "The only fragile antiques in our house are us!" and "If you're nervous, stay home. That's your loss."

The consensus is that the people coming into your home for a vacation visit are no longer strangers. "This is a social exchange," is the way a Frederick, Maryland, couple puts it. "We have invited guests for dinner, so to speak; we just aren't there to greet them. Would you hide the silver from your dinner guests?" They go on to say, "The job of the prospective partners is to ascertain through correspondence, phone calls, photographs, videos, and any available means of communication that each is dealing with responsible, interesting, mature people of a similar educational level and like interests."

"The key word is *trust*. We trust them to care for our home, and they trust us to do the same," writes a Saint Croix artist. "Going through the process of establishing what I guess might be called 'blind trust' prior to the exchange and then making the pleasant discovery of new friends is a wonderful experience—both as an example to our children and as a renewal of our own faith in people," declares a Portland, Oregon, teacher.

Trust is one of the most frequently used words in any discussion about vacation home exchanging. Exchange partners seem to develop a sufficient amount of trust in each other to exchange keys to each other's homes and often their cars, too. Where does this trust come from? It is the result of "talking with other exchangers," "sharing photographs," "exchanging correspondence," "telephone conversations," and "it seems to develop with exchange experience."

"After all that communication and research," the Portland exchanger goes on, "we don't feel our exchange partners are strangers anymore; they have become true and trusted friends, and our exchanges are simply cases of two friends enjoying each other's homes for family vacations. No big deal."

Collectively, home exchangers report that communication (the exchanger's "homework") is the keystone of this trust—the most important factor in the relationship. It does not result from one letter, one phone call, one fax, then "Here we are!"—kids, suitcases, and key in hand. A writer, an exchanger from Maryland, puts it this way: "I think that the exchange of letters offers an opportunity to sense the character and personality of those with whom we might exchange. Writing is, to begin with, a solo act requiring some serious prior thought. Thus, as readers, we should be able to decipher certain things about the letter writer: How do these people present themselves? What are their interests? Would we want them as friends if they lived on our street? Or if not intimate friends with whom we would spend a lot of time, are they at least considerate of our interests? Do we seem to understand each other's feelings and ways of thinking?"

All the elements of in-depth communication are essential to genuine trust. In an almost uncanny fashion, this correspondence—which may go on for months—makes friends out of strangers and trusted and trusting exchangers out of apprehensive ones. Often, the resultant exchange evolves not only into warm friendships but lifelong, close relationships.

"I think a particular type of person goes to the trouble of trying for a vacation home exchange," writes a teacher on the Isle of Mull, Scotland. "I guess we have quite a bit of faith in the human race and look for the best in other people until proven wrong." A Warwick, Bermuda, architect with a family of four sent in this thought: "It's a matter of trusting people. Life is a gamble. To have new and interesting life experiences, you sometimes have to take chances."

From Laguna Beach, California, a bank vice president and his dental-hygienist wife write, "By the time we write, phone, and exchange references and photos, we no longer feel we're dealing with 'strangers.' No, we're not at all nervous having exchangers occupying our home."

If people are really nervous about having strangers vacationing in their homes, home exchanging is probably not for them. "People who lock up their VCRs and good china—who record the liquor levels, quantities of foods and detergents, rolls of toilet paper, etc.—should not even think of exchanging. Generally speaking (and fortunately for the rest of us), they don't," comments a New Yorker, among others. "It's a small miracle that in this day and age, full of aggression and lies, this vacation home exchange system—almost totally based on trust—actually works," is the sentiment of two Belgian teachers.

Another teacher, from Bois Colombes, France, perhaps best captures the feel of exchanging. "Home exchange is something magic. You are living another's life: you are, in truth, your partner. His neighbors, friends, and shopkeepers are your neighbors, friends, and shopkeepers; his car, his appliances, his books and magazines are yours; the postman gives you his mail. In the end, you come to truly know and appreciate these persons, even though your respective exchange travel schedules may prevent your meeting them face-to-face."

In summary, while it does take a certain amount of courage and confidence to firm up that first home exchange arrangement, probably the "stranger" question is best answered by this exchanger in Hancock, New Hampshire: "It's true—we have strangers in our house, but our exchange partners also have 'strangers' in their house: Us!"

CHAPTER 30

Finally, More People Who Tried It . . . and Liked It

Residing in Santpoort-Noord, Netherlands, René Nossin is project manager in the Automation Department of KLM, the national Dutch airline, where he has worked for twenty-five years. Ria Nossin is associated with a telemarketing company in Haarlem. These exchangers have two sons: Emile (twenty years old) is studying to be an airline pilot, and Michel (eighteen years old) is a student of information technology.

Before becoming home exchangers, the Nossin family members were accustomed to vacationing at rented holiday homes in Switzerland or Austria. Because they generally found this type of vacation quite expensive, the Nossins responded positively to a 1983 home exchange-related radio program. Soon thereafter, they were off to a holiday fair in Utrecht to learn more about this unique holiday concept. This was in January 1984.

Some years later, the Nossins appeared on Dutch television, introducing the home exchange concept to viewers of a program focused on holidays.

Ria and René Nossin write:

Hearing that radio program—an interview with Mr. Renger de Ruiter, director of the Dutch home exchange organization (LOVW)—and going to Utrecht to learn firsthand all about holiday home exchanging at the LOVW exhibit convinced us that this type of holiday might be just right for us and our two sons.

Why? Well, many reasons. First, the luxury of staying in a private home or apartment. Second, no rent! Among the other good things we learned about home exchanging arrangements was the security it would provide for our own home being occupied by our home exchange friends at the same time we would be occupying their home.

Also important were the facts that the exchanging of cars (and even bikes) is often a part of the arrangement (big savings there, no car rental); that home exchange locations are usually not in tourist areas; and that new friendships are made while on holiday with the neighbors of our exchange partners. And our boys would have built-in friends. Family holidays are so much more beneficial and enjoyable for all if the children can make friends with others their own ages. Fun time for the kids every day.

So, yes, we were excited when we arranged to have our home listed in an international home exchange directory and even more excited when, through this listing, we arranged for our very first home exchange: two weeks in Biella, in northern Italy.

As we looked forward to this summer 1984 first home exchange holiday, we became a little bit nervous. Would our new friends take good care of our home? Would we be happy in theirs? All our questions were answered when we met the family with whom we would be exchanging. We knew then we had made the right decision. We had a great time in their Biella apartment, and they enjoyed our Dutch home, garden, and bikes.

Since then, we've had another fifteen exchanges, varying from one to five weeks each in Sweden, Germany, California, Ontario, British Columbia, England, Belgium, Colorado, Washington, Singapore, Washington, D.C., and two shorter exchanges right here in Holland. Most of these exchanges were during the summer school holidays. Generally, we prefer to go to different places, but in several cases we have had repeat exchanges.

In the summer of 1994, after ten years of rent-free holidays, we actually paid rent during our holiday. Our efforts to put together a home exchange in South Africa did not succeed, so we did the next best thing. We rented a beautiful holiday home at the seaside near Durban, South Africa, from a home exchange family. Later we rented a camper and visited many interesting places in South Africa.

In Singapore and the rest of the Far East, it is rather difficult to arrange a home exchange. That's why we contacted the general manager of KLM in Singapore, who made contact via the Dutch club with a Dutch family looking forward to visiting their family in Holland and having their own home base in Holland during that period. For us it was an interesting exchange because we had a servant in our Singapore home who helped us with the housekeeping, cooking, washing, and ironing. This may be a normal situation for some exchangers, but for us it was quite an unusual experience.

Earlier we mentioned that our exchange partners' neighbors and family and other friends too were a very important part of the home exchange experience. Those who are nervous about exchanging must realize that living in someone else's home doesn't mean you are stranded in a big house way out in the middle of nowhere. In our sixteen exchanges, we have been amazed at how friendly and helpful our new-found neighbors and friends have been. Questions about appliances (sometimes difficult to operate in a foreign country), places to shop, things to do, places to see. The answers to these and dozens of other questions are as near as your exchange partners' neighbors.

Just the other day, we were recalling neighbors near Stockholm. One day they asked us to join them for a visit to their second home way out in the country in a forest where even bears could appear. We said yes and had a wonderful time together in their small wooden cottage with no electricity and no running water. But we managed—fishing, hiking, and truly enjoying nature at its very best. Does this sound like a conventional holiday? I should think not. Indeed, friendship between our families flourished, and both adults and young people had great fun.

In 1990, our Seattle, Washington, exchange partners (Dutch emigrants) had lots of friends, many of them also Dutch emigrants. It was a great experience for us to be hosted at parties, on speedboat trips on Lake Washington, and other special events by friends of Dutch heritage right in the United States. A Seattle home exchange member, who was soon to depart for an Amsterdam (Holland) home exchange, called us because he wanted some information about the Netherlands and invited us to a barbecue at his home. We had a cheerful evening and agreed to see each other in our Dutch home after our return. They loved our home, and we spent another nice evening together—this time in Holland.

As we go about arranging our exchanges from one year to the next, we prefer to allow as much time in planning as possible. We always start to contact those with whom we might like to exchange as soon as the first edition of the directory appears; usually this is in January or early February. We have our listing, with an accompanying photo of our home, placed in this first directory, as it's usually the one with the most listings and is referred to by the largest number of potential home exchangers. If an exchanger communicates with a large number of home exchange possibilities, following through with appropriate correspondence to the final arrangement (or arrangements) can easily take months. Special consideration in firming up arrangements must be made if intercontinental travel is involved, since one can enjoy a considerable savings by making early travel reservations. Also, the arrangement letters back and forth take more time.

We know that different exchangers follow different procedures in making initial contacts with each other. We have found the best procedure for us is to make the first contact by telephone. Obviously this saves time, and we get a direct response. We get a no if it's unlikely this particular exchange possibility is viable. But if we get a positive answer from the initial telephone call, then we send letters, photos, and often faxes. Occasionally, we make the initial contact by letter, following up by telephone after several weeks, during which the receivers have had time to consider our offer. But whatever the procedure, we strongly advise exchangers to move as quickly as possible through the communication stages. Do not wait. Be active!

Both parties must be totally honest with each other—and seriously interested in the exchange itself—during the communications stages, right up through the point of coming to an agreement. It is vitally important that exchange partners have a sense of mutual trust, because we believe the foundation of home exchanging is trust. Perhaps we should add here that in none of our sixteen highly successful exchanges have we ever had any problems of any kind in the areas of honesty, reliability, and trustworthiness in our relationships with exchange partners.

Our exchange partners have included teachers, a car mechanic, a bakery manager, an insurance broker, a psychotherapist, a real estate broker, a professor, a journalist, a medical doctor, and others representing a range of careers and professions. All, however, had one thing in common: they were very nice, very careful with other people's belongings, and were excited about the many advantages of the holiday home exchanging concept.

We thought too that readers might be interested in "seeing" home exchanging through the experiences of the younger generation—our eldest son, Emile.

I am twenty years old now, and I can say that I found the time I spent with my family home exchanging, when I was still a teenager, was .always very exciting and educational. I'm sure that home exchanging from a young age on (I was ten when we started it) has given me a better look at other cultures than I would have had if we had been staying in hotels or apartments in tourist areas. The experiences we have had varied from living in an Italian apartment to an American oceanview villa, a Dutch farmhouse, and so on. Every house had new toys, new surroundings to discover, usually new neighborhood friends, and sometimes new pets for my brother and me to take care of. I still find myself having an edge in a conversation or discussion over someone who went to the same area or country but stayed in a hotel or rented apartment.

The second thing Michel and I (actually the whole family) liked and still like about home exchanging was having a place to come back to after trips: a "home base"—not having to miss home during the holidays (especially important for smaller children) and having a place to relax for a few days, too. This is very nice after a long trip, and it is something you don't easily do in a hotel. It is during these "relaxation" periods that you get to know the other way of life. You find out what kind of things people normally do when they are at home or what kind of activities there are in the neighborhood: swimming, hiking, cycling, going to the beach, the shopping mall, a market, a street festival, and so on.

I still go on holiday exchanges with my parents, mainly because I can't afford to go to all those exotic places by myself yet, but also because it's a unique way to get acquainted with another way of life—among the greatest advantages of being a part of the international holiday home exchange community.

In 1970, John Price spotted a newspaper advertisement for holiday home exchanging—this after holidays beset with house moves, pregnancies, and staying with family members. There were the occasional hotels and other rental accommodations, but no toys and sometimes no safe arrangements for the three (then) young Price children.

Their first home exchange in Brighton, England, introduced a breath of fresh air into the Price family's holiday experience—the first of twenty-four annual home exchange holidays.

Specializing in personal injury work, John is a partner in a large law firm with offices in Exeter and Plymouth, England, his home city. Decidedly a people person, Pat Price enjoys working at the local college bookshop—a job that brings her into contact with students, faculty, and administrators. John is a reader and rugby fan; Pat is a collector of old glass and a gardener. They share an interest in walking, bridge playing, cycling, traveling, and holiday home exchanging.

The Price's eldest son, Andrew, is a law student. His brother Richard is an accountant. His sister Louise is in hospitality management training in both England and France.

Pat Price writes:

After our first holiday home exchange success in Brighton, our confidence in this new holiday concept grew, and soon we decided to risk the Continent—France, in particular, followed by holidays over the years in Sweden, Spain, Greece, Belgium, and the United States. In the States, our exchanges were in Los Angeles, Seattle, and Connecticut. We would very much like to revisit Vashon Island, Washington, and Yosemite National Park, as well as trying some new places—possibly in the Rocky Mountains, elsewhere in the States, or destinations not yet visited in Europe.

Among our home exchange partners to date have been a bank manager, an accountant, a factory manager, a retired vicar, lawyers, engineers, teachers, and others representing a broad range of professions and occupations. Reflecting over those with whom we have exchanged, all were family oriented, responsible, both inexperienced and experienced home exchangers, and what we would call like-minded people.

With the exception of our exchanges in the United States, for the most part it has not been our custom to swap cars. We do so in the States because the distances are so vast and because the auto insurance policies there are more or less standard in covering both the owners and drivers of autos. Further, to bring our own car from England would be prohibitively expensive, and the outlay for renting a car in the United States is too much for our budgets.

I do recall, however, swapping cars with a French family once. Our first stop at a garage resulted in John's filling up the car's tank, then his shoes, and then the driveway. This had nothing to do with insurance; it was simply a matter of John's schoolboy French letting him down when he could not find a way to switch off the pump.

Aside from the fact that we love our home here, we are fortunate in that Plymouth is an extremely popular holiday resort, appealing to vacationers from Europe and overseas. In making our exchange contacts, we simply list our home in one of the top home exchange directories and then sit back confidently, awaiting the deluge of inquiries that come immediately after the directory is released. Exchangers who are off the beaten path have to work much harder in consummating exchange arrangements. While people usually write us, at least three of our holidays would never have happened if potential exchangers had not telephoned us, building a rapport and interesting us in the details of their home and family situations before mailing us a descriptive selection of brochures and other material. We believe the telephone makes the contact much more personal and seems to give an added dimension to our impressions about families, their homes, their areas, and their needs. After all, we want our exchange partners to enjoy their holidays at our home as much as we want to enjoy our holidays at theirs.

Home exchangers around the world rate the people part as being among the most important elements in home exchanging, and we certainly agree with this. Some years back, John took a six-month sabbatical. Having previously enjoyed several exchanges in the States, we decided to return there. This time, we started in Connecticut, then went to Chicago, where we met people from a previous exchange in Sweden, and eventually ended up spending most of our time on the West Coast. We met our two previous American exchange partners and stayed with their neighbors on Vashon Island, before hiring a car and touring the Pacific Coast from Seattle to San Francisco. Americans have to be the most generous and warm-hearted people we have ever met.

On another occasion we were delighted when a French family with whom we had swapped contacted us to see if we could assist their son who was interested in law. This young man came to live with us and spent two months working at John's office. We have since seen him, his wife, and their new baby (who happens to be the same age as our grandson). We wonder if this home exchange connection will continue through the babies!

We exchanged daughters with our hosts the year after our Spanish exchange—very successful—and, indeed, had another recent get-together with them.

The Swedish exchange resulted in our putting up two girls for three years running—young people who wanted to improve their English; later we met their parents and one of their fiancés and still later attended their wedding in Sweden.

We have revisited our Greek home exchange partners on a B&B basis and hope they will stay with us next time they are in England.

Quite often exchangers get to know their exchange partners' neighbors better than their exchangers. Indeed, we found this to be so on Vashon Island. These neighbor friends have visited us twice, and we have been back to see them as well; now we are talking of traveling together in Spain sometime in the future.

With the passing of more than two decades of holidaying in the wonderful world of holiday home exchanging, we can recall only two wrinkles, so to speak. The first of these was a problem of washing-machine repair. The repairmen were there all right, but the language problem made it all rather embarrassing, and we never did get that washing machine sorted out properly. On another occasion, we left a man painting the outside of our house while we were away. We had not realized that this would be an inconvenience for our home exchange partners, and we will certainly not do this again.

John and I are every bit as enthusiastic now as when we first started to exchange . . . and, I must say, we experience the same excitement when the home exchange–related letters start to arrive year after year. We expect to continue exchanging in the years ahead and look forward after retirement to great possibilities of making more than one swap annually.

We think a personal testimony to the validity of the home exchange holiday is that, to our great delight, our son has caught the home exchange vision. He and our daughter-in-law are now arranging their first home swap—more links in our family's home exchange chain.

Born and raised in Pasco, Washington, Virginia Stanton, after graduating from college, spent thirty-five years in personnel and employee relations for industry and government and on her own. Never a biological parent, about fifteen years ago she sponsored a young family into the United States and is now known as their American mother and grandmother, depending on which generation is speaking.

Her first exchange in 1974–75 was both to celebrate her retirement (she's retired twice since then) and to encourage the emotional healing necessary following the death of her husband. A year or so before, they had read about home exchanging, and after some diligence, Virginia was off on a twenty-year exchange adventure.

When she remarried in 1985, she and Stan had a wonderful home exchanging honeymoon in California. Their marriage— sadly cut short by Stan's bout with cancer—was enhanced by a number of exchanges on the East Coast and in Canada.

Nearly all her exchanges took place while she lived in suburban Washington, D.C. As she puts it, "An ideal base for exchanging. Everybody wants to visit Washington at some time or other."

Since 1987 Virginia has lived in a retirement community of single-family homes in Southern California.

Virginia Stanton writes:

Some of my most enjoyable home exchanges have started with the hosts still at their homes to enlighten us on the idiosyncrasies of the house and car and to instruct us on where to go and what to see and do. In Germany, our Hamm hosts met us at the Frankfurt airport with a picnic lunch to eat on the way home. After insisting we take a short jet-lag rest, they showed us around the house and introduced us to their children and friends before serving all of us a superb dinner. The next day they took us around town, introducing us to people in the bank and markets who spoke English and also helped us make arrangements for a side trip we had planned. When they departed, they left the nicest gift of all a few doors down the street, staying with friends—their son, who was of invaluable help whenever we had questions to ask about the house, its immediate area, and about sightseeing.

Some years ago, I arranged a trip around the United States—mainly by home exchange—for friends of mine from what was then Rhodesia (now Zimbabwe) and me to celebrate our retirements (again!). Their twenty-two-year-old daughter went with us.

We left Rockville, Maryland, in August and returned in time for me to vote on November 3. Of the sixty-eight nights we were on the road, we spent thirty-one in seven home exchanges and ten nights in six hospitality exchanges. Through home exchange listings, we also rented a penthouse on San Francisco's Nob Hill for two nights. We stayed with friends for two additional nights. That left only twenty nights for which we needed hotel or motel rooms. Through home and hospitality exchanging, we had the finest of accommodations plus the added ambience of being expected and warmly welcomed. It was an incredible experience.

Our exchanges went from four one-night stands to stays of four to six days each. The longer stays were in Estes Park, Colorado; in Sequom, Washington, on a golf course; in Santa Barbara in a home so elegant it was featured in *Sunset* magazine; in Las Vegas (my favorite exchange house); and in Atlanta in an artist's paradise. Probably the most exciting were our "cowboys and Indians" days in and around Pinedale, Wyoming (a hospitality exchange), that ended with sleeping overnight in a tepee in the Tetons at a hunting camp readied to open for bow-hunting season. Our Pinedale host will never be forgotten for showing us deer and antelope at play and making the Wild West leap to life for my guests from Africa.

To set up this trip, I mailed more than a hundred letters five months ahead of time to addresses around the nation near the tourist areas I wanted to see and show my friends. I received twenty interested responses. I took these to AAA, where I was assisted by a woman I knew who had worked there for thirty years. Her help in working out our itinerary and routing was invaluable.

My main job was the correspondence. I worked out a schedule for seven families to use my home while we were away—not necessarily on the same dates we were occupying their homes. Only one family expressed any disappointment in my home: it was farther from the downtown metro than they had envisioned. Our accommodations were all just perfect.

The hospitality exchanges were great, too. (If we had any negative comment, it would be that we felt we had to be on our best behavior while we were entertained by so many strangers, and the strain of that can become a bit wearing.) I am puzzled by the fact that only half of our hosts ever claimed their part of the bargain. There was never a cross word or a dull moment, but I still owe hospitality to three families, and this bothers me.

On a West Coast exchange, I picked up the key to my hosts' Honda Civic as prearranged and proceeded to the behemoth parking facility to find it. I got in. Hmmm, stick shift, and not the traditional H-shape I learned so long ago. Oh, well, here goes. On the dash were instructions to their house. First, I was to get on the Santa Monica Freeway, then traverse what appeared to be miles of surface streets, stopping and starting at so many traffic lights I lost count. I started the car and made a few hairy practice runs, shifting gears, around the parking area. Finally, I aimed at the freeway. With the good Lord at my side, I made it. I have the pretty clear impression that I scared the wits out of more than one unwary California driver before finally getting to our host's street and driveway.

Another car story makes a good point about car exchanges. On one exchange, we were to use our hosts' diesel Mercedes, so they suggested that I take a lesson from a dealer in my area before we left. Once we got there, I did get the car started, but it was pouring rain when we got off the plane, and none of us could figure out how to get the windshield wipers to work. Of course, we finally did (when all else fails, look in the owner's manual), but I was exceedingly thankful for my earlier driving lesson.

My first exchange on my own, so to speak, was to Port Antonio, Jamaica, and it set the stage for almost all the rest. (I cannot help but feel that the majority of the time I've come out on the better end of the deal!) When the chauffeur drove us up to the front door, a lineup of appropriately costumed staff—houseboy, cook, gardener, laundress—greeted us. During my six-week stay, friends flew in and out, all of us relishing a life we had never known or even dreamed of. We even had our own snorkeling and diving instructor.

Not all exchanges have been quite so exotic. Once I somewhat hastily obliged a young professional couple from the West Coast in exchange for their very small garage apartment. "Small" I didn't object to in the slightest; "squalid" I did not expect.

With whom have my exchanges been made? By far the most have been with executives and managers in both government and industry, followed by educators, social workers, artists and writers, engineers, real estate brokers, ranchers and farmers (including vintners in wine country), a concert pianist, a machinist, an airline pilot, a military officer, an estate officer, accountant, minister, nurse, sports outfitter, and others just as diverse. I tend to remember them as people more than I do for what they did for a living. It's truly an amazing spectrum.

My advice to those new to the home exchange adventure?

1. Be totally honest with fellow exchangers.

2. Don't try to lure a potential exchanger with exotic descriptions of your home.

3. Leave your place clean and neat.

4. Make space for your exchangers' things.

5. Trust your exchange partners.

6. Never exchange "in haste."

When my friends and I exchange, I insist we play a game called "Leave this place exactly as we found it." The idea is for the exchanger to come home and never know we were there—except, of course, for the letter of thanks, a nice meal in the refrigerator, and a welcome-home gift.

When I was on the long tour around the country—in our last exchange prior to returning to Washington, as a matter of fact—I got a call from the exchangers in my house. "How many exchangers have been here while you've been gone?"

"You're the seventh," I replied.

"That's incredible! This place is immaculate!" And when we got back five days later, it still was.

CHAPTER 31

The Ultimate Disaster

EVERY WORTHWHILE FIELD OF ENDEAVOR HAS ITS
very own parade of possible catastrophes, and in this respect,
vacation home exchanging is no exception. Some, obviously,
are worse than others. A teacher in Saint Croix, Virgin Islands,
wrote a rather plaintive note at the end of her survey response: "Our
home exchange career came to an abrupt halt—-at least for a while—
when our home blew away during Hurricane Hugo."

But most home exchange catastrophes, bad though they may seem
at the time, are more like these. An American turning right into a
clockwise-traffic English roundabout in his host's brand-new Mercedes.
A nonsmoking exchange host who returns home to find his living room
drapes yellowed from the smoke of his guest's daily dozen cheap cigars.
The Portuguese host who failed to leave proper instructions on lighting
the propane stove and returned home to find his oven had blown up. A
teenager, scheduled to leave the exchange home with her parents the
next day, who leans on the sink to get a little closer to the bathroom
mirror and pulls the sink completely off the wall. Vacation home
exchanging is no freer of catastrophes than any other part of life.

But the ultimate disaster in home exchanging (short of someone's
death or having a home blown away)—the really bad one—is perhaps
most succinctly described by a ten-time Atlanta exchanger: "A French
family backed out of our exchange only days before we were to leave
for Europe. We were stuck with airline tickets for my wife, our three
children, and me. It was just dreadful."

A Sutton, Ireland, aircraft engineer, his registered-nurse wife, and
their three children share this unfortunate story: "We were in the
middle of arrangements, almost finalized; all we had to do was arrange
for car insurance covering our partners. The expected reply to our last
letter never materialized. So, about five weeks before Exchange Day, I
called and got the shock of my life when our supposed partners

informed me that they'd changed their minds and were going to Spain instead. They said they had written a letter of explanation, but it never came. At that stage it was too late for us to make alternate arrangements. Our holiday was ruined."

"We had two back-to-back exchanges set up," writes a retired airline captain in Bradenton, Florida. "About a month before the exchange dates, both our 'partners' changed their minds, leaving us completely in limbo—airline tickets to nowhere, etc." An irate Virginian tells of being canceled two days before E-day "on what, to me, was a very flimsy excuse."

Dreadful!—Shock of my life—holiday ruined—in limbo—letter never came—flimsy excuse. Fortunately, these negative experiences are rare occurrences with vacation home exchanging. All of these exchangers had been careful each step of the way in their planning and correspondence and were looking forward to exchanges in several parts of the world—only to learn their "partners" had become nonpartners. Their experiences underscore in the best possible way the vital importance of exchangers fulfilling their commitments to each other. Just because a plan revolves around a proposed fun-filled vacation doesn't mean that the obligation to follow through with the plan is any less serious. In the normal course of events, there is no place for "Dear John" letters in vacation home exchange correspondence.

On rare occasions plans must be changed. People die, children and adults become seriously ill, and changing job situations may well have to scrap vacation plans—home exchange or otherwise.

So you get the bad news. You think some evil thoughts about your nonexchanging partners and may even blue the air with a few choice comments. After a night of fitful sleep, in the light of the new day, you come to realize that under different circumstances the canceling party might have been you.

Airlines and hotels have the luxury of being able to overbook to cover cancellations, but that is not an option for home exchangers. It is surprising how often a jilted home exchanger can pick up the pieces of a cancellation and arrange an alternate exchange vacation. For one thing, the person canceling on you may well hold the key to straightening out your dilemma. For example, an exchanger in Arlington, Virginia, writes, "Just before one of our exchanges, my wife became seriously ill, making our home unavailable to our exchange partners. As it happened, our next-door neighbors were to be out of town at the same time our guests were to be coming here, and they generously offered to have our exchange partners stay in their home. It worked very well, and we were thankful that (1) we had such good neighbors and (2) we didn't ruin our partners' plans."

There is an obvious solution available to exchangers who have to cancel if they have an available second home in the general vicinity of the original exchange home. "Our exchange partner in France changed his mind about coming here, but let us use his second home."

"Our exchangers were enjoying our New York City apartment when the man's father died, and they had to return to Spain. Although we grieved with him over his loss, we were thankful that we were in their vacation cottage, not their primary residence."

Another New York couple, having exchanged all over the world, were distressed when their Italian partner called to say he had to cancel his trip to New York. "The upshot was that, although he couldn't leave the country at the time, he and his family were able to go elsewhere in Italy while we spent a month in their palazzo in Rome—housekeeper, car, and all. Later, they came to visit us in New York, and we've been great friends ever since."

If you ever have to cancel a vacation home exchange arrangement, there are two initial steps to take, each vitally important: (1) advise your partner by telephone, wire, cable, or fax immediately—as soon as you know you will not be able to carry through with the exchange plan, thus giving your partner the maximum amount of time to make other arrangements—and (2) make every effort to provide an alternate plan. Do you have a second home? Do you have a relative or friend in your area who has a second home available? Do you have a relative or friend whose home might be available? If reasons other than illness are causing you to cancel and you will, in fact, be at home during the period in question, can you handle your partners as house-guests (a hospitality exchange instead of a simultaneous exchange)? Could you make such an arrangement with someone else if you can't do it? Can you find an inexpensive rental for your partners—perhaps even splitting the rental fee? Remember, your exchange partners have been planning to stay in your home, so it behooves you to do everything you possibly can to arrange a substitute plan for them, even a rental. In a situation like this, any port in a storm is better than leaving your partners adrift.

Occasionally, exchanges can be postponed, especially if the cancellation circumstances are known far enough ahead of time. Some airline tickets can have the dates changed for a modest fee. Exchangers in Portland, Oregon, and Washington, D.C., were going to switch homes for a month one summer. "It was all worked out. Then, because my mother who was to travel with us became critically ill, we had to abort the exchange. Fortunately, mother recovered, and we were able to make the exchange the next spring."

If your exchange partner cannot go through with the exchange and offers no acceptable alternate plan, reach for a legal pad and draw up a list of possibilities. The key issue here is the amount of time you have left in which to make your substitute arrangements.

1. Communicate by telephone your plight to some of the "near misses" you might have had in the weeks or months before the cancellation—persons you corresponded with but with whom you couldn't quite work out an exchange. Possibly

some of them may not have firmed up their exchange plans yet.

2. Possibly arrange to rent a motor home in or near the area in which the exchange was to have taken place.

3. If there is time, go back to square one: Get out the exchange directories and (again by telephone) try to put together a last-minute substitute exchange.

4. Perhaps you can postpone to a later date, the way the Portland, Oregon, exchangers did—perhaps with your original exchangers.

5. The absolute last resort: If you have the resources, try to arrange a conventional vacation at a hotel or rental facility near where the exchange was to have taken place.

Mid-exchange disasters can happen, but seldom (survey results confirm this) do exchangers really get stuck. A couple in Hawaii exchanged for a large house on the mainland and made all the arrangements with their host for family and friends to join them for their twenty-fifth anniversary. "After only two days the homeowner's father died, the family returned home, and we all had to leave. Motel costs for the planned vacation time were astronomical! Always, somehow, somewhere in the back of your mind, have a Plan B!"

A couple from the Lothian region of Scotland reiterates this last point as they tell about their somewhat different kind of disaster. Although he is a town planner and might have expected to be informed about major projects affecting his neighborhood, he was not notified that the road department was to dig up the street in front of his house during the time his exchangers were there. Not only did the equipment and oceans of mud almost imprison his guests on the property, but the road crew somehow managed to block all the drains in the house. "Our exchangers left early, we had to leave their house and go elsewhere, and our guests threatened to sue us. If possible, always try to have extra money with you along with some idea of an alternative plan," is their recommendation. As in the case of the New Yorkers vacationing in Spain, the availability of a second home or vacation cottage could have solved these two problems but not everyone has the luxury of a second residence.

If your vacation plans go up in smoke, get creative. As the old used-car adage goes, "When stuck with a lemon, make lemonade!" "When our partners canceled out on us, we had already purchased nonrefundable airline tickets, so we wrote to a bunch of people in England listed in the directories, asking for help. We received two offers of vacation cabins at very low rents, and we took one—in Lyme Regis." That from a retired engineer in New York City, an eight-time exchanger.

Those who are experienced in vacation home exchanging year after year often have gut feelings that, sooner or later, some emergency situation will cause a cancellation. They are prepared to roll with the punches. There are pluses and minuses to any situation. Exchangers in Eastleigh, England, had to leave their Myrtle Beach, South Carolina, exchange home a couple of days early, but, by so doing, they missed Hurricane Hugo, which slammed into Myrtle Beach two days later.

A Maryville, Tennessee, couple had finally worked out the details of an exchange on Dauphin Island off the coast of Alabama. In fact, plans had been completed for six months. "A couple of days before we were to leave on a weeklong, leisurely, sightseeing drive down there, the people canceled on us. We were furious. Less than ten days later a fierce hurricane wiped out Bayou La Batre, obliterated the causeway from Cedar Point to the island, and split Dauphin Island itself in two."

Anticipating that one day he might be confronted with a cancellation, the Eastleigh businessman writes, "We were able to extend the usual holiday insurance to include the expense of substitute accommodations in the event that our exchangers could not follow through on their commitments. Our experience shows how vital this insurance is, yet no one in England appeared to have even heard of such coverage. It took a lot of time, telephone calls, and research on my part before we found an insurance carrier willing to provide it" (see chapter 16).

"We've had cancellations only twice in more than twenty-five times out," writes a Coloradan. "Both times my husband stomped around, ranting and raving about these revolting developments . . . inconsiderate people . . . and never doing this again! But we've had such great fun vacation home exchanging that, when he simmered down, we arranged another. Then another and another. We're working on two for this summer and next year hope to do a six-week chain of exchanges in Europe. Those will take our adventure list well over thirty."

With a reasonable mix of understanding, patience, and flexibility, any person, couple, or family group can look to vacation home exchanging as the answer to that perennial question, "What are we going to do for vacation this year?"

CHAPTER 32

A Funny Thing Happened . . .

IT WOULD APPEAR FROM THE NUMEROUS STORIES related throughout this book that vacation home exchangers are subject not only to memorable experiences but seem to have a built-in sense of humor and an almost slapstick sense of the ridiculous. Even a couple's perspective on home exchanging itself and the question of strangers in their homes can be wry: It's a balance of terror! I'll exchange my shack for your chateau anytime! I tell my friends it's sort of a hostage situation—your home for mine! I'll pretend to trust you if you'll pretend to trust me!

One European responded to every question on the survey very precisely, except the one asking people to relate any funny experiences they had had. "I had funny experience," he said, "but I speak so bad English!"

Some of the stories that were submitted deal with the places exchangers have visited over the years.

On our very first day in Burlington, Ontario, I ventured out in our exchange car and soon found myself hopelessly lost. On a long, winding country road I managed to flag down the only living soul I had seen for some time and started to ask directions back to our vacation home. Before I could even get my question out, the young man said, to my utter amazement, 'You must be the folks at the Knowltons'.''

"Uhhh, yes, but—"

"Well, you're driving my father's car. I'm Michael Knowlton."

Now the population of Burlington and its surroundings is somewhat more than 112,000 people. I wonder what the odds are on this kind of thing happening?—Kingston, England

A Littleton, Colorado, couple tells of their first exchange—a well-equipped cabin in an isolated area of Wyoming. "Since shopping was quite far away, our exchangers told us to help ourselves to the food in their large freezer. We found out quickly that elk meat does not taste like beef—we had no idea whatsoever what to do with it. We ate a lot of pasta and cereal that week."

A European exchanger tells of the time he and his family exchanged in Nairobi, Kenya. Their skepticism had been assuaged by assurances that there was a more-than-adequate water supply where they were staying, but they wound up having to bribe someone to bring them water in a tanker.

Friends from our hometown in Signal Mountain, Tennessee, visited us once when we were on an exchange in Ventura, California. They loved the area, they loved the house, they loved the ocean—all of it. They even called a real estate broker to inquire about any houses for sale in the area. They were told there was one that would be on the market as soon as the owners returned from vacation, but they didn't want anyone to know it yet. They took down the address and were urged not to linger too long in the area. "Avoid looking like potential home buyers," were the broker's words. They came out of the office, got back in the car with us, and we geared up for our surreptitious survey of the property. The address? The exchange house we were all staying in!

Hindsight tells us that our exchange in Amsterdam was somewhat unusual, although, at the time, it simply seemed exciting to us "jaded" New Yorkers. The apartment was smack in the middle of the red-light district with its many attractions, and the place was "owned" by three very neurotic cats.

In Ireland some of the long, very narrow, winding roads are edged on both sides with rock walls. It was on just such a road that we, in our exchange host's small car, came face to face with an enormous bus. (Well, it looked enormous.) With no place for either of us to pull off, the resourceful bus driver and some of his equally brawny passengers simply picked up our car and moved it to within millimeters of the wall. The bus squeezed past, and we were each on our way.—Ocean Ridge, Florida

One year a Plymouth, England, couple did a "double," a back-to-back pair of exchanges—first to the Canadian Rockies, then to Arizona. It so happened that they left Canada in the midst of a snowstorm and stepped off the plane in Phoenix a few hours later to blazing sun and 112°—in September.

Other tales relate to exchange partners—their families, their homes, or their friends and neighbors.

A couple now living in Coral Springs, Florida, writes, "One of the family members staying in what was then our home on Cape Cod in Massachusetts called us one day (during the peak-rate period, of course) with the following question: 'We went to the beach and the tide was out. Can you tell us how to get to a beach where the tide is in?'"

In England, I walked each day to the local post office and newsstand to get the paper, and I got to know the shopkeeper and his wife pretty well. They knew I played golf every couple of days, and I kept them informed of our local sightseeing excursions, some of which they had recommended. On the spur of the moment one Thursday night, we decided to take a long weekend in Paris, leaving early Friday morning and returning late Sunday night. Monday morning I went for my paper at the usual time and greeted my two friends, who went quite gray and appeared close to fainting when they saw me. "You didn't die? We heard you'd had a heart attack and died on Friday!" "Hardly," I said, "we went to Paris for the weekend." It seems that an American had died on the golf course, and I was the only American golfer anyone knew was visiting in the area.—West Chester, Pennsylvania

We're from Northampton, England, and when my daughter was six we exchanged with a family in Asheville, North Carolina. I listened rather proudly as my little one was explaining to our exchange neighbor's six-year-old son, Morgan, about the time difference between England the eastern United States. "We're six hours in front of you in England," she said. Whereupon Morgan promptly asked, "Well, when does that mean you people go to bed?"

My wife and I were in Glasgow, Scotland, on an exchange. Every time we left the house and each night, I locked the door. One day, as I was going out to pick up the newspaper, I noticed that there were additional keys on the table. I thought about burglars, but nothing seemed amiss. I asked my wife if she had put the keys there. No. I was astonished because this was a completely different key chain and set of keys.

My surprise was even greater when I almost plowed into a young man in pajamas in the upstairs hall. He seemed as amazed as I was. I asked how he got in the house. He asked me the same thing, adding that it was his parents' home. Hearing that, I breathed a sign of relief and introduced myself. He didn't appear satisfied. I explained as briefly as I could about home exchanging and told him that his parents were in our home in Oran, Algeria, while we were in theirs. He finally laughed, and with a big sigh, said, "I've been in India for a year and came home as a surprise for their anniversary." Sad to say, not quite the surprise he'd envisioned, but we had a great time together.

When we returned to our home in Silver Springs, Maryland, from our European exchange, the neighbors reported that the large family staying in our home had occasionally carted the dining room table, chairs, and all the related paraphernalia out to the front yard for dinners on the lawn. Other neighbors had invited them over for a backyard barbecue to which they came dressed to the nines. High heels, jewels, elaborate hairdos, and chiffon party dresses adorned the women. Crisp white suits, silk ties, and highly polished shoes were sported by the men. But all of this splendor paled, we were told, beside the vision of the absolutely stunning teenage daughter sunbathing at our neighborhood pool sans bikini top!

As usual, we went to a lot of trouble leaving information about our home, shopping, restaurants, getting around in London, and so on. Our exchange partners assured us that they had done the same, but all we found at their home was a large sheet of paper on which they had laboriously converted centigrade into Fahrenheit.

An occasion arose in Italy where we needed to contact the person whose name had been left for us in case of an emergency. The gentleman was very helpful and afterward invited us out to dinner.

For some reason, my wife suspected that his companion was not quite his wife. This was later confirmed when my wife, who speaks some Italian, had occasion to call his home. When a lady answered, my wife greeted her with "Hello, Sophia!" Our friend called back shortly afterward quite agitated and excited and said, "Please, please, do not call my home and ask for Sophia."—Cranbury, New Jersey

"Our European exchanger was completely baffled by the garbage disposal," writes an exchanger from Honolulu, Hawaii. "They left a note expressing their concern that they might have broken it, as they had never figured out how to empty it."

The greatest exchange-related offer we ever had was from our Irish exchange partner who said, "The tap over there beside the washing machine is the beer. Help yourself!"—Vancouver, British Columbia

While researching future home exchange possibilities in London, England, a Mahwah, New Jersey, couple visited a home that had no microwave oven but did have most of the other amenities—plus, in the kitchen, two thriving marijuana plants.

The best visuals can probably be found in some of the tales exchangers tell about their experiences with animals.

You try transporting four large dogs (boxers, to be exact), all in need of acute care at the same time for some kind of virus, to the veterinary clinic in Zimbabwe in an economy-size car!—Hertfordshire, England

This was one of the directions in the ring-binder home information kit left by our hosts in Cleveland, Ohio: "After flushing downstairs toilet, please leave seat up so cat can have access to drinking water."—Abilene, Texas

For our first home exchange, my engineer husband and I traveled afar: from the West Midlands of England to the Midlands of the States—a ranch house on two acres near Cedar Rapids, Iowa. There the corn grows tall . . . and the cattle just grow. We liked to walk among the cornstalks but kept our distance from the cattle, until early one morning when an especially neighborly bull poked his head into our bedroom window.—Salihull, England

"Hey, get this," said a Brooklyn, New York, restaurant waitress to a co-worker. "An old guy comes in, sits down, and tells me he's from Florida—does home exchanging. Sez he's not too hungry. Seems nice enough, 'til he asks me if we give senior citizens a discount off the children's menu!"—New York, New York

A couple from Troon, Scotland, found it incredible that they were regularly seeing mice scampering around their beautiful exchange home in Southern California a few years ago. "Incredible, that is, until we happened to hear on the news that the whole area was infested with field mice. The irony was that our exchange partner was a pest-control man (obviously retired)."

As a Bridgeport, Connecticut, family was trying to work out dates for a New Orleans exchange, their potential host suggested that they wait 'til August; by then he'd have the doghouse air conditioned and they could bring along their dog.

A severe rainstorm in the Dordogne area of France brought frogs from the lake at the bottom of the garden up toward the house by the thousands, unbeknownst to us. We had been suffering through a heat wave, and at 10 P.M. the doors were wide open as we ate supper and played cards. Suddenly, the advancing storm cut all the electricity. As we were stumbling around searching for candles, we realized that there were frogs everywhere—leaping up our legs, all over the floor, the furniture, everywhere. A lot of shrieking, squealing, and laughing, but we bravely rounded them up and cleared them out of the house. It seemingly took forever. I must admit, I slept somewhat fitfully that night, fully expecting to be awakened by one of "those things" using me as a landing pad. We never mentioned it to our hosts, although I have often wondered how many frog carcasses they eventually found hidden behind or in pieces of furniture.—London, England

Teaneck, New Jersey, exchangers won't soon forget the Night of the Wild Boars. The setting? An isolated country home in Trifels, Germany. Their Scrabble-with-brandy evening was suddenly interrupted by a high-pitched squealing and loud thrashing in the bushes just outside the house. "With fear and trembling (and a pretty feeble flashlight) we sallied forth into the moonless night, fully expecting to confront a herd of wild boars.

"Stealthy tracking of the ever-louder squeals led us to the sudden discovery that our herd of wild, ferocious pigs was, in fact, four gentle, very frightened deer. Apparently, they had jumped the fence and were shrieking in panic as they crashed through the bushes looking for a way out of the yard."

And some incidents just seem to happen—nurtured, perhaps, by the nature of the particular exchange or Murphy's Law, or who knows what.

"Picture, if you will," writes a Transvaal, South Africa, exchanger, "watching the front door of your vacation villa in Spain blow closed in the wind—knowing for a fact that the only spare keys are in Norway."

We were set to fly out from Heathrow the next morning for Connecticut when my husband discovered that his passport was out-of-date. The airline put us on a flight the following day, we called our partners to explain, then spent the next day in the passport office. Our partners came in very late that night, but we had moved to an airport hotel.

Believe it or not, our return trip was equally eventful: ten minutes before departure, our commuter flight from Hartford to New York was canceled, and the airline tried to send us instead to Chicago, then London. To this added delay we (rather politely, I think) said no. We figured, at least if we stayed, we'd have the opportunity to meet our partners. The only hitch was that our luggage was already on its way to Chicago; we had only the clothes we stood up in. When I finally met our exchange partners I was wearing one of their large "Save the Whales" towels!

Prior to leaving Washington, D.C., on one exchange, we wrote ourselves a note to hide the wine and pasted it on the inside of the front door so it would be the last thing we'd see and do before leaving the apartment. (We had some really nice vintages we'd collected that we wanted to save for special occasions.) However, in our rush to leave, we completely forgot about the note.

On our return home some weeks later, the first thing we saw as we entered the house was the note on the front door. Embarrassed? You bet we were!

During our holiday, my husband and I learned how to milk a goat and drive a tractor, became addicted to corn on the cob, and stood in for absent members of a league bowling team, among other things. I went to a naughty nightie party; my husband went out with a fellow joiner (carpenter) for the day and wound up showing his new friend how to put up a traditional roof. These kinds of things don't happen on a "normal" holiday.—Nottinghamshire, England

From Caudan, France, comes the tale of the traveler who made a mistake about his return date and, at midnight, had to break into his own home (still in use by his Italian exchange partner) as if he were a burglar. His family of eight slept in the one tiny, unoccupied room.

On the first day of our first exchange, all the way from Cologne, Germany, to the California coast, we went for a long walk along the beach. After about an hour, we sat down on the sand to enjoy the waves and surfers, then walked for another hour. All of a sudden, it dawned on us both that neither one had the house key. "This is the end," we thought and had visions of begging the police to break into a home that was not ours. We had neither passports nor other documents with us.

We headed back—very slowly, very sadly—and, suddenly, I felt something besides sand under my left foot. Believe it or not, I had actually stepped on the key—our key! We both dropped to our knees, not knowing whether to laugh or cry.

Once when we were exchanging homes with an English family, we had the services of their Chinese housekeeper. Several days after our arrival, my brother came to visit. Unaware of the housekeeper's presence in the house, when he heard noises, my brother went to investigate. He found a person, dressed from head to foot in black, emerging from the salon with two filled shopping bags, obviously intent on leaving the premises. He grabbed and held her, yelling for us to call the police. When we were able to calm them both down, we showed him the ironing she was taking home in the shopping bags to finish. Both parties were frightfully embarrassed and apologetic (especially my brother); the rest of us were absolutely weak and crying from laughing so hard.—Las Vegas, Nevada

You want to see something funny?! Watch a couple of fifty-ish hospitality exchangers hand-bail a garden pool after inadvertently leaving the water running into it all night before their hosts get home from work. And be cleaned up and spiffy (ready to share a relaxed glass of sherry with them when they got there) before going out to dinner!—Cambridge, England

Soon after arriving at our home exchange in Florida, our partner called from California. Of course, my first reaction was panic—earthquake? fire? what? Not to worry, however. "In our hurry to leave, we forgot Mother. Have you seen her?" He took an obvious breath and continued, "Mother's in the closet behind the vanity."

Finally, all in a rush, he explained, "You see, Mother passed away this year, and her ashes are in a cardboard box on the closet floor. We want to honor her with a memorial service here by San Francisco Bay with her California grandchildren. Would you mind shipping Mother out here?"

We FedEx'd Mother the next morning.

Reference Section

1. Organizations That Serve Home Exchangers

Having heard about vacation home exchanging from friends or having read about it in books or newspaper or magazine articles, today large numbers of people are asking, "How does our family get started?"

Chapters 7 and 8 deal in depth with the recommended steps to take in making vacation home exchange arrangements. First and foremost, of course, are the resources home exchangers utilize in contacting each other. Happily, the worldwide home exchange community is served by organizations—oftentimes called clubs—that compile, produce, and release listings of home exchange opportunities in directories, booklets, and newsletters. Generally, these are distributed during January and February each year, when vacationers begin to think seriously about holiday plans for that year. Some of these clubs offer supplementary listings at regular intervals during the year.

The listings, which are quite similar to advertisements, provide a wealth of information—everything one needs to make the all-important where-when vacation decision. For example, each listing provides the name, address, and telephone number of the member seeking a vacation exchange. Further, this information includes the location of the member's home, the number of bedrooms and bathrooms, and the home appliances available. In most cases a photograph of the house is included. Each listing also shows the member's preferred destinations and vacation dates and the number of adults and children in the group. Other information describes the attractions of the member's local area as a holiday destination. Car exchange is a popular option sought out by many members.

Those interested in having their homes listed in one or more of the home exchange directories should contact the organizations by letter, telephone, fax, or e-mail, requesting complete listing information and a listing application. The listing fees are reasonable—even more so when the member realizes his home is brought to the attention of thousands of other vacationing home exchangers and that he has at his fingertips an equal number of viable vacation contacts throughout the world.

From their personal home exchange experience—more than eighty home exchanges throughout the world—the authors recommend, first and foremost, HomeLink International—the exchange club acclaimed by the survey participants as number one in the field.

Established in 1952, HomeLink has more than eighteen thousand members, and its annual directory covers fifty countries. Homes of all types are represented, ranging from small apartments in cities to large homes on private estates. HomeLink is a worldwide exchange club with offices in more than twenty countries. Each national office provides home exchange listings from its respective country to a central point, at which these listings are compiled prior to the production process. Then the completed directory is produced and distributed simultaneously to all the members. Readers who wish to find out more should contact the HomeLink office in their own (or nearest) country for an information pack. Listed here are the HomeLink offices in seven leading English-speaking countries.

• *Internet:* HomeLink International now has its own Internet central address. Any person sending e-mail to HomeLink will get a response and more details about this worldwide organization, as well as the address and phone number of the relevant associate. The Internet e-mail address is exchange@homelink.org. Or contact HomeLink's Worldwide Web site at www.homelink.org. HomeLink may be contacted through e-mail directly from the Web page.

• *Country offices:* The following addresses are for the HomeLink affiliates in each country.

Australia
HomeLink Australia
34 Franklin Street
Malden
Victoria 3463
Australia
contact: Julie Gittus
phone: (61) 54752 829
fax: (61) 54751 078

Canada
HomeLink Canada
1707 Platt Crescent
North Vancouver
British Columbia V7J 1X9
Canada
contact: Jack Graber
phone: (1) 604 987 3262
fax: (1) 604 987 3262

Great Britain
HomeLink Great Britain
Linfield House
Gorse Hill Road
Virginia Water
Surrey GU25 4AS
England
contact: Heather Anderson
phone: (44) 1344.842642
fax: (44) 1344.842642

Ireland
HomeLink Ireland
95 Bracken Drive
Portmarnock, Co. Dublin
Ireland
contact: Marie Murphy
phone: (353) 1 846 2598
fax: (353) 1 846 0305

New Zealand
 HomeLink New Zealand
 1 Higham Ferrers Place
 Red Beach
 Hibiscus Court
 New Zealand
 contact: Neil Smith
 phone: (64) 942 64084

South Africa
 HomeLink South Africa
 P.O. Box 23188
 Claremont
 Capetown 7735
 South Africa
 contact: Connie Booth
 phone: (27) 21 794 3433
 fax: (27) 21 794 3433

United States
 Vacation Exchange Club*
 P.O. Box 650
 Key West, Florida 33041
 contact: Karl Costabel
 phone: (1) 305-294-1448
 fax: (1) 305-294-1448
 (toll free, U.S. only)
 phone: (1) 800-638-3841
 fax: (1) 800-638-3841

 *affiliated with HomeLink
 International

Included in the following worldwide list of organizations that have been serving the vacation home exchange community for many years is Intervac International. For decades, Intervac has produced an annual directory, followed by supplementary listings during the year.

Australia
 HomeLink Australia
 34 Franklin Street
 Malden
 Victoria 3463
 Australia
 contact: Julie Gittus
 phone: 1 (61) 54752 829
 fax: (61) 54751 078

 Intervac Australia
 57 Sydney Road
 Manly
 NSW 2095
 Australia
 contact: Gerd Willmer
 phone: (61) 2 9777 100
 fax: (61) 2 9777 682

Austria
 HomeLink Austria
 Juchgasse 30/27
 A-1030 Wien
 Austria
 contact: Otto Stebel
 phone: + (43) 222-7124789

 Intervac Austria
 Pestalozzistrasse 5
 A 9100 Volkermarkt
 Austria
 contact: Hans and Ingeborg Winkler
 phone: (43) 423-2323838

Belgium
 HomeLink Belgium
 Onderbergen 51
 B-9000 Ghent
 Belgium
 contact: Jan Küssendorf
 phone: 1 (32) 9/223.23.10
 fax: 1 (32) 9/224.31.44

 Intervac Belgium
 Lindenberglaan 26
 B-1933 Sterrebeek
 Belgium
 contact: Jempi de Cooman
 phone: (32) 2/731.52.02
 fax: (32) 2/731.52.02

Brazil
 Intervac Brazil
 Ave. Rio Branco 245
 Room 1805
 CEP 20040 Rio de Janeiro (RJ)
 Brazil
 contact: J. V. Almeida
 phone: (55) 21 27 43 521

Canada
 HomeLink Canada
 1707 Platt Crescent
 North Vancouver
 British Columbia V7J 1X9
 Canada
 contact: Jack Graber
 phone: (1) 604-987-3262
 fax: (1) 604-987-3262

Intervac Canada
606 Alexander Crescent N.W.
Calgary
Alberta T2M 4T3
Canada
contact: Suzanne Cassin
phone: (1) 403-284-3747
fax: (1) 403-284-3747

Caribbean Islands
HomeLink Caribbean Islands
Sta. Rosaweg 116
Willemstad
Curacao, N.A.
contact: Ester Maduro
phone: 1 (599) 9-374420
fax: 1 (599) 9-371210

Costa Rica
Marilyn Root
SJO 053
P.O. Box 025369
Miami, Florida 33102
U.S.A.
phone: 1-506-220-1762
fax: 1-506-220-1762

Cyprus
Intervac Cyprus
B.P. 1069
Kato Paphos
Cyprus
contact: Anne Sophie
Hadjialexandrou
phone: (357) 6 245 789

Czech Republic
HomeLink Czech Republic
Zitomirská 39
10 100 Praha 10
Czech Republic
contact: Dr. Alena Klirová
phone: + (42) 2-722856

Intervac Czech Republic
Podstanci 25/603
10200 Praha 10
Czech Republic
contact: Antonin and Lenka
Macháckovi
phone: (42) 2-757250
fax: (42) 2-7860061

Denmark
HomeLink Denmark
Trangårdsve 64
Box 53
DK-2900 Hellcrup
Denmark
contact: Peter Ebert
phone: 1 (45) 31 610405
fax: (45) 31 610405

Intervac Denmark
Svenstrupvang 17
DK-4622 Havdrup
Denmark
contact: Jens C. H. Lauritzen
c/o Bodl and Leif Bigler
phone: (45) 42 134380

Finland
Intervac Finland
A-lomatry Kellosilta 7
F00520 Helsinki
Finland
contact: Pentti Jankala
phone: (358) 0 1502484
fax: (358) 0 145706

France
HomeLink France
Bel Ormeau 409
Avenue Jean Paul-Coste
13100 Aix-en-Provence
France
contact: Lilli Engle
phone: + (33) 42 38 42 38
fax: + (33) 42 38 95 66

Intervac France
Note: for information about France,
Morocco, and Tunisia, contact
Lucien Mazik as follows:
230 Boulevard Voltaire
F-75011 Paris
France
phone: 1-(33)- 43 70 21 22
fax: 1-(33)- 43 70 73 35

Germany
HomeLink Germany
Herausgeber Seehofstrasse 50
D-96117 Memmelsdorf
Germany
contact: Manfred Lypold
phone: 1 (49) 951-43055
fax: 1 (49) 951-43057

Intervac Germany
Verdiweg 2
D-70771 Leinfelden-Echterdingen
Germany
contact: Helge and Dieter Günzler
phone: (49) 711-7546069
fax: (49) 711-7542831

Great Britain
HomeLink Great Britain
Linfield House
Gorse Hill Road
Virginia Water
Surrey GU25 4AS
England
contact: Heather Anderson
phone: 1 (44) 1344.842642
fax: 1 (44) 1344.842642

Intervac Great Britain
3 Orchard Court
North Wraxhall
Wiltshire SN14 7AD
England
contact: Rhona Nayar
phone: 1 (44) 1225.892208
fax: 1 (44) 1225.892011

Worldwide Home Exchange Club
50 Hans Crescent
London SW1X ONA
England
contact: Mildred J. Baer
Phone: 1 (44) 0171-823-9937

Greece
HomeLink Greece
Montzarou 5
106 72 Athens
Greece
contact: Michael Lucas
phone: + (30) 1-36.26.994
fax: + (30) 1-36.00.389

Intervac Greece
Fintiou 20
Athenes 11253
Greece
contact: Despina Anagnostopoulos
phone: + (30) 1-86.78.917

Hungary
HomeLink Hungary
6 Tinodi u.6.sz.
4200 Hajdùszoboszló
Hungary
contact: László Sóvágó
phone: 1 (36) 52-361778
fax: + (36) 52-361778

Intervac Hungary
Bognár u 3b
1021 Budapest
Hungary
contact: Janos Rusz
phone: (36) 11-760494
fax: (36) 12-516010

Iceland
HomeLink Iceland
Seles 19
700 Egilsstaoir
Iceland
contact: Iirefna Iijalmarsdottir
phone: 1 (354) 471.2588
fax: 1 (354) 471.2588

Intervac Iceland
Nÿbÿlavegi 42
200 Kópavogur
Iceland
contact: Elisa M. Kwaszenko
phone: 1 (354) 554.44684
fax: 1 (354) 557.74301

Ireland
HomeLink Ireland
95 Bracken Drive
Portmarnock, Co. Dublin
Ireland
contact: Marie Murphy
phone: 1 (353) 1-846-2598
fax: + (353) 1-8460305

Intervac Ireland
Phillipstown
Ballymakenny Road
Drogheda
Ireland
contact: Frank Kelly
phone: (353) 1-4130936
fax: (353) 1-4130929

Israel
HomeLink Israel
6 Days Street 49
97804 Jerusalem
Israel
contact: David Hamburger
phone: 1 (972) 2-812726
fax: 1 (972) 2-811178

Italy
HomeLink Italy
Via Trilussa 6
06063 Magione (PG)
Italy
contact: Marie Teresa Barettini
phone: + (39) 75-843491
fax: + (39) 75-843491

Intervac Italy
Via Oreglia 18
40047 Riola (BO)
Italy
contact: Gaby Zanobetti
phone: (39) 51-910818
fax: (39) 51-912028

Japan
Intervac Japan
4-20-13-401 Sekimachi Minami-
Nerima-ku
Tokyo 176
Japan
contact: Ted Fotos
phone: (81) 339 299927

Luxembourg
Intervac Luxembourg
B.P. 3
L 8201 Mamer
Luxembourg
contact: Lone Lauritzen
phone: (352) 313580
fax: (352) 313625

Mexico
Intervac Mexico
Calz. de Los Leones 248-5
01710 Mexico
D.F. / Mexico
contact: Leticia Muris
phone: (5) 660 6279
fax: (5) 680 0598

Netherlands
HomeLink Netherlands
Kraneweg 86A
9718 JW, Gronigen
Netherlands
contact: Renger & Ton de Ruiter
phone: 1-(31) 503-133535
fax: 1-(31) 503-133177

Intervac Netherlands
Paasberg 25
6862 CB Oosterbeek
Netherlands
contact: Willemien & Roel Eissen
phone: (31) 85 343272
fax: (31) 85 343276

New Zealand
HomeLink New Zealand
1 Higham Ferrers Place
Red Beach
Hibiscus Court
New Zealand
contact: Neil Smith
phone: + (64) 942-64084

Intervac New Zealand
36, Roys Road
Plimmerton
Wellington
New Zealand
contact: Ann Delany
phone: (64) 477-0388
fax: (64) 477-0388

Norway
HomeLink Norway
P.O. Box 95
Kjelsås
0411 Oslo 4
Norway
contact: Henning Halversen
phone: 1 (47) 22-158019

Intervac Norway
Fagerlivegen 9
N-2800 Gjovik
Norway
contact: Ivar Solli
phone: (47) 6117 9185
fax: (47) 6117 7899

Poland
HomeLink Poland
u1.Obornicka 269/271
60-650 Poznan
Poland
contact: Maria Walkowiak
phone: + (48) 61239741
fax: + (48) 61233971

Intervac Poland
Rogi 49, 38-430 Miejsce
Piastowewoj.
Krosno
Poland
contact: Barbara Zakrzewska-
Trzcinka
phone: (48) 536 40

Portugal
HomeLink Portugal
Chacara dos Lobos
2750 Janes/Cascais
Portugal
contact: Julie deWolff
phone: 1 (351) 1-487-2478
fax: 1 (351) 1-487-2455

Intervac Portugal
Rua Inacio de Sousa 23, R/C Do.
1500 Lisboa
Portugal
contact: Antonio St. Aubyn
phone: 35-1-1-785179

Slovakia
HomeLink Slovakia
Limbová 18
831 01 Bratislava
Slovakia
contact: Ing. Dana Dráboá
phone: + (43) 7 377103

South Africa
HomeLink South Africa
P.O. Box 23188, Claremont
Cape Town 7735
South Africa
contact: Connie Booth
phone: 1 (27) 21-794-3433
fax: 1 (27) 21-794-3433

Spain
HomeLink Spain
C/Fuencarral 146
28010 Madrid
Spain
contact: Wladimiro Muños
phone: 1 (34) 1-447 5140/28
fax: 1 (34) 1-447 50140

HomeLink Spain
Obispo Sastre 14
Santa Eugenia
07142 Mallorca
Spain
contact: Helen Courtney-Lewis
phone: + (34) 71-620603
fax: 1 (34) 71-602960

Intervac Spain
Consell de Cent 226
1, 3, 08011 Barcelona
Spain
contact: Maria Angeles Sas
phone: (34) 34-533171
fax: (34) 34-513024

Sweden
HomeLink Sweden
Tranegårdsvej 64
Box 53
DK 2900 Hellerup
Denmark
contact: Peter Eberth
phone: + (46) 31 610405
fax: + (46) 31 610405

Intervac Sweden
Storskiftesvägen 32
S 291 73 ônnestad
Sweden
contact: Anki & Karl Gemfeldt
phone: (46) 0 44 70270
fax: (46) 0 44 70080

Switzerland
HomeLink Switzerland
Brückengasse 5a
CH-8280 Kreuzlingen
Switzerland
contact: Tina Roy
phone: 1 (41) 77 97 69 04
fax: 1 (41) 7531-22804

Intervac Switzerland
Oberdorfstr. 7
9524 Zuzwil
Switzerland
contact: Iso and Claudia
Niedermann
phone: (41) 73 28 27 79

Turkey
Intervac Turkey
Agora Ltd., Güvenlik Mah.
Mimar Sinan Cad. 24/B
Bayrakci Apt.
07050 Antalya
Turkey
phone: (90) 2423 442047
fax: (90) 2423 341570

United States
Vacation Exchange Club
P.O. Box 650
Key West
Florida 33041
contact: Karl Costabel
phone: 1-(305) 294-1448
fax: 1-(305) 294-1448
(toll free, U.S. only)
phone: 1-(800) 638-3841
fax: 1-(800) 638-3841

Intervac U.S.
P.O. Box 590504
San Francisco
California 94159
contact: Lori Horne and Paula Jaffe
phone: 1-(415) 535-3497
fax: 1-(415) 435-7440

Kimco Communications
4242 West Dayton
Fresno
California 93722
contact: John C. Kimbrough
phone: 1-(209)-275-0893
fax: 1-(209)-275-8642

Loan-a-Home
2 Park Avenue, 6E
Mount Vernon
New York 10552
contact: Muriel Gould
phone: + 1 (914)-664-7640

Teacher Swap
P.O. Box 454
Oakdale
New York 11769-0454
contact: Ron Frevola
phone: 1-(516)-244-2845
fax: 1-(516)-244-2845

**Worldwide Home
Exchange Club**
806 Brantford Avenue
Silver Spring
Maryland 20904
contact: E. Levy
phone: + 1-(301)-680-8950

Zimbabwe
HomeLink Zimbabwe
P.O. Box HG 630
Highlands
Harare
Zimbabwe
contact: Bernard Hayward
phone: + (263) 4-786430
fax: + (263) 4-786430

Finally, the most recently established organization serving home exchangers is the International Home Exchange Association (IHEA). The IHEA is a union of eighteen independently owned and operated home exchange clubs, worldwide. Some of those affiliated with the IHEA have been offering listings of home exchangers in one format or another for some years, while others are relatively new in their services to the home exchange community. Readers can receive information about the IHEA by contacting the following:

Ann Pottinger
Vacation Homes Unlimited
and Director, IHEA
P.O. Box 1562
Santa Clara
California 91386-0566
phone: (toll free) 1-(800)-VHU-SWAP
phone: 1-(805)-298-0376
fax: 1-(805)-298-0576

2. Suggested Letters for Use in Vacation Home Exchange Correspondence

Throughout this book it has been emphasized that once a contact has been made, the correspondence between the two potential exchangers is of paramount importance in determining whether a particular exchange is workable. To aid exchangers in communicating with one another, what follows is a series of model letters focused on the fact sheet, the initial contact, hospitality exchanging, and other subjects that generally are a part of home exchange correspondence. These letters should demonstrate the honesty, thoroughness, and flexibility that characterizes successful home exchange correspondence.

Fact Sheet _____

The fact sheet is an overview of the exchanger's home and the area around it. It includes pertinent information about the exchanger and his family and/or others traveling with him. Some exchangers say this is the most important single document in the exchange correspondence because the fact sheet is really a sales tool, promoting a particular home and home exchange family (see chapter 7). Always enclosed with the initial contact letters, the fact sheet should motivate potential exchangers to want to follow up the contact.

Regarding the Stedmans' condominium on Sanibel Island, Florida:

For thirteen years we have owned a luxury condominium on Florida's Gulf Coast. This second home is occupied by vacationing home exchangers, family members, and occasionally ourselves.

Our condo is at Loggerhead Cay, a large, first-class resort on Sanibel Island, near Fort Myers, Florida. This condo is one of the two most desired condos at Loggerhead Cay—this because it is on the top floor, Gulf front, and faces south with a 180° panoramic view of the sandy beach below and the Gulf of Mexico.

A few steps from the parking space, you will take the elevator to the fourth floor and find the condo has a large master bedroom with a king-sized bed, a second bedroom with twin-sized beds, two baths, and a large living room with a couch that converts into a queen-sized bed. The dining area is connected by a pass-through to a full, modern, eat-in kitchen—appliances include a microwave oven, a dishwasher, and a garbage disposal. The condo's large screened-in porch overlooks the Gulf of Mexico and miles of sandy beach; its sun balcony overlooks the garden and a private swimming pool.

Further, the condo is newly furnished and fully air-conditioned. It has two cable television sets, a radio, and a VCR. Finally, it has ample linens, cooking utensils, dishes, flatware, and all amenities required for comfortable vacationing for a family of up to six persons.

Loggerhead Cay has a beautiful beach, a large private swimming pool, and private tennis courts. There are several public golf courses nearby. In addition to being an ideal, year-round resort, Sanibel Island is famous for its beaches (number three in the world for shelling); its surf, bay, and deep-sea fishing; its wildlife sanctuary; its miles of cycling paths; and its fine shops and restaurants in every price range—fast-food to gourmet. The island's lack of high-rise, high-density buildings and its preservation of tropical trees, plants, and flowers help to make Sanibel one of Florida's most beautiful islands.

Sanibel Island is just thirty minutes by car from Southwest Florida International Airport at Fort Myers—one served by most major airlines.

Recent vacationers from Geneva, Switzerland, write: "We have just had the best home exchange ever at Loggerhead Cay, Sanibel Island, Florida!"

Now in our early sixties, Harry (a retired airline executive) and Mary have had many home exchanges in the United States and Europe. Generally, there are just the two of us traveling, although occasionally we do have another couple along. Because this condo is our second home, we have flexibility in our exchange scheduling, though we prefer to travel in the spring. We are nonsmokers and have three married children and eight grandchildren.

Initial Contact

This letter is designed for use by the person who hopes to arrange an exchange with another person after seeing the latter's listing in one of the exchange directories. Enclosed with this initial contact letter should be a fact sheet, several photos of the exchange home, and photos of the people participating in the proposed exchange. Because the fact sheet will be photocopied, it is important that this initial contact letter be typed and hand-signed or handwritten. Thus, it will not have the appearance of every other, easy-to-toss-out form letter.

Dear Mr. and Mrs. —:

We saw your listing in the Vacation Exchange Club's current directory and note your interest in exchanging somewhere along Florida's west coast. Our condo is on Sanibel Island, three miles (by causeway) from Fort Myers. Your home there in Vancouver, B.C., sounds just perfect for my wife, Mary, and me. So perhaps we might be able to arrange a home exchange for two or three weeks next spring—perhaps in May or June.

The enclosed fact sheet and photos will give you information about our condo, its location, and ourselves. We should add that in recent years we have had six exchanges—four here in the States and two in Europe. We neither smoke nor drink, and we generally exchange cars; we offer a 1995 four-door Honda Accord.

After looking over the enclosures, we hope you will be interested in spending some time at our Sanibel Island condo next spring. We are quite flexible as to dates.

Assuming you think there is a possibility of an exchange between us, please send us complete information about your home and the area in which you live. Feel free to contact us about our condo, this part of Florida, or any other questions you might have.

Very cordially,

Follow Up _____

The initial contact letter was well received by the potential exchangers in Vancouver. Indeed, within a week they responded with a letter of their own, enclosing information about their home and themselves (both retired), photos, their willingness to include their car in the exchange, and suggesting a date. Various questions were asked. So here is a suggested followup letter.

Dear Mr. and Mrs. —:

Thanks for getting back to us so promptly on this possibility of our working up a home exchange next spring. We appreciate your giving us so much information about your home. The photos are great. While we do have a few more questions, at this point we feel there's a likelihood we might well be able to exchange with you folks next spring. Finally, we may get to see Canada!

But first, your questions:

1. Your suggested dates sound just fine to us: three weeks beginning May 23.

2. Our Honda has an automatic transmission.

3. It is possible to rent bikes on Sanibel Island, and the condo complex has a covered rack for storing locked bikes.

4. There are two supermarkets on Sanibel Island. One is a mile from our condo, the other about two miles.

5. May/June is offseason at Sanibel Island—no traffic problems. Shopping is easy; there's no need for reservations at restaurants or tennis courts or at golf courses—a big plus for tennis players and golfers!

6. Our spring weather is ideal—daytime temperatures between 75° and 80°, low humidity (not like August!), and lots of sun, a gentle breeze, and an occasional late-afternoon shower. Pool temperature: 80°; Gulf temps: 75–78°.

7. On the matter of cleaning, if you wish to have the condo

cleaned weekly (or at the exchange midpoint), maid service is available; our exchangers pay for this cleaning service. On the day you depart, however, we arrange for the condo to be cleaned—our expense.

Now, we have a few thoughts and questions. As it happens, our guest room and guest bath are separated from the rest of the condo—almost like a little apartment. We would very much like to meet you folks and show you the ropes at our place and introduce you to our neighbors and our condo community. It would be great if you could plan to arrive at Sanibel Island a day or so before we leave for your place. Would this be possible?

Other questions:

1. As we would be making quite a few phone calls back to the States, how do you prefer to handle long-distance calls?

2. Is it possible to take one- or two-day excursions in the waters north of Vancouver?

3. Would it be okay with you if at the last moment our son and daughter-in-law should decide to be with us during the last week of our stay at your home?

I'm sure we'll have other thoughts and questions in the weeks just ahead, but I'm anxious to get this letter off to you without delay.

Very cordially,

There may well be three or four exchanges of correspondence— and perhaps a phone call or two—leading up to the eventual consummation of a home exchange arrangement. Chapters 7 and 8 present at length many of the exchange-related details that should be addressed by all parties to a vacation home exchange. It is covering and agreeing upon all the aspects of the exchange before the dates of the exchange that makes for the most successful home exchange.

It's a Deal

With all questions, and other exchange matters taken into consideration, there comes that point during each exchange correspondence that a deal is either made or not. If both parties to the correspondence agree that everything is in order for the exchange, then one or the other should confirm this fact in writing, such as the following:

Dear Harriet:

It was good talking with you over the phone the other day, because that gave us both an opportunity to discuss the home and car insurance matters—this after talking with our respective insurance agents, to answer our pool-cleaning query, and to deal with various minor aspects of our exchange arrangement.

So now . . . we agree with you: It's a deal! When we started corresponding with you several months ago, there seemed to be so many exchange arrangements to be made that Ed and I wondered if we'd ever get everything squared away. I guess part of our apprehension was because this is our first home exchange experience.

Even though our exchange date is three months away, I'm very glad we started our exchange arrangements early. It would be awful to leave all of that stuff to the last minute.

Probably in the weeks ahead we will have a few arrangement afterthoughts. We can clear up those matters in due course. Also, later we can make house key and final arrival arrangements. You know my brother and sister-in-law will be meeting your flight and then bringing you to our house here—also getting you fixed up with our car—and introducing you to several nearby neighbors.

The other day a friend of mine asked: "Aren't you folks nervous about having some total strangers living in your home?" We said that we have no concern whatsoever about you folks occupying our home. After getting to know you through all these letters and telephone calls we consider it a privilege to be hosting you here.

Ed and I send our special greetings and best wishes.

Very cordially,

Hospitality Exchange _____

Chapter 25 deals in depth with all elements of hospitality exchanging.

Dear Dr. and Mrs. —:

I have just noticed your hospitality exchange listing in the recently received HomeLink directory. This is interesting because for some months my daughter has been urging me to get back into exchanging and to try a hospitality exchange—"get back into," that is, because my husband and I thoroughly enjoyed a dozen or more regular home exchanges over a ten-year period up until his recent passing.

A widow now for the past year and a half, I'm beginning to get out and around more. I would just love to have a hospitality exchange in London sometime in the next four to six months.

I am in my early sixties and maintain my own home here in San Francisco. I consider myself fairly independent—but not sufficiently so to want to do a "solo" regular home exchange with a family—that is, for them to be occupying my home while I would be alone at theirs.

My kids seem to come often for dinner, so I guess they like my cooking. Aside from an unhappy shoulder (due to a fall last year), I'm in good health. My diet includes just about anything (and usually too much of everything). I like the theater and concerts—not big on ballet, though—reading, playing bridge, watching television game shows, sightseeing (and there's so much to see in London and San Francisco). I stopped smoking decades ago but have no objection to those who still do. I'm not adverse to a glass of wine with dinner but can do very nicely without it. Here's a recent photo— my two daughters, their husbands, and assorted grandchildren. I promise not to bring the grandchildren with me.

I've lived in San Francisco, high on this hill, for the last twenty-three years. The house is really too large for me at this point—four bedrooms, three baths, and lots of space. I have my own car. Love to drive. And would be happy to tour-guide you folks anywhere in California. Well, enough about me.

If you would like to spend a couple of weeks in San Francisco some-time in the months just ahead, I'd love to hear all about you and your home in Chelsea, my favorite part of London. Do you have any pets? We had dogs for years, but now I have only one very lovable cat.

I'm looking forward to hearing from you at your convenience.

With best wishes,

Accumulating Credit in Home Exchanging

As has been emphasized throughout the preceding chapters, the scheduling—selection of mutually acceptable exchange dates—is more often than not the most challenging part of making home exchange arrangements, especially in the cases of simultaneous exchanges. Exchangers with second homes have a decided advantage here because they can agree to exchanging on different dates. The key to this type of exchanging is the "banking" of exchange arrangements by one of the exchangers. For instance, Exchanger A spends two weeks at the mountain home of Exchanger B in the spring. Thus B has banked or is holding a credit for two weeks at one of A's two homes—perhaps two weeks in the fall. A suggested letter that might be appropriate to one of these banking exchange situations follows.

Dear Mrs. —:

With so many letters and so much home exchange-related information going between us in recent months, I really feel like we know each other— a longtime friendship.

And so I am particularly sorry to report that our son's June marriage rules out our living at your home later that month. This certainly is sad, because we know you are anxious to take your vacation during this same time. But perhaps all is not lost. In my initial letter, we included complete information about and a photo of our home at Long Beach Island, New

Jersey. This is a great place—a natural for a restful vacation in June. So instead of your coming to our home here, why don't you arrange to spend those two weeks at our home on the shore?

And how about us? Well, at some later date we can spend a couple of weeks at either one of your homes—coordinating, of course, our schedule with yours. At this point we don't have any particular dates in mind, but we are thinking about early spring or fall of next year.

In home exchange parlance, I think they call this "banking" a two-week exchange. In other words, because you will have been at our second home this coming June—and we will not be at your place at that point—you "owe" us two weeks at one of your homes. We know there are some disadvantages in owning two homes, but there is at least one advantage—the possibility of using the second home to "untangle" home exchange scheduling!

We hope you'll like this suggestion and look forward to hearing from you soon.

Very cordially,

Agreement _____

Generally speaking, home exchangers do not enter into formal home exchange "contracts." They consider the contents of their correspondence as covering all of the important aspects of the exchange arrangements. Nevertheless, as indicated in chapter 8, some exchangers are accustomed to drawing up an informal letter of agreement related to the exchange. The following suggested agreement includes many of the elements that experienced, agreement-making exchangers feel are important in a document of this nature. The elements of these agreements vary from one exchange situation to the next, but this suggested agreement should be considered as a guide and modified to meet the requirements of a pending home exchange arrangement.

HOME EXCHANGE AGREEMENT

It is the intention of the undersigned persons to engage in a "home exchange" arrangement. That is, we will occupy each other's homes simultaneously during a predetermined time period.

Basically, we agree with the generally accepted and long-standing principle of home exchanging: We will treat our home exchange partner's home in the same way we will expect him to treat ours. Specifically:

1. We will provide each other with detailed information about our homes, including instructions for those appliances we will be using.

2. We will provide each other with the names and telephone numbers for plumbers, electricians, and others to be contacted in emergency situations.

3. We will provide each other with the names and information about the closest neighbors.

4. We will clean the home regularly and comply with the arrangements regarding cleaning on departure.

5. We will lock the home and put security systems (if any) in place when we are away for any period of time.

6. We will provide each other with information as to such overnight periods when we may be away from the home and with information about such overnight guests as we may have.

7. We will adhere to such arrangements as are made regarding the use of the telephone and the handling of long distance telephone charges.

8. We will provide each other with ample closet and drawer space for clothes and other personal items.

9. We will respect the privacy of each other's closets, drawers, desks, files, and so on. We will not snoop.

10. We will not use golf clubs, bicycles, wine cellars, deep freezing units, and/or other items not considered to be a part of the exchange.

11. We will replace such staple food items as coffee, sugar, condiments, and so on as we use during the exchange.

12. We will endeavor to take special care of our partner's glassware, china, utensils, and other household items. Should any of these be broken during our stay, we will replace them in kind or in money.

13. While we understand the host partners will be responsible for normal, basic repairs to the home and its appliances, we will reimburse him in full for such damage as we may do to the home and/or its contents.

Agreed   Agreed

_____   _____

Name   Date   Name   Date

Automobile Exchange _____

Increasingly, automobiles are becoming an important part of the home exchange experience. Currently, 75 percent of those exchanging homes also exchange cars. Chapter 23 deals with various aspects of car exchanging, and much of chapter 16 focuses on insurance requirements for a car exchange. For easy reference, the glove compartment is the ideal place for auto documents—in particular, registration and insurance information. In addition, it's recommended the exchange-driver be given a letter from the owner stating that the exchanger is authorized to drive the car. This most appropriate letter we've come across is one being used by an Akron, Ohio, home and car exchanger.

To Whom It May Concern:

This will advise you that (insert name and address of exchange-driver) is authorized by me to drive this vehicle.

This driver has in his/her possession a valid automobile operator's permit, along with this car's registration and insurance document.

(signed) Homer Exchanger, Owner _____

(address) _____

_____

Vehicle Identification # _____

Vehicle License (tag) # _____

Cancellation _____

Chapter 31 addresses the vacation cancellation dilemma and suggests several alternatives in which a vacation might be put back on track. The following letter may be of some help to an exchanger who has to be the bearer of exchange-cancellation news.

Dear Erik:

It's with great sadness I must tell you that Alice and I have decided to sell our home here and move to New York City, where I've just accepted a new position in my field of advertising.

This has been an agonizing time for us: uprooting the children from their schools here, selling this home, renting an apartment in New York until we decide where we'll wish to live permanently, leaving older relatives, and so on.

And, of course, an especially sad part for us, this means we'll not be able to carry through with our long-planned home exchange with you and your family.

We have spent so much time and effort in working out every detail of our exchange—with you folks coming here to the Washington area and our going to your home in Oslo—that we are especially sorry to be giving you this news now.

You have gone more than halfway putting together our proposed exchange and will be disappointed to get this word from us—"disappointed," a masterpiece of understatement!

In the past few days, Alice has been in touch with no fewer than six good friends and three relatives, all of whom live in this general area. With certainty we can say that we've got you covered: You and your family will be able to stay in the home of one of our friends during the same weeks you had planned on being here. Fortunately, masses of people around here hurry off to vacations during the month of August.

Time is a little short, so we'll have to select the home in which you'll be staying. I will share with your new host our correspondence file, and then he'll be in touch with you, probably first by telephone.

Your responsibility to him? Nothing. You see, we will arrange with your host family to occupy our rented New York apartment next spring while we'll be in Barbados for a month.

And our trip to your home in Oslo? Well, that will have to be put on hold for a while, though we hope to be there sometime late next year. We'll keep in touch with you on this. If you are to be away on vacation next year, perhaps we could occupy your home at that time, or maybe at some other time convenient to your vacation schedule. At this point, frankly, I am not so worried about our coming there as I am about your having an enjoyable exchange experience here in Washington.

Finally, we're sorry to have had to back out of our arrangement, but, Erik, you have my word that you will be every bit as happy in the home we select for you as you would have been here in our home. This we can assure you.

Even though you won't be staying at our place, of course, we'll be keeping in touch. Soon after your arrival in the States, we'll be calling you. I'm sure we'll be able to get down to Washington to meet you folks during your stay.

Alice and I send our greetings to you and Ingrid.

Very cordially,

Departure _____

> **During the exchange period, the partners to the exchange often wonder how things are going back home. Are our**

> exchange friends enjoying their vacation? Have they had any
> problems with our appliances? Or the car? Any disasters
> with the burglar alarm? These and other matters pertinent
> to the exchange can be dealt with in the departure letter,
> generally left in the home at the time of departure.

Dear Harry and Alice:

Aside from the fact that the weather was not too cooperative, we had a great time at your condo! We can't believe we've been here three weeks. It's seemed more like ten days.

The information you left us was most helpful, especially when we couldn't figure out how to work that fancy clothes dryer you've got.

In our previous three home exchanges, it seems we always had a minor problem or two—the car, the plumbing, or something. Not here, no problems. In fact, we didn't even break a dish.

Your shopping suggestions were great. We did most of our food shopping at Bailey's. And we sure worked over your restaurant list. On our twenty-fourth wedding anniversary we splurged and went to The Bubble Room. We also did Chadwick's, The Timbers, and even Bangkok House.

We're so glad you suggested the Fort Myers Broadway Palm Dinner Theater. We took friends and had a supergreat evening—eating everything in sight and enjoying "Born Yesterday."

The museums, the art gallery, the shell shops—we did them all. But best of all is this lovely condo of yours.

Now we just hope you enjoyed our place half as much as we enjoyed yours!

With best wishes,

P.S. In the refrigerator are a few welcome-home goodies.

3. A Checklist for Home Exchange Partners

Hermann Lippold of Mainz, Germany (see chapter 22) provides his home exchange partners with detailed, all-encompassing information about his home and property and the area in which he lives. The Lippolds' many exchange partners have found the information to be extremely useful during their visits.

Using Hermann's outline as a guide and including related suggestions from other experienced home exchangers, we present the following outline—one recommended for use by home exchange partners. While, of course, the details of such a list will vary from one exchange home to another, we feel this is an excellent checklist of important information for home exchange hosts to leave for their exchange partners.

I. House
Living Room
1. Television, channel list on back of remote control
2. VCR, instruction booklet on top of set; videocassette library to right of unit
3. Stereo equipment, the switch LS1 on the main amplifier V2000 is for the loudspeakers in the living room. The switch LS2 is for the loudspeakers in the kitchen, bathroom, basement, and master bedroom. In some of these rooms there are separate control knobs. The output of the tape deck is on the switch "Monitor on." Please feel free to use any of our CDs (near cassette library).
4. Sofa-bed, when cushions are removed, this folds out easily into a queen-sized bed; pillows and linens near door to porch

Kitchen
1. Appliances—all electric; instruction booklets in drawer next to fridge. Special note: water must be on when using disposal
2. Utensils
   1. Pots, pans, etc. in various drawers and cabinets
2. Larger pots in garage cupboard
3. Dishes, unbreakable and microwave OK, in cabinets for regular dining; for candlelight dinners use white and gold set in dining room; best that the Wedgwood not be used
4. Glassware for regular use in kitchen cabinets
5. Silverware for regular use in top drawer; for "good," second drawer
6. Countertops cannot be used for carving or slicing; use cutting boards
7. Soaps, cleansers, sponges, and other supplies on top shelf in broom closet; vacuum cleaner in there, too—also new vacuum bags
8. Dish towels, washcloths in drawer below miscellaneous drawer (corkscrew, measuring spoons, matches, rubber bands, bag ties, etc.)
9. Garbage container below sink; always use garbage bags (different sizes in boxes in garage)

Dining Room
1. Chairs and table, indestructible, but use hot pads on table
2. Water, wine, and liquor glasses, "good" ones, in cabinets
3. Carpet under tables/chairs can handle normal wear and tear, but must be vacuumed regularly
4. Wines and liquors, basic stocks in small rolling bar; use and replace

Master Bedroom
1. Linens in hall closet
2. Bed set up for electric blanket; controls in drawers of bedside tables, right and left
3. Bedside reading lights, dimmers underneath the headboard

4. Air conditioning, turn fan control to "auto" and set desired temperature

5. Closets and drawers, ample room for clothes in dressers and closet

Bathrooms

1. Medicine chest empty for your use
2. Bathroom supplies, linens, soap, Kleenex, toilet paper, etc. in cupboard and drawer
3. Exhaust fan switch to right side of toilet; shuts off automatically after a few minutes of use

Guest Bedroom

1. Linens on shelves behind curtains
2. Iron, main switch behind curtain near the window; ironing board in closet
3. Clothes, closet space available

Sewing Room

1. Marked off-limits
2. Contains certain personal items of the host, including clothing

Sauna

1. Instructions mounted on the front of sauna
2. Warm-up time, it takes one hour "on" before this is ready for use

Garage

1. Car, use smaller car (see Section III)
2. Workbench area, wall racks contain most tools

II. Exterior of House

1. Lawn, the electric lawn mower is in the shed. The electric outlet on the patio is normally currentless. The switch for the outlet and the patio light is inside the living room to the left of the patio door. The electric outlet for the front garden is in entrance hall. Lawn should be mowed weekly; grass cuttings can be spread in wooded area.
2. Arrangements can be made with lawn service to handle mowing (call Steve: 978-1337)
3. Watering, built-in sprinkler system; if it's very dry for two weeks, sprinkler should be turned on for an hour; on/off valve near light switch in garage.
4. Gardening tools in shed
5. Barbecue, heated by propane gas in tanks, in shed

III. Car

1. Glove compartment: insurance papers, vehicle registration, accident report, permission-to-drive letter, owner's manual, and instructions for air conditioning and radio

2. Fuel, car uses only unleaded gas—regular (cheapest)
3. Key, duplicate set on hook near light switch in garage
4. Repairs, local Honda Service Center (Jack Harrison 555-2963)
5. Driveway parking, OK for car to be parked in driveway during day-time; at night, it should be in locked garage

IV. Other Matters

1. Ring binder in kitchen, has an alphabetical listing with complete information about following:

banks	repairs
emergencies	restaurants
heating	shopping
insurance	telephone
keys	utilities
mail	waste disposal
places to go/things to see	

2. Neighbors. Should questions arise about any aspects of the house, the property, the area, emergencies of any kind, contact the following persons:

name _____

address _____

phone # _____

name _____

address _____

phone # _____

name _____

address _____

phone # _____

These neighbors know home exchangers are occupying the house and will be happy to be of assistance.

Bill Barbour, a former CEO of a book publishing company, and Mary Barbour, a former administrator of educational programs for disadvantaged children, have traveled throughout the world on vacation home exchanges that have taken them as far west as Hong Kong and as far east as Switzerland.

Readers desiring to know more about vacation home exchanging may write the authors at the following address:

Bill and Mary Barbour
Vacation Home Exchange
Services International, Inc.
16956-4 South McGregor Boulevard
Fort Myers, FL 33908 U.S.A.